An Administrator's Guide to Better Teacher Mentoring

William L. Fibkins

A SCARECROWEDUCATION BOOK

The Scarecrow Press, Inc.
Lanham, Maryland, and London
2002

A SCARECROWEDUCATION BOOK

Published in the United States of America
by Scarecrow Press, Inc.
A Member of the Rowman & Littlefield Publishing Group
4720 Boston Way, Lanham, Maryland 20706
www.scarecroweducation.com

4 Pleydell Gardens, Folkestone
Kent CT20 2DN, England

British Library Cataloguing in Publication Information Available

Library of Congress Cataloging-in-Publication Data

Fibkins, William L.
    An administrator's guide to better teacher mentoring / William L. Fibkins.
      p. cm.
    Includes bibliographical references (p.) and index.
    ISBN 0-8108-4401-X (alk.) ISBN 0-8108-4280-7 (pbk : alk. paper)
      1. Mentoring in education—United States—Handbooks, manuals, etc. 2.
Teachers—In-service training—United States—Handbooks, manuals, etc. 3.
School administrators—United States—Handbooks, manuals, etc. I. Title.

LB1731.4 .F53 2002
371.102—dc21   2002020081

♾ ™ The paper used in this publication meets the minimum requirements of
American National Standard for Information Sciences—Permanence of Paper for
Printed Library Materials, ANSI/NISO Z39.48-1992.
Manufactured in the United States of America.

Contents

Acknowledgments

This book is dedicated to my mentor George Forbes. George was principal of Bay Shore Junior High School, Bay Shore, Long Island, New York, during the 1970s and 1980s. Bay Shore Junior was a large school with a population of over 1,600 students with a multicultural population. Given these large numbers of pre-adolescent students at the school, it was not an easy setting to administer. However, George helped create a safe, caring, and hopeful learning environment. He was a kind but strong administrator who believed in collegiality and involving every staff member in the education process. George also understood what good teaching was all about and he didn't hesitate to address poor teaching and discipline practices. He did whatever was necessary to help prevent his teachers and students from drifting into failure patterns. He wanted everyone to succeed.

As such he had finely honed mentoring skills, he successfully modeled these skills in every school venue. He knew how to listen, be non-judgmental, and encourage new ideas and approaches. But he also could accept criticism and understood how to overcome resistance to new projects. He was available to his staff, students, and parents in times of professional and personal crisis.

George understood he couldn't be a model and mentor for every teacher on his staff. He delegated responsibility and helped other staff members gain needed leadership experience and exposure. In my case he encouraged me to develop a school-day teacher-training center in conjunction with the State University of New York at Stony Brook. In a real sense he invited me to become his partner in training teachers in the school. He was not threatened by my new role or the involvement of a university. He understood the need for a shared intervention if the teaching staff was to grow professionally and avoid burnout. He couldn't do the job on his own and without help.

In closing let me say that George's intense involvement with teachers, students, and parents probably came at a cost. Being accessible, available, and continuing to know and understand each staff member as they move through the various stages of their careers takes great energy, will, determination, and time. When teachers find a mentor from whom they can get help, support, and develop new skills, the floodgates open. Word is spread among the faculty that "really he listens and understands what is happening in my. . . ." Teachers no longer feel alone or without support. In this mentoring process, my guess is, George had to give up some of his personal life so he could complete his mission of helping each teacher and student be all they can be. The good news, and reward, is that he succeeded with me and my colleagues. Who knows what would have happened to our careers if a George Forbes weren't around to teach, advise, and guide us.

Foreword

Since the middle of the 1980s public attention has been drawn to the debate over the quality of America's schools. One repeatedly used indicator, common to every public, private, or parochial school in our nation, is the effectiveness of the classroom teacher. An effective teacher, in the minds of many Americans, is one who enables students to learn while simultaneously advancing individual students to the next tier of their achievement. Perceived as a collective, renewable resource, teachers continue to be upgraded through a deliberate and thoughtful process defined as a professional development continuum, a guided sequential progression that begins with mentoring.

Research documents that teachers who know a lot about teaching and who work in environments that allow them to know students well, are the critical elements of successful student learning. The question plaguing school boards and administrators today is how best to elevate beginning teachers to a satisfactory level of effectiveness while stabilizing attrition rates. One educative solution is offered by Bill Fibkins in this book, a process plan for total school involvement in an expanded and enriched set of experiences designed to nurture, support, instruct, and incorporate an entry-level teacher into the working life of a school and district. He does not suggest that mentoring is easy or a quick fix; however, he does reiterate that it is worth doing.

The stated goals of the book are to give direction to the selection and preparation of mentors, design a mentoring curriculum, and monitor a school-based mentoring program. It is a practical step-by-step approach to establishing a program, a logical approach to a complicated process, one of many to be sustained and managed by a building or district administrator. Yet a mentoring process, such as the one described by Bill, is a program that will demonstrate annual gain as incentives for retirement become available and as pressure builds on local boards of education to reduce class size. While a greater need for novice teachers continues so does the need for an induction program, a complex set of tasks comprehensive and instructional in nature. Mentoring as a school improvement initiative, which is Fibkins's thrust, is based on the logic of mutual benefits among and between the major constituencies active in the public schools: teachers, administrators, parents and students, and unions. It is a process expected to benefit others in the school organization by improving the quality and ownership of decision making, reducing resistance to change and, ultimately, impacting student achievement. Mentoring grows ever more important as alternate teacher certification programs expand and teachers, entering classrooms without the benefit of supervised field experiences, are expected to perform at levels of competency.

Discouraged and disillusioned, many teachers quit, with half leaving the profession within five years. One purpose of mentoring, aside from offering support, encouragement, insight, and practice, is to retain new teachers within the education system. The residual effects of teacher-mentor programs most often are related to the quality of the mentor–mentee relationship, a relationship with an intense and specific life expectancy. During that designated time a mentor is expected to encourage the beginner to reflect upon the professional, social, and cultural issues of the school community.

Attributes and characteristics of an effective mentor include the ability to provide focused and frequent communication. Communication includes feedback, listening, and responding, useful skills to support the transition of teachers into their professional capacities within a school. This verbal and, on occasion, written give-and-take tend to work particularly well when communication focuses on the improvement of teaching and student achievement.

School leaders and university deans continue to explore ways in which they can partner in the preparation of pre-service and in-service teachers. One such partnership could revolve around mentoring and supporting the beginning teacher, helping to dispel the professional loneliness that comes with the job while providing opportunities to expand their knowledge base of best practices for classroom success. Other partnership activities might include school-based teacher education programs, cohort placements of field experience students, and co-teaching campus courses by P–12 teachers.

During this decade, schools will hire two million new teachers. How well new teachers are selected, educated, and introduced into the schools may be the most important factors in the success or failure of public schools. Without well-educated and freshly motivated teachers, schools cannot succeed. New teachers start their work charged with idealism, committed to making improvements, and may find their innovative ideas stifled by tradition-bound colleagues in the schools. Mentoring will not solve all the ills of the American education system; however, it is one process that has made a difference in the life and work of new teachers. It is a process that makes a deliberate and sustained commitment to the education of educators.

Martha M. Mobley, Ph.D.
Director, Teaching Performance Center
Kean University

1

The Pressing Need for Administrators to Take on a New Mentoring Role

We live in a world in which mentoring, coaching, team building, and empowering have become standard practices for many successful corporations and corporate leaders. Concerned and committed employees want to learn how to be successful and play an important role in building their company. They expect their CEOs to make ongoing training easily accessible in order to prepare them for their ever-changing roles. As Michael Hammer and James Champy suggest, ongoing training to constantly assess the needs of customers and to learn new skills to address these needs are top priorities for successful corporations.[1] "Change is constant" is a given theme. In fact, many Americans work in a rather democratic setting in which skill is what counts, not dress, degree, or background. Collegiality, the sharing of authority among colleagues, is promoted, as is the theme that each member of the corporation must be a constant learner if the organization is to thrive.

I believe this process embraced by so much of corporate America needs to be adopted by future-looking educators as well. If any place has constant change, it is America's schools. Students, parents, and community members look to schools to solve the academic and, increasingly, nonacademic or personal problems of students. Education opens doors; it is the ticket to a seat in our highly competitive society. Yet ongoing mentoring for teachers, investing time and money in their professional development, has not caught on in the same way that it has in corporate life. Some would say the reason for this lack of a national effort to establish school-based teacher mentoring programs is a lack of funding and resource allocation. They have a point, of course, because schools always need more resources. However, I believe additional, more complex reasons keep lo-

1

cal schools from establishing ongoing mentoring programs led by successful and respected local educators. Here are five reasons:

1. Many school administrators are very busy people. They rightfully say they do not have time to mentor every teacher in the school. Crisis resolution, budget preparation, overseeing curriculum development, and carrying out state education department testing mandates are just a few of the many complicated tasks that are the responsibility of school administration. When teachers and community members think of the role of administrator, these are some of the tasks they associate with the role. Like it or not, many administrators are locked into a traditional role in which convention dictates that they are primarily business leaders and problem solvers, not mentors of teachers.

   Unfortunately, this limited conception of the duties of administrators keeps them from developing a mentoring program to better prepare teachers to meet the needs of their changing customer population—students and parents. Don't administrators have enough on their plates already? Assuming total responsibility for another major program, one in which they would be mentoring every teacher in the school, may seem too much for beleaguered administrators. And they are correct. Given the limits of their time and ability, they alone cannot institute a mentoring program.

2. Many administrators also rightfully say that even if they had the time, they would still lack the necessary training and methodology to acquire skills to help them become effective mentors. Many are not accustomed to working in intimate, one-on-one relationships in which they help teachers, situations that call for behaviors and skills such as building trust, being patient in order for change to occur, and offering ongoing support. While much literature exists about teachers as mentors for students, I believe critics pay less attention to what it takes for administrators to be effective mentors for teachers.

3. There are few role models for administrators to emulate if they indeed did have the time to become effective mentors for their teachers. How does the administrator as mentor behave? The role of an administrator is a powerful role that involves quick reactions, decision making, and politicking. Mentoring is different. It is a shared

role that requires delicate and caring intervention and feedback. It is a slow process built on mutual trust and self-respect. It works only when both parties, the mentor and the protégé, clearly understand the areas that need improvement and how the mentor can be useful. It is a teaching position carried on in the classroom setting, a far cry from the administrator's often crisis-centered and chaotic office. The mentoring setting is not without the conflict or resistance that comes with helping teachers change, but the conflict is subtler. It requires new, tactful approaches and skills. Mentoring also requires the belief that change is possible with patient and trustful intervention.

4. If the administrator had more time, opportunities for skill acquisition, and a model to follow to become an effective mentor, would he or she be willing to take on this "different" role? In all likelihood, teachers, students, parents, and community members at first will be confused with this new mentoring role, and resistance may run high. People may talk, saying things such as, "Why is the administrator spending so much time helping teachers? Doesn't he belong back in the office?" Change is difficult, especially when the head of the school begins to take on a new role that is not in keeping with tradition, assumptions of the past, and conventional wisdom.

5. Even if all of the above needs are met, administrators need to come to terms with the issue that providing mentoring for every teacher is a serious move. It is not small change. Will they get the support and resources needed from the central office? Being out of the office trying to forge new mentoring relations can take administrators out of the political issues of the school. While they may be more visible to teachers, they would be increasingly out of the office, not dealing with the self-promotional aspects that are key to survival in the highly politicized world of school administrators. They may even learn to value mentoring above the more crass aspects of their work that politicizing requires. Shining one's light all day can be draining, but being out of the picture can be dangerous to one's career. Making mentoring a major part of an administrator's work can be risky business if pursued with too much enthusiasm.

I believe these reasons are all valid. Administrators are busy. Many lack mentoring skills and a model to follow. A risk is involved in taking on a "different" administrative role that may leave them vulnerable to those who want a more traditional, office-centered administrator. But I believe these risks are overshadowed by the growing public demand for teachers who are well prepared. These demands are a driving force in helping administrators take a hands-on role in retraining their teaching staff. I agree with David A. Gilman and Barbara Lanman-Givens when they suggest that school districts need to restructure the principal's role to allow them to focus on student learning and instructional leadership and to face fewer demands for management tasks.[2] Principals will be able to devote more time to improving instructional leadership and student learning when they can delegate some managerial duties to an assistant principal or office manager.

But change is slow and sometimes requires small, incremental steps. I argue that school administrators can proceed to play a major leadership role in developing a mentoring program without totally restructuring their daily job requirements and becoming completely immersed in a new role. Here is how:

1. While administrators cannot do much about the demands of their job and time requirements, they can teach themselves mentoring skills. They can prepare themselves for the mentoring role.

2. Knowing they cannot establish and maintain a mentoring program alone, administrators can form a mentoring team made up of an assistant principal, department chairperson, teacher leader, and counselor leader. The administrator will have a place in the mentoring process but will be joined by a competent team made up of educators who are known and respected in the school.

3. The administrator can train this team to be effective mentors and ongoing sources of support and training for each other.

4. The administrator can lead the way in promoting the mentoring program. In selling the program, simple questions work best. For example, "Wouldn't it be better for our staff to be well-trained and better prepared than to be resting on our laurels, waiting for the next crisis?"

5. The administrator can encourage teachers who have been mentored to take on a mentoring role with colleagues, thereby widening the mentoring circle and creating new opportunities for renewal. This

process will create a new role for teachers—mentors for colleagues as well as teachers of students.

6. The administrator can encourage the mentoring team to pass on their skills to support staff and students, thereby creating a school-wide mentoring process in which all members of the school community have the opportunity to be learners and begin a new way of operating, leaving past failures and setbacks in the past where they belong.

This plan allows administrators to create a mentoring program and thereby escape the self-defeating illusion that they are the only resource for training and renewal in the school. This mentoring plan can create a freeing process for administrators, altering their role in a subtle but clearly defined way. In the process of being a mentor leader and mentor, the administrator is moving away from a traditional supervisory role and acting as a facilitator, an enabler, and someone whose job includes the development of people and their skills. The mentoring program is also an acknowledgement that America's schools are experiencing a time of great change and the roles of educators must change with these demanding times. In turn, the role of teachers in today's world is multidimensional and dynamic. It is a role that requires intellect, a desire to learn and take risks, emotional and physical wellness, and openness to personal and professional change. This is not a slot that can be filled by just anyone with a degree, completed coursework, and certification—a "warm body," as they say on the frontlines in the schools—sent naively into the battleground of the classroom.

Effective mentoring tears away the faulty assumption raised by critics that teachers' work involves simple, easily achievable tasks. A teacher is a warm body, not exactly a rocket scientist, some would say. To the contrary, as any effective teacher knows, teaching involves interacting with many, sometimes hundreds, of students and staff each day. Much of this interaction is complicated because it requires the teacher to know the needs of the many students he or she is trying to serve and how to make use of the best skills to meet these needs. To be effective, the teacher must be aware of each student's personality, home life, motivation level, physical and emotional condition, relationship with peers and other teachers, and most importantly, the student's goals and dreams. Each student has his or her own story that needs to be understood and respected. Contrary to the public's widely held vision of a soft job with summers off, teaching is a very demanding role. As I often stress, teachers need to be in excellent physical, intellectual, and emotional shape if they are to do this important job well. They also need a mentor who is able to listen to their needs, concerns, and fears, a mentor who can help keep them up to date and master the skills they need to be at the top of their game.

Initially, teachers themselves often are reluctant to become involved in professional renewal development programs. In the busy world of teaching, teachers are constantly dealing with the present, with the daily issues of students, parents, colleagues, and administrators. Learning new skills that can help them deal with emerging issues is not a reality in most schools because there is no mechanism in place to make it happen. While many teachers admit that they feel the need to learn new skills, nothing much happens unless schools make clear, easily accessible, attractive, ongoing, and trusted intervention programs available. Also, teachers' skills do not stay the same, but get better or worse over time. Leaving teachers without opportunities for mentoring is hazardous and undesirable.

Leaving teachers without opportunities for mentoring is not cost effective. Poorly trained teachers can be problematic and even harmful. As a result, administrators in some schools continually find themselves in a reactive mode of trying to dig themselves and their staff out of ill-advised interaction between teachers and students. It is a daily, time consuming, and dismal practice trying to right problems related to poor, sometimes inept student disciplining, parent communication, staff relationships, and unprofessional practices. Rather than taking a proactive role in mentoring and training teachers, many administrators find themselves caught in a catch-22 situation: they have no mentoring program in place, so they have no proactive mechanism to help troubled teachers become effective. The constant stream of rectifying the problems caused by teachers who, as one would naively expect should know better, is debilitating. But in fact, some teachers do not know better and it is not their fault. They are, for the most part, simply untrained to handle the problems and issues that are part of their duties in America's changing schools, whether they are new, midcareer, or veteran. Untrained teachers are problems waiting to happen and everyone in the school—administrators, fellow teachers, students, and parents—usually knows their plight.

Here is an example of what often happens when teachers are left without effective intervention and mentoring. Anyone who has been a classroom teacher knows teaching has many emotional pitfalls. One can easily lose one's way going down new roads without experience and direction. As Dr. Seuss suggests—and it certainly applies to the lives of teachers— "You will come to a place where the streets are not marked. Some windows are lighted . . . but mostly they're darked. Simple it's not, I'm afraid you will find, for a mind-maker-upper to make up his mind."[3] When teachers enter the field they are often unaware of their own conflicting values and feelings about students. It's new territory with no past experience to guide them—the "windows are darked"—except for their own limited personal and professional backgrounds. Teachers tend to make their job comfortable by spending more time with students who are like them, avoiding students who are different and whose physical appearance, background, personality, or behavior inexplicably stirs up unwanted, hostile feelings in them. Spend time observing teacher/student interactions and no doubt you will see many teachers directing their questions and gravitating toward certain students, usually the brightest and the best behaved. They seem at home with these students because they pose no threat.

When teachers gravitate toward a certain type of student, this means that there are many other students whom they seem to avoid, seemingly afraid to make contact for fear of rejection. What do teachers do when confronted with students who may reject them, who are not willing to play their game? They hesitate and stumble, looking for the right response that usually doesn't come, drawing a line between them and the resisting student. A sort of battle begins and teachers are usually alone with the problem. Do they share it at a faculty meeting or in the faculty room? This usually is not the place they can get help with their problem, so they think it is better to keep it to themselves. Maybe no one will notice. In many schools, teachers know they are on their own. Help and intervention are things they talked about in college courses. It is not a reality for them. Once again, the role of a teacher reminds us of what Dr. Seuss says, that at times you will be, "*All alone!* Whether you like it or not, alone will be something you'll be quite a lot. And when you're alone, there's a very good chance you'll meet things that scare you right out of your pants. There are some, down the road between hither and yon, that can scare you so much you won't want to go on." Being alone, these teachers watch the clock, waiting for the period to end, telling themselves to keep the students busy and under control. Tomorrow is Friday. TGIF! I've survived another week. June is three months away. Maybe next year's classes will be easier. The other teachers say this is the toughest class in years. Maybe it's not me. Maybe it's them.

I believe this example is common all too often in our schools. Is this a natural condition? Yes. The classroom really is a battlefield. It is a place to test the teacher's skills, courage, will to win, compassion, and endurance against some students who by nature will resist and act out. Yet it is the teacher's responsibility to win these students over and get them on track to a good education. It is the teacher's ballgame to win or lose. It often is not peaceful, calm, and correct. It is a heated chess game. The teacher makes a move and the students counter it. If the teacher is unskilled or lacks the will to win or the compassion and the endurance to go the distance with these students, problems will arise. Courage plays an important part. Teachers invariably experience a classroom situation that can, as Dr. Seuss depicts it, scare them and make them not want to go on. Doing battle and losing can bring about surrendering and letting the students do what they want. One hears from a teacher, "It's not my job to straighten them out." Often, crying burnout and casting blame on the students can be all too easy. Finding the courage to regain control in difficult classroom situations is not easy, especially when the teacher is alone or does not know how to ask for help when the ship is sinking.

Left unaddressed and unresolved, a hostile classroom can limit the positive impact the teacher can have on *all* of the students in the class. To be effective with all students, the teacher needs to understand complicated student/teacher interaction and learn the necessary skills to make contact with each student in the room. It is important to understand that all teachers bring their own biases into the classroom that either enhance or interfere with the teaching and learning process. As I mentioned earlier, factors such as the students' gender, race, culture, personality, and behavior, can unexpectedly set off conflicting feelings within the teacher that spring from personal biases and limited background. These conflicting feelings often go unspoken. The myth that teachers are supposed to like—even love, some say—and support *all* of their students usually prevails in the schools and hides the real mentoring work that has to be done. Spending too much time with some students and avoiding others is not a cost-effective strategy and does a disservice to each group. The students who are unconnected and left out may personalize the rejection and consider it their problem, not the teacher's. Effective mentoring can help teachers develop a set of skills that will help them avoid the classroom polarization that usually sets in when they are unaware of and unprepared to deal with students who come from different cultures and ways of behaving.

Traditionally, many schools have not made mentoring and supervising teachers and investing in their continued improvement, a top priority. The mentoring process that exists usually involves a few classroom observations followed by a conference and written evaluation. It is a process to get out of the way as fast as possible for both the administrator and the teacher. In their meetings they often engage in little or no conversation about how to improve the teacher's skills and do not point out specific teacher/student interactions that need to be addressed over time. They also infrequently discuss the teacher's own fears and questions. Why is this teacher uneasy with certain students? Why does he seem to discipline certain students more harshly? Why does he lecture so much and leave little time for students' participation? In this hurried evaluation process, the teacher and administrator do not ask questions that would bring the hidden concerns and needs of the teacher out in the open to be addressed without judgment. Most likely they do not have time set aside for the administrator to model new classroom techniques and approaches and suggest other sources of support and training within both the school and community, truly to be a teaching principal.

What does take place in these so-called supervision and mentoring conversations often focuses on what I call the business aspects of teaching. The administrator makes sure that the teacher has enough materials, is current on testing schedules, is ready for parent conferences, knows when grades are due in the office, and so on. To use a basketball analogy, the administrator does not blow the whistle unless there is some flagrant violation going on with students and parents. The administrator is there to make sure that everything is under control and keep things from getting out of hand. The process is often apologetic: "I'm sorry, Tom, I hate to intrude, but you know I have to make these yearly evaluations. Let me come in for a few minutes during third period. I'm sure there are no problems."

When it takes this form, teachers often view supervision and mentoring with sarcasm and dark humor, a game to be played but without much substance. It becomes an interaction guided by the words, "Let's not make this a problem for each other; we are busy people." Clearly this is not a model that creates conditions for helping teachers identify problem areas and learn new skills. This is not to say that administrators in this role are not caring or that they are disinterested in their teachers' professional development. Of course not. But the mentoring role described above keeps them in an observing, not a teaching, role. It is a process in which both the administrator and the teacher settle for less. What presents itself as an opportunity for real dialog and change is downgraded to a chore. It is a lose-lose situation for both the administrator and the teacher. Teachers remain stuck using skills that are out of date and tend to produce failure. It is a bit like giving them World War II rifles to fight a war in which the opposition has modern electronic weaponry. Administrators remain stuck as well, using supervisory skills and a process that robs them of real interaction with teachers.

I believe these conditions can be changed. The mentoring plan I suggest can alter the way teachers continue to grow and learn, and it can also bring needed change to the way administrators view their role in improving their teachers' performance.

The potential for professional growth involved in effective mentoring is not just for teachers. In developing a trusted mentoring role with teachers, administrators also create a teacher-learner climate in which they, too, become open to examining their own skills. Where are their strengths as a mentor? For example, are they an effective listener, nonjudgmental, able to offer constructive feedback, successfully model the behaviors they are asking their teachers to take on? Just as important, where are their skills lacking? What areas do they need to improve? Remember, the skills of the administrator, like those of his teachers, do not stay the same. They either get better or worse over time. Without reflection and positive, nonjudgmental feedback, administrators can get stuck as well, using and relying on skills no longer relevant in today's schools. In this intimate mentoring relationship, they too, like their teachers, become aware of the barriers that threaten and undermine their work. For example, they become aware of those teachers whom they avoid and whom seem to threaten their role as administrator. And like teachers with their students, mentors need to work hard to overcome these barriers by being in touch with their teachers and their personalities, home life, motivation levels, physical and emotional well-being, relationships with peers and colleagues, students and parents, and most important, their goals, dreams, and fears. I believe all teachers dream of being something special in the classroom. In the mentoring process, the administrator begins to become aware of these dynamics and focuses on the new skills he needs to get teachers committed to the process. Also, administrators usually don't receive truthful and direct feedback concerning their work. Being a mentor opens up the possibility of direct feedback from teachers.

Clearly, mentoring is an extremely useful and helpful way for administrators and teachers to stay on top of their game. In very pragmatic ways, mentoring also helps define where we need to put our resources: in teacher improvement. By zeroing in on a way to provide teachers with ongoing skills acquisition and renewal throughout their careers, we are avoiding vague, illusive definitions such as "school reform." Michael A. Ballin— president of the Clark Foundation, a foundation whose mission is to help improve schools and the education of children—questions whether the millions his foundation has spent on large-scale reform programs have had lasting impact:

> Talk about something that is hard to do . . . try to change a system. Even under the best of conditions it can absorb or co-opt the energy of the reformers. It matters relatively little whether we can craft great institutions out of existing schools. Schools, after all, are institutions; education is the work of educators, not the work of schools. Good schools help; great schools help more; but great teachers are a far more precious commodity. As the Clark Foundation has discovered, addressing the system rather than the specific actions of individual teachers leads us to commit the cardinal sin of educators . . . confusing treatment with the cure. For the Clark Foundation, for the massed armies of school reformers . . . I have only one bit of advice to aid escape from the futilities of school reform. Stop trying to make schools great schools and take up the task of trying to make teachers great teachers. We engage in school reform teacher by teacher.[4]

Mentoring also provides schools with a way to avoid teacher turnover and attrition. As the National Education Association (NEA) suggests, more than a million veteran teachers are nearing retirement.[5] Twenty percent of first-time hires leave their teaching jobs within three years. In urban districts, nearly fifty percent of newcomers leave the profession during their first five years of teaching. America will need two million new teachers in the next decade and experts predict that half of the teachers who will be in public school classrooms have not yet been hired. By 2006, America will educate almost three million more children than it does today—more than fifty-four million youngsters. We will need intervention to help new hires and also cut down on unnecessary turnovers. The NEA recommends that newly hired teachers be assigned a mentor who will assist them with everything from classroom management to student assessment. An effective mentoring program can also address turnover and attrition. A report issued by Public Agenda, "A Sense of Calling: Why Teachers Teach," found that seventy-six percent of the nine hundred teachers polled contend that they are made to be "scapegoats" for problems in education.[6] Moreover, a majority told pollsters that they don't see opportunities for career advancement nor do they feel appreciated for the work they do. The teachers also reported that their jobs are made more difficult because they lack the skills to maintain classroom discipline. Six in ten teachers said that most take over classrooms without the requisite experience in handling them. The study found keeping capable teachers in the classroom depends on improving each educator's quality of life during the school day rather than increasing their paychecks.

The issues raised in the Public Agenda report—scapegoats, feeling unappreciated, little opportunity for advancement, lack of needed skills—can be addressed. If they are left unaddressed, we should not be surprised by the fact that twenty percent of new teachers flee the classroom after three years and that fifty percent leave urban schools after five years. Teachers are telling us what they need, not only to survive but also to become great teachers. Let's give them what they need: skills, accolades, support, career novelty. Mentoring can help produce this change.

I believe David C. Berliner captures the value of mentoring when he suggests the following:

[M]entoring programs are promising for two reasons. First, they cut the dropout rate of teachers from roughly 50 to 15 percent during the first five years of teaching. Without mentoring our [teacher] shortages will grow. The second reason we need mentoring is a moral, not a pragmatic, one. We must not abandon beginners who have been placed in the complex world of teaching. Through apprenticeships novices can learn from masters. Mentoring helps new teachers think about their experience, and it helps them to handle the emotional side of teaching. Teaching is an emotionally draining experience. Teachers get caught up in the lives of kids and their parents. They need to know what a healthy response is and when to put up boundaries. They need clear advice about how to do something better or different the next time they teach it.[7]

I believe there are two additional benefits from the mentoring process. Well-trained mentors are also ideally positioned to advise and guide mid-career and veteran teachers who run into difficulties as their careers evolve. Renewal opportunities need to be available for all teacher groups in the school setting. Secondly, master teachers benefit immensely in their new role of advising and guiding newcomers. They are able to use their hard-won classroom experience in a positive way, instead of being isolated in their classrooms with no opportunity to be a teacher of teachers. Teachers as mentors of colleagues can act as catalysts to reinvigorate experienced teachers and create a sense of novelty and change, a chance to show others how they have learned from many setbacks and failures over time. This is a major change.

Berliner also accurately describes where we are in developing school-based mentoring programs when he suggests:

> Mentoring is not widespread enough. Here at Arizona State we mentor more than 1,000 teachers in their first two years of teaching. About 300 teachers from the school districts mentor these new teachers. . . . Every state really needs a program like this. It costs a few hundred dollars per teacher per year for the first two years of the teacher's professional life. It's the pragmatic and morally right thing to do.

I suggest the same applies for midcareer and veteran teachers, as well.

The mentoring process presents school administrators with a unique opportunity to help every teacher become more effective in his or her classroom. How do they proceed in this important mission? An important first step is to better understand what it is like to be a competent teacher. Administrators need to observe master teachers to help them identify a model of an effective and competent teacher. This understanding can help educators focus on what kinds of teacher behaviors and skills create, foster, and support these models. I believe that it is important for educators to understand how professionals in other fields such as music, dance, and sports become successful in their craft. What can we learn from their successful careers? What barriers and obstacles do they face? What are the parallels between their successes and those of teachers?

NOTES

1. Michael Hammer and James Champy, *Reengineering the Corporation* (New York: HarperCollins, 1993), 28.

2. David A. Gilman and Barbara Lanman-Givens,. "Where Have All the Principals Gone?" *Educational Leadership* 58 (8) (May 2001): 73.

3. Dr. Seuss, *Oh, the Places You'll Go!* (New York: Random House, 1990).

4. Peter Temes, "The End of School Reform," *Education Week* 4 April 2001, http://www.edweek.org/ew/ewstory.cfm?Slug=29temes.h20 (4 April 2001).

5. National Education Association, Teacher Quality Fact Sheet, "Teaching," http://www.nea.org/teaching/shortage.html (20 April 2001).

6. Julie Blair, "Teacher Idealism Tempered by Frustration, Survey Finds," *Education Week* (31 May 2000), 6.

7. David C. Berliner, "Improving the Quality of the Teaching Force," *Educational Leadership* 58 (8) (May 2001): 10.

2

A Vision of the Competent Master Teacher

Before we proceed to examine how administrators can understand and implement a teacher mentoring plan, I suggest we consider the qualities of the model teacher we are trying to create in an effective mentoring process. What is our picture of a competent teacher? What are the parallels between a competent teacher and performers in other fields such as athletics, dance, music, stage, and film? What can we learn from other professionals about issues related to skill acquisition, renewal, failure, success, commitment, aging, courage, and the ongoing battle to ward off extinction? Teachers and administrators are, after, all, performers. They work live on stage each day. Their performance is closely watched and critiqued by colleagues, students, parents, and community members. This audience assesses the teacher and forms an opinion and, like criticisms of Broadway actors and actresses, some are not kind. Teaching, like other performing arts, is risky business. If teachers fail to deliver a good performance, their worth and value are diminished. They may keep their job, but skill-building opportunities and chances for renewal are not always easily available or desired. Dr. Seuss reminds us that "unslumping [ourselves] is not easily done," and it is no easier in teaching and the arts. Stephen Sondheim, the great American composer, suggests, "What I found out in my work is that everyone is talented. It's just that some people get it developed and some don't. Developing your talent takes work."[1]

In this chapter I share my vision of what competent teachers looks like: the hard work that they must put into the process and the realities that they must face to ward off the ever-present forces of failure and extinction. This picture will hopefully add to our understanding of why the leadership of school administrators in the mentoring process is so important. Not letting one teacher fall through the cracks of failure is an achievable goal, one made easier with the recognition that the craft is demanding and requires ongoing hard work and commitment. There are no easy days. Teaching, like the other performing crafts—music, acting, dance, and athletics—requires a special set of skills that are honed and refined over a professional's lifetime. Teachers who successfully develop their craft understand that the process is evolutionary and includes many failed experiences in the search to become an effective teacher. It takes a skilled craftsman to know how to connect the dots of the past and the present—the visible and the hidden—and find the pattern. In the classroom, teachers use their craft to show their students that the world is safe, even with all the violence, and manageable. The students may come from homes that are abusive, even violent, but in the classroom (literally a home away from home), they fit, they are safe, and they belong. The teacher, for the duration of the school day, is the parent/mentor they need to show them the way. He or she gives students the necessary skills to move through life's challenges. A teacher makes students feel useful, optimistic, and confident that they have a role to play in the world.

A competent teacher's daily work is meticulously crafted, from the first hello in the morning until the yellow school bus heads home after class. If one observes teachers closely, one sees a form to their work and a process in how they go about creating a classroom climate in which every student can learn. Of course, they are affected by events beyond the classroom—calls for education reform, budget battles, issues the administration has with the union, family problems that affect students, and cries of teacher burnout from colleagues. But their main focus is the classroom. Successful teachers know they have to shield themselves from the external distractions that are kindling outside the classroom. They discipline themselves so they do not fall prey to these distractions that may sap their energy and spirit. In a sense they are like athletes intent on getting to the Super Bowl, the World Series, or the Final Four. They must tune out the external noise, conserve their energy, and stay focused.

Of course, teachers are not at all immune to events in the school, the district, the educational community, or the struggles of fellow teachers to be more effective in their work. They just do not allow these events to rule their life and get in the way of their major goal, to be the very best teacher each day for the students and to serve as a role model for peers—some who say they want to better their craft and others who seem satisfied to be less than they can be. Teachers understand that peers, many of whom have settled for mediocrity and rebuff every effort to raise their level of skill, *can* be coached into more training given the right intervention. The teacher does not reject or judge these peers. They are available to help these teachers and include them in the ongoing work of improving the craft of teaching. Teachers make sure to avoid cynicism and the debilitating effect it has on his craft. They are akin to dancer Twyla Tharp when she says, "Cynicism is very de-energizing. And dance needs energy to go on. You have to believe that what you are doing is important . . . so there is no point in being cynical if you want to dance. So get over it."[2] Teaching also needs energy to go on. The model teacher walks a fine line, being available to peers who are cynical about teaching but not taking these words to heart. Good teachers can't afford cynicism. They get over it.

In the laboratory of the classroom, model teachers view themselves as having the skills and desire to teach *every child* who enters the classroom. They continually work at their craft and over time develop a unique style, one that showcases their talents. When it comes to education reform, competent teachers listen but do not stop their work or change their style to wait for the next round of proposals. They do not hold their breath and wait for change to come to them. Instead, they see themselves as agents initiating change in the place where it counts most, their classrooms.

For teachers like Ana England, a sixth-grade math teacher in Watsonville, California, little is expected to change in the current debate over education reform. "I've looked at the state standards [in science and math] and the things the Board has crossed out are words like 'analyze' and 'explain your thinking.' But there's nothing in the standards that says you can't teach that. A good teacher is going to do that, in addition to teaching the basic skills." Nathan Tarkov suggests that any attempt to dictate a solution (to teachers) is doomed: "Whatever the curriculum, ultimately it comes down to the teacher, especially the teacher's energy and character, and sense of humor and ability to relate to young people, and not just the policies the teacher follows."[3] The question successful teachers always ask when it comes to innovation and reform is, "How does it improve learning in my classroom?"[4]

A teacher's own failure and resistance are also major factors in developing a unique teaching style. Much of what teachers do each day results in failure. Becoming better at the craft leads a teacher down many roads, some of which are dead ends. Failed lesson plans, failed approaches to resolving a student's personal problems, the discouragement of a bad day when everything seems to backfire—all of these can lay a teacher low. Getting some students to do what they don't want to do—work harder, get better grades, have hopes and dreams—is no easy task! It is tough work, a demanding labor not unlike the assembly line's constant pressure. Even the best teachers can lose their way and face a dead-end. Constant reassessment of what is going on in the classroom—is what I am doing right now working?—is a critical skill for the competent teacher.

Becoming a successful teacher is an evolutionary process that requires work, discipline, focus, overcoming failure, developing a style, and refining that style so it continues to work. It means continually searching for new approaches and giving up what once worked but is no longer effective. It is a constant, though not always conscious, process of addition and deletion. It means taking risks, giving up the tried and true for a glimpse of a distant vision. Effective teachers are like musicians who are constantly improvising with new lyrics and notes so they don't become outdated. The career of the competent teacher is no different from that of other performing artists and athletes. Teachers improvise to meet the individual needs of each child and create the conditions under which each child can learn. In the words of jazz pianist Keith Jarrett, "When you are improvising, you can play anything, and you can make it work somehow."[5]

Changing and improvising take work, practice, and discipline. As composer Stephen Sondheim suggests, it is a process that one works at to become better. Sondheim reports that the first music teacher he had at Williams College, Robert Barrows, "made me realize that all my romantic views of art were nonsense. He taught me that art is something to be worked at." And so is teaching. Many teachers have talent, but some get developed and some don't.

Woody Allen, actor and director, suggests that to stay at the top of your craft, "You just have to work. You can't read your reviews."[6] Frank Sinatra, perhaps the greatest popular singer of our time, gives us a glimpse into his work at developing the Sinatra style.

> I began swimming in public pools, taking laps under water and thinking song lyrics to myself as I swam holding my breath. Over six months or so,

I began to delineate a method of long phraseology. Instead of singing only two bars at a time . . . like most other guys . . . I was able to sing six bars, and in some songs eight bars, without taking a visible or audible breath. That gave the melody a flowing, unbroken quality, and that's what made my sound different.[7]

Much the same can be said of the sound of the great trumpet player and singer Louis Armstrong. It is often said that his singing is a direct extension, a kind of mirror, of his playing. In fact, he never sang out of tune or put accents or notes in the wrong places. He knew how to articulate and how to set each song, no matter how trifling, into focus. And so do competent teachers. They too know how to articulate, set each lesson plan, no matter how trifling, into focus.[8]

Performing artists, like teachers, face bouts of failure and self-doubt throughout their careers. Some overcome these barriers and move on to fulfill their promise. Others get stuck and finish out their careers unfulfilled and jaded. Visit any school and you will find teachers who have overcome barriers and are seen as stars of their craft. You will also find teachers who got stuck and have not developed. In the passage that follows, I describe examples of how the battle to stay at the height of one's career is fought by famous performing artists and athletes. I believe their stories of achievements and setbacks can help would-be mentors understand the precariousness and risk that are a part of the craft of education as well. Performing, being in front of the crowd, doing it well—this is hard work. Done daily, five days a week, invariably leads to some wrong roads, misdirection, even breakdowns among the successes.

Frank Sinatra. Singer and actor. Frank Sinatra suffered a series of setbacks in the early 1950s. No one would hire him. "I was in trouble. I was busted . . . I did lie down for a while and had some large bar bills for about a year. Then I said, 'OK, holiday's over . . . let's go back to work.'" But his comeback was slow. In an age of rock 'n' roll he had to travel—Australia in 1959, the legendary Melbourne concert—to work and stay connected to a live audience. He even announced his retirement in 1970. But he began to hit his stride again in 1973 with the release of the aptly titled album *Ol' Blue Eyes is Back.* His comeback was complete when he gave a concert, *Sinatra: The Main Event . . . Live,* to a sold-out crowd of 20,000 people at Madison Square Garden on October 13, 1974. His opening comments at the concert are poignant: "Thank you. It's my great pleasure to be back in New York and to be able to work again. . . . I'm ready and I'm set."[9]

Twyla Tharp. Dancer and choreographer. Tharp is troubled and a little exasperated by a dark mood that has seemed to settle over dance recently.

> My business is simply the work I do . . . but I must say I have little patience for what I basically think is the disregard for the abundance of good things that we've had from the dance world in our lifetime. The depression in the dance world is totally debilitating. I can't afford it. I've worked too hard my entire life to have to endure at this point. I'm not interested in seeing dance die. . . . You have to believe that what you are doing is important. You really have to believe that you are of some use to people and that what you have to offer has something good for them. I've always believed that a dance evening energizes an audience, that an audience goes out feeling chemically stronger and more optimistic. This is what I understand about dance. And this is an important thing. We need this. Our culture needs it. Cynicism is very de-energizing. And dance needs energy. You have to believe that what you are doing is important. So there is no point being cynical if you want to dance. So get over it.

Pete Harnisch. Baseball pitcher in recovery from depression. For Pete Harnisch, free agency could not have come at a worse time. Harnisch missed most of the 1997 baseball season with the New York Mets after falling into depression in April. After his return to the Mets in August, he was traded to Milwaukee. Interest in Harnisch had been lukewarm, as he explains it. "I'm in kind of a 'prove it' year. I know what I've got to do and I'll go somewhere and pitch 200 innings and make my start. Obviously, I would have hoped to be signed by now." Harnisch was not sure whether his bout with depression muted interest in him. "It wouldn't surprise me if there was some concern, but I don't walk around every day wondering if it's going to happen again." Harnisch said dealing with depression was the most difficult thing he had ever been through. "But in a way it makes you stronger. I know it's kind of a cliché, but now it's like, what's worse out there? You can't hit me with anything else."[10]

Louis Armstrong. Singer, trumpet player, and first black superstar. Near the end of his career, Armstrong was senselessly overbooked and overworked. His trumpet playing became stenciled and tired. The wear showed. He was down a wrong road that sapped his energy and talent. But still you knew that when you went to see Armstrong, you were listening to the great Louis Armstrong, the first black superstar, and you'd better pay attention because he might suddenly stop you with an impassioned "Sunny Side of the Street." Sadly, celebrity status, as in Armstrong's case, is often mindlessly conferred when the celebrated can no longer do what makes him famous or when what he invented has become buried and forgotten under accumulated applause.

Cecil Taylor. Jazz pianist. In a conversation with jazz historian Nat Hentoff, Taylor reported that he had some terrible times when he first started playing as a professional. Hentoff reported, "He told me he hadn't worked in six or eight months. He said he held imaginary club sessions in his room, to keep himself from forgetting what it is like to play in public. . . . "[11]

Keith Jarrett. Jazz pianist. "If I play a poor concert, I'm ruined. I've given myself toxin."[12]

Miles Davis. Trumpet player. Davis, world-renowned trumpet player, presents a vivid picture of himself as a craftsman who hit a dead end when he began using drugs. "I lost my sense of discipline, lost my sense of control over my life and started to drift. It wasn't like I didn't know what was happening. I did, but I didn't care any more. I had such confidence in myself that even when I was losing control I really felt I had everything under control. But your mind can play tricks on you. I guess when I started to hang like I did, it surprised a lot of people who thought I had it all together. It also surprised me."[13]

Phil Simms. Sports announcer and former New York Giants quarterback. "Sometime in your life, you're going to experience something difficult, like being a back-up quarterback. The thing is never to get comfortable with not playing. If you do, it'd be hard to keep your skills. By not playing, there's a greater chance of things going downhill."[14]

Chris Mullin. Basketball star for the Indiana Pacers and recovering alcoholic. For Mullin, the secret to fulfillment no longer came with what he was capable of doing inside the arena. "You know basketball is very unbalanced . . . you win, you feel good. You lose, you feel bad. I can't rely on that. I've been through so much the last four years, so much insecurity, that basketball isn't the rock. It isn't the foundation for me right now. I find it hard to get excited and upset. A lot of times it's just an empty feel-

ing . . . I know time will make it better, help me focus. I can't say I see
the light at the end of the tunnel. Maybe I can see the tunnel."[15]

Neil Young. Singer, songwriter, and actor. Young's career was always
subject to surprises and unpredictability, mainly because of his frequent
shifts of mood and mind. Every statement Young makes, he may someday retract; every style of music he plays, he may eventually disavow,
only to return to it again in the future; every musician he plays with, he
may some day desert. The only sure statement one can make about his
next step is that it won't be anything like his preceding one. As Young
suggests in his famous song, "Hey, Hey, My, My," "It's better to burn out
than fade away."[16]

Jason Robards. Actor. The popular actor Kevin Spacey saw Jason Robards as a mentor-figure. He says, "Actors know a great performance when
they see one because inside every actor is a great performance. A thousand
things come between most actors and their dreams. There are only a hand-
ful like Jason who are given the chance, and have the courage, to give audiences the best and the worst of themselves. Again and again. So actors
live through a performer like Jason Robards. He was brave. He adored the
craft of acting. He clung to it and honored it. Actors can tell the difference
between those who respect the written word and serve the material and
those who set out to serve themselves. Jason fought to be the best. . . . "[17]

Bob Brookmeyer. Musician. "I've got a wonderful band and I'd like to
write about three CD's worth of large-ensemble jazz music for them.
They've given me a fresh palette. There's another place waiting for me. I
don't know where it is yet but it's where I have to move."[18]

Paul Schrader. Film writer. "Having done fairly early on work I thought
was valuable and I thought would endure was an enormous relief. I knew
that I had done something in life. I know people my age who still have not
had the sense of personal artistic rewards. And it gets to be a hard and bitter thing in your 50's and 60's never to have had the sense of 'I did something.' . . . Most artists have seven hot years and then there are seven
shadow years. And the rest of their lives are living off that. Except for
some. Some artists are able to reinvent themselves with second lives."[19]

Carl Yastrzemski. Baseball player. Walter Hriniak, a close friend of
Carl Yastrzemski and Boston Red Sox batting coach, had this to say about
Yastrzemski: "He worked at hitting practice until his hands bled. In the
rain, in good weather, at 8 o'clock in the morning before anyone was out

in the ballpark, at age 38, 39, 42. Younger players saw it and will never forget it."[20]

Andre Previn. Pianist and conductor. "There are many evenings, though, when I come home and start talking to the furniture. I'm offered invitations but usually I can't accept. I spend my evenings studying, working, preparing, and the times I have a casual evening off are rare. A career in music, when you get to a certain point, it takes all your efforts just to stay there."[21]

Merce Cunningham. Dancer and choreographer. Cunningham was asked why audiences no longer see him in his famous plastic bag routine. "Because I was in it once," he replied. *Because I was in it once.* For Cunningham, dance remains a continuing exploration of movement, a process rather than a fixed and reachable goal. "Every artist should ask, 'What is the point of doing what you already know?'"[22]

Don Sutton. Hall of fame baseball pitcher. He was willing to move to pursue his art and passion, willing to accept being third or fourth or fifth pitcher on his staff. That's how he got to win 324 games. He pitched in a style he called "crafty."[23]

Larry Bird. Former Boston Celtics star. "In high school my coach told me, 'Larry, no matter how much you work at it, there's always someone out there who's working a little harder . . . If you take 150 practice shots, he's taking 200,'" Bird recalled. "And that drove me. In the pro's, that someone was Magic Johnson. In my head, in my dreams, he was the one I was always competing with."[24]

For the competent teacher, there is always the fear of extinction, insignificance, and running out of energy, ideas, and emotional gas. In a real sense the risk of diminishing or losing the essence of one's craft is what drives the competent teacher to take risks and discover new approaches. A good teacher is on the edge and can go either way, drift away like Miles Davis or rebound like Frank Sinatra. Yet the process of adapting, refining, and seeking new approaches to fuel one's creativity is a slow process. It is a continuous process of asking, as Merce Cunningham does, "What is the point of doing what you already know?" It is also a process, as artist Bruce Nauman points out, of "avoiding what is too easy."[25] Cecil Taylor describes the process well: "Sometimes I will work on my material two years before I play it. I get rid of some pieces right away, because they aren't very good. I put some away for a year, then go back to them and see how they sound. I am relaxed with the idea that not every piece I write is perfect. You improve in the smallest steps. At the end of a year, maybe you've developed an inch."[26]

Competent teachers, like Cecil Taylor, develop by inches. When you walk into their classrooms you sense the slow development that is characteristic of the competent teacher. What you observe is a setting that belongs uniquely to that teacher and defines what his or her work is all about. The furniture, the pictures, the sense of activity—all contribute to the choreography of that classroom. It is impossible to imagine this room without his or her presence and command. A good teacher is like the dancer Merce Cunningham: "He is not a figurehead but a doer . . . even when offstage, he stays in the back of your mind, wise and discreet, an inscrutable observer, without whose supervision everything would fall apart."

One has to adapt to succeed at a craft. John Cassavetes, the late film director, put it well when he said, "You have to fight sophistication. You have to fight knowing, because once you know something, it's hard to be open and creative."[27] Some teachers, through a process of self-analysis, awareness, understanding today's children, and constant skill-building and seeking new approaches evolve into competent teachers. This evolution is both a tangible and an intangible quality that observers *see* and *feel* when they walk into the teacher's classroom. It is tangible in the sense that they can *see* the skills the teacher is using to motivate the students to learn. It is intangible in the sense that the observer *feels* the excitement, energy, and element of risk as the competent teacher pushes, pulls, confronts, and cajoles students to stay engaged in the learning process. No one is exempt; everyone is in the game. Everyone is seen as a valued learner and participant. Everyone has a place and is safe. It is a physically, emotionally, and intellectually demanding craft—no different from that of musician, actor, dancer, athlete—that often leaves the teacher spent at the end of the day. It goes on five days a week, eight to twelve hours a day, with preparation, teaching, advising, and teaming with colleagues. As Nathan Tarkov suggests, the success of the craft depends very much on the teacher's energy, sense of humor, and ability to relate to young people. These vital qualities are not givens for every teacher entering the teaching field. They have to be attained and nurtured through a daily regimen of self-care, self-awareness, and ongoing professional development. Surprisingly, when we talk about education reform and encouraging teachers to increase their level of competency, there is little mention of the important need for teachers to be in excellent physical, emotional, and intellectual condition throughout their careers in order to get the job done each day.

Often, competent teachers succeed in an environment where some peers reject their all-out zeal, their giving one hundred percent. What competent teachers do in the classroom seems beyond others' skills and creativity. These teachers react, naturally, by being defensive and distancing themselves from the competent teacher model. They allow and even encourage detractions in the school's politics to become the main focus of their daily work. The classroom and the students take on a secondary role, becoming a place that the teacher has to go to. It is like playing for a last place team: you play the game but you are never a winner. The work is drudgery and the only relief comes outside the classroom, perhaps in the faculty lounge where the talk often is about burnout, school politics, the next teacher contract, or notorious student behavior.

I believe that a major, often overlooked reason for the seeming lack of hard work and commitment to improving skills on the part of many teachers is that the craft requires much more physical, emotional, and intellectual energy than they expected when they first entered the profession. Keeping up, let alone getting better, requires personal and professional discipline. It requires a commitment to self-care, such as being in good physical condition and keeping one's personal and professional life in order. It requires self-awareness so one can remain flexible and open to new directions and approaches when needed. It also requires taking advantage of ongoing opportunities for professional development. It requires a willingness to say, in the words of Frank Sinatra, "I'm ready and I'm set"— every day.

I believe these seemingly disinterested teachers long to be more like competent teachers, to acquire the skills they need to be successful in their teaching role. I believe *all* teachers want to better their craft, to view themselves and to be viewed by their colleagues as gifted and talented teachers. They want to be *shown* how, not *told* how. There is no more painful scene than to observe a teacher failing to teach and communicate with students. The teacher knows failure is setting in and the students are aware. Everyone in the classroom watches the clock. When will the torture end? Students act out and learning gets lost in the teacher's battle for control and survival. Many teachers experience this situation every day.

The class period and the school day can't end soon enough for them—or for their students. They are looking for ways to become better, not failures. Too often, any help available to them takes the form of *telling* teachers how to correct what is not working. But *telling* does not *show* them how to go about improving their craft. This action is unsubstantial lip service, not being our brother's keeper, not taking him by the hand and leading him through the steps, not teaching by example. Supervision, whether it is administrative or peer supervision, does not work if it is limited to *telling* someone what to do rather than *showing* him.

Our task is to find ways to help teachers reach their goal of improving. It is a worthy goal. In a real sense we are our brother's keeper. When we see fellow teachers and their students floundering, it is our professional responsibility to help them better their craft. When students are performing poorly, we tend to do whatever it takes to get them back on track. Teachers are learners, too, and when they experience failure, we need to get them back on track.

I believe there are few *naturally* competent teachers. Those who truly master their craft do so because they understand that they are involved in a career-long creative process. Like successful musicians, actors, dancers, and athletes, they understand that the process to get good and stay good takes dedication and commitment to ongoing skill acquisition.

A competent teacher possesses some specific characteristics. Here is a summary of those characteristics:

1. He works hard, understands that his craft is very demanding, and he is physically, emotionally, and intellectually ready each day.
2. He develops a set of skills and a style that works to help his students learn. He sees his classroom as his laboratory in which he must experiment and change.
3. He sees himself as having the skill and desire to teach every child who comes through the classroom door. His mission is dedicated to helping all his students be successful.
4. He understands that failure, resistance to change, and embeddedness are necessary experiences in developing his craft.
5. He experiences self-doubt and needs affirmation and feedback about his work from students, peers, parents, and supervisors.
6. He is able to relinquish outworn approaches and seek new ones.

7. He is focused and disciplined and does not allow detractions and events outside the classroom to interfere with his, and his students', work, growth, and creativity.

8. He is wary of too much good publicity about his work, which can lull him into complacency.

9. He seizes every opportunity to be a mentor for colleagues and include them in his work. He has the skill, as musicians do, to perform solo so that his peers can observe firsthand how the competent teacher goes about his work. This means not rejecting colleagues who rebuff his interventions and believing that every teacher can be brought to a higher level of performance.

10. He is loyal to his colleagues who are floundering and getting more than their share of criticism. The work of the competent teacher is to help them get better, to build on their existing skills and uniqueness. Ineffective teachers need to feel safe and nurtured before they can set out to risk new approaches. The musician, craftsman, and jazz pianist Cecil Taylor puts it well: "It's rare to find musicians who are loyal and protect you and give you the space to be yourself. You learn to value them highly and give them the same space they give you. Each musician has to play his world in the framework you design for him. Improvisation is the blood that makes music go. It's a way to prepare yourself to talk responsibly with others in a musical community."[28]

11. He is tough, has the will to win and the fire in his belly, but can be soft when needed. The classroom is an environment filled with cross currents—who is in control, who is competing with whom, who is well liked, who is on the outs. It is often not a civil, orderly place, in spite of our efforts to make it so. It is explosive, as one would imagine when one puts twenty or thirty students together in one room. The competent teacher understands this phenomenon, embraces it, and avoids the naysayers who constantly wish it weren't so. Having the skill to get students to learn amid these cross currents is a must.

12. Like dancer Twyla Tharp, the competent teacher understands that "You have to believe that what you are doing is important, that you are of some use to people and what you have to offer has something good for them."

I believe that we have many competent teachers in schools throughout the country. But usually we don't hear their stories of how they developed their craft and made it work. How did they arrive at a stage in their teaching career in which they were able to look at their craft with pride and say, "I've created something and done something significant with my life"? How do they face tough classes, students, failures, and still manage to press on? Let's match a real-world persona with our model of a competent teacher. I believe we have such a teacher in Irmgard Williams, a teacher in South Heights School in Henderson, Kentucky. What is she like? A semifinalist in 1995 for the Teacher of the Year in Kentucky, Ms. Williams typifies what it takes to be a competent teacher. She may not identify herself as a competent teacher but I believe the label fits her very well. Following is a snapshot of Williams's personality, skills, and approach to teaching:

1. Williams says, "I'm here to do a job . . . whatever you give me, I'll handle it. I really feel like my classroom is my ministry. And her dedication has rewards. She was semifinalist for Kentucky's Teacher of the Year award and was selected as KERA (Kentucky Education Reform Act) Fellow, a faculty member on loan to other schools in the state.

2. Williams acknowledges that her teaching methods are different—better, she thinks—than they were years ago. She attributes it to a combination of new ideas generated through staff training and her own instincts about what works best for young children. She doesn't follow education reform like a zealot, however. She prefers a balanced approach that doesn't ask her to toss out tradition with the trash.

3. Williams believes, "If some children can't learn one way, they can learn another."

4. Like a talented artist, Williams knows that good teaching requires a continual refinement of the craft, an ability to adjust techniques as circumstances change.

5. In her classroom (a multi-age primary program with twenty-four students, mostly six- and seven-year-olds, among them a child with spina bifida, a child with autism, three children with attention deficit hyperactivity disorders, four children taking Ritalin, and one child

with, she suspects, Tourette's syndrome), Williams, standing five-feet, two-inches tall, barely rises above some of her students. Yet she is clearly in control. She sings, she dances, she even dons costumes on occasion, but she never lets fun and excitement give way to disorder. Like many grandmothers, Williams knows that children often need a soft lap to sit on and a homemade cookie to soothe their hurts, but they also need a steady hand to guide them. When a child misbehaves, Williams pulls him close to her side, cupping his chin in her hand with a gesture that mixes affection with discipline. She is effusive with praise, almost jolly at times, as she moves among her pupils, and she is always proper.

6. All her colleagues didn't praise her success as a classroom teacher. "Well," one teacher sniffed, "how did you get to do that?" The letter Williams received from the state about not winning the Teacher of the Year award was polite but perfunctory; it didn't provide the extensive feedback that Williams so desperately wanted. "I keep wondering what I did wrong," she said. Like so many of her peers, Williams was so unaccustomed to praise that she clung to every word.

7. Whatever pats on the back Williams missed in her years of teaching, she wasn't stingy with her praise for others. "You can have the mechanics, but if you don't have teachers with heart and a passion to teach, what do you have? From the top down, there ought to be something we do to show people we're proud of them. It might make better teachers if more recognition were given."[29]

Ms. Williams embodies many of the characteristics present in so many of the competent teachers:

1. She works hard. She says, "I'm here to do a job."
2. She believes she can teach any child who walks through her classroom door. She says, "If some children can't learn one way, they can learn another."
3. She has commitment and passion about her work, referring to the classroom as her "ministry."
4. Her teaching methods have improved over time. She knows that good teaching requires a continuing refinement of her craft.

5. She trusts her own instincts and experiences about what works best for the children. She doesn't rely solely on the advice of education experts.
6. She is in charge. She is the chief choreographer in her classroom.
7. On top of these characteristics, she is human and has self-doubt. She is hurt by snide comments from peers—"How did you do that?"—and by a lack of praise and affirmation from her administrators and KERA officials. Education leaders in Kentucky tended to take the loyalty and the morale of converts for granted and concentrated their efforts on resisters. As a result active reformers such as Williams often received few strokes and trivial snubs became magnified.
8. She is cognizant of her fellow teachers and wants to help them improve their craft. She understands the importance of affirmation in this process.

How can a team composed of a principal, department chairperson, teacher, and counselor leader mentor teachers so they evolve into competent teachers like Irmgard Williams? The following chapter focuses on the characteristics of an effective mentor. Clearly competent teachers and mentors are more alike than different and operate with similar skills. They work in different contexts—teachers serve students and mentors serve teachers—yet a common thread runs through their efforts.

NOTES

1. Stephen Schiff, "Stephen Sondheim." *The New Yorker* (8 March 1993): 77.

2. Jennifer Dunning, "Twyla Tharp Finds Virtue as a Cause for Dancing," *New York Times,* 12 January 1995, C1, C13.

3. Jacques Steinberg, "Class Wars; Clashing over Education's One True Faith," *New York Times,* 14 December 1997, 1, sec. 4.

4. Ibid.

5. Andrew Solomon, "The Jazz Martyr," *New York Times,* 9 February 1997, sec. 6, 35.

6. John Lahr, "The Imperfectionist," *The New Yorker* (12 September 1992): 68.

7. John Lahr, "Sinatra's Song," *The New Yorker* (3 November 1997): 77.

8. Whitney Balliett, "King Louis," *The New Yorker* (8 August 1994): 69.

9. Lahr, "Sinatra's Song."

10. Steve Jacobson, "Complex Illness Hit Harnisch," *Newsday,* 6 August 1997, A71.

11. Whitney Balliett, "Cecil," *The New Yorker* (5 May 1986): 104.

12. Soloman, "The Jazz Martyr" 34.

13. Whitney Balliett, "Miles," *The New Yorker* (4 December 1989): 156.

14. Bob Glauber, "Simms: I'd Retire If . . . ," *Newsday,* 19 October 1991, 85.

15. Harvey Araton, "At Age 30, Mullin's World Takes Strange New Twists," *New York Times,* 14 January 1994, C6.

16. Steve Erickson, "Neil Young . . . On a Good Day," *New York Times,* 30 July 2000, sec. 6, 26.

17. Kevin Spacey, "An Example, a Mentor, an Actor Above All," *New York Times,* 4 January 2001, AR 6.

18. Terry Teachout, "Still Full of Jazz, Still Pouring It Out," *New York Times,* 19 December 1999, AR 44.

19. Bernie Weintraub, "Looking Back at Two Classics," *New York Times,* 23 January 1998, E8.

20. David Faulkner, "For Yastrzemski, the Fire Still Burns," *New York Times,* 14 October 1986, C3.

21. Helen Routtencutter, "Andre Previn," *The New Yorker* (12 January 1983): 113.

22. Alastair Macaulay, "Happy Hooligan," *The New Yorker* (27 April 1992): 89.

23. Steve Jacobson, "A Complement to Sutton's Life," *Newsday,* 7 January 1998, A75.

24. Ira Berkow, "The Legend Continues . . . Bird Shoots for Coaching Greatness," *New York Times,* 10 August 1997, sec. 8, 1.

25. Andrew Solomon, "Bruce Nauman," *New York Times,* 5 March 1995, sec. 6, 28.

26. Balliett, "Cecil."

27. Philip Lopate, "Learning to Love the Ardent Chaos of Cassavetes," *New York Times,* 17 August 1997, H11.

28. Balliett, "Cecil."

29. Holly Holland, "KERA, A Tale of One Teacher," *Kappan* 79(4) (December 1997): 265–71.

3

Characteristics of the Effective Mentor

The major goal of a mentoring program should be to help every teacher be highly skilled, self-aware, inclusive, energetic, and creative, and to carry a zest for teaching into the classroom every day. These are big goals and not easy to achieve. Nevertheless, they are important goals if we are to help all children be all they can be—intellectually, emotionally, and physically. Perhaps it is easier to put a face to these goals by describing what a successful classroom looks like. I believe visual descriptions help because they give concrete meaning to the word "teacher." Here is my vision. When you walk into a successful teacher's classroom, there is no aura of giving up, boredom, lesson plans yellowed with age, or a teacher longing for retirement. These enemies of good teaching are not present. If by chance they emerge, as they are sure to do on occasion, the teacher fiercely challenges them because they are hazardous to effective teaching. In an effective teacher's classroom, we sense the slow development of a building art form, a continuous process of trying out new material and discarding old. We observe a setting that is uniquely his and defines what his work is about. The furniture, pictures, flowers, space for quiet time, sense of activity, of something important going on—all contribute to the choreography at work. The teacher is in a real sense the choreographer at work. His words, actions, and focus all convey a message, a lesson to be learned. He is not unlike the dancer Merce Cunningham, whose presence and power are described by Alastair Macaulay in an earlier chapter: "He is not a figurehead but a doer . . . even when offstage he stays in back of your mind, wise, discreet and an inscrutable observer, without whose supervision everything would fall apart." This picture presents a person involved in something worthwhile and important, a person with a gift to create conditions in which students feel at home, energized, and committed to learning and to each other. Without this teacher's presence—in the hands of a less skilled, less caring, or less committed person—everything would indeed fall apart.

Teachers have a great responsibility to be prepared for the many challenges that arise each day. Children are our greatest natural resource. Our work as educational and community leaders is to make sure they are well prepared and up to the task of learning. This also means not letting one teacher be less than excellent because of lack of skill, support, or encouragement. School leaders talk a great deal about not letting one student fall through the cracks. Why not do the same for teachers? Many of them, as every reader of this book knows, need intervention and help to improve. I believe teachers want to be successful with all their students, even those who are openly or covertly resistant to help and training. All teachers go down wrong roads and experience failure and burnout. Teachers make mistakes because of inexperience, lack of skill, or faulty assumptions about children, parents, colleagues, and school culture. But as film director Mike Nichols suggests, we must keep in mind that "nothing is written . . . it's all in the future . . . things can change . . . shift your weight . . . believe in change."[1] I believe teachers can overcome their lack of experience, skills, and self-awareness with caring intervention by mentors who can dignify their worth and at the same time help them learn new, effective approaches. The lyricist Cy Coleman's song, "It's Not Where You Start, It's Where You Finish," provides a useful metaphor for the important work involved in helping teachers renew themselves:

> It's not where you start, it's where you finish.
> It's not how you go, it's how you land.
> Remember, if you start at the top you're certain to drop.
> If you're going to last, you can't make it fast.
> Nobody starts a winner.
> Give me a slow beginner.
> Easy does it,
> Take it rung after rung.[2]

The focus of this book, then, is to tackle the question of how to develop and nurture effective teachers within the school setting. In Cy Coleman's

words, we must take it "rung by rung." It is about how we can proceed to
make mentoring easily accessible to teachers so they can learn how to
maintain a high level of skill, ongoing commitment to their own professional development, and a caring zest for their important work. It is about
creating mentoring opportunities for teachers in every career stage—beginners, those at midcareer, and those veterans in their final years of
teaching. We must remind them that they share a common bond: a desire
to be at the top of their professional life and successful in educating all of
their students. Teachers are more alike than different. Beginners and those
finishing their careers alike want to be effective and recognized as people
who make a difference in the lives of children, parents, and colleagues.

Ongoing mentoring of teachers at all career stages is the best way to
help all teachers be master teachers. Just what is a mentor and why should
this role be championed by administrators and others in leadership positions in the schools? What is the interaction like between a mentor and a
teacher? What are the key elements in the process that a successful mentor must understand to guarantee success? Webster's Dictionary defines a
mentor as a wise, loyal advisor, a loyal friend, teacher, and coach. Each
of these words—*wise, loyal, advisor, friend, teacher, coach*—represents
critical aspects of the mentoring role. Let's talk about their role in the
mentoring process:

THE WISE MENTOR

What are the characteristics of wise mentors?

1. They are people who have experienced and understand the realities of
   teaching and classroom dynamics. Clearly every teacher could benefit from having a wise mentor in his corner throughout his career,
   someone he can count on to be there for him in good and bad times.
   He needs a supportive and intimate relationship with a mentor who
   knows firsthand the struggles, failures, and fleeting successes that
   mark the daily life of a teacher—someone who has been in the
   trenches, has the battle ribbons, and is a frequent visitor to and observer of the real world of teaching. Mentors should be people who
   are known and welcomed, bearers of gifts, not grief, someone who

knows the sounds and smells of the classroom without abandoning the reality that a teacher's day involves many different and demanding responses: confrontation, care, deflection, encouragement, reprimand, and more. Mentors might best be described by lyricist Stephen Sondheim in his *Follies* hit song "I'm Still Here." Remember the lyrics? "Good times and bum times, I've seen them all . . . and I'm still here."[3] The wise mentor knows how to create a successful classroom environment and is aware of the dangers that can befall wellintentioned but poorly prepared teachers. His own career probably has had failures and low points. It helps a mentor to speak from real experiences that helped him come to terms with his own lack of skill, prompting him to reassess and learn new ways of teaching. It does take one to know one.

2. Mentors are people who understand that teaching is hard work and that renewing oneself is not easy. On the path to becoming effective, teachers may succeed for a while without hard work but it will catch up with them. The actress Charlotte Rampling puts it well when she suggests, "As you go through life there are cycles you have to live through. There is so much apprenticeship about life that quite a lot of time you're walking in mud. Everything seems to go wrong but you keep on walking because you have to survive. Then there is a moment when things come together, as if by magic, though it's not magic. It's mostly hard work."[4] It is hard work that has a special risk to it. The French actor Phillippe Torreton has the right idea. Torreton has a starring role as a kindergarten teacher in the film *It All Starts Today*. He suggests that being an actor prepared him to perform in front of a class but being a teacher was more challenging. He says, "A teacher is never forgiven. As actors, we perform in front of people who have bought tickets and even if they're bored, they're unlikely to make a fuss because they have paid good money. But for a teacher facing pupils who don't want to be there and are thinking only of recreation, the smallest mistake, the tiniest slip of attention, is punished. It's terrible exposure."[5]

3. Mentors are people who know that improving one's skills calls for taking risks and forging new directions. The wise mentor knows that in the work to change old habits and acquire new skills, the familiar, trusted ways of doing things are tenacious. Teachers, like all people,

resist change. It is a normal state of mind. As in a bad marriage, we often stay with what we know even if it is not working. As the late film director John Cassavetes advises, "You have to fight sophistication. You have to fight knowing because once you know something it's hard to be open and creative."[6] It takes courage, even being afraid that the old ways are killing you personally and professionally, to change. And the reality is that when we begin to try out new ways and new lessons, we often stumble. Our minds and bodies refuse to cooperate. We should not be surprised by this reaction. We are, after all, accustomed to the old, worn ways, like that mothballed sweater we refuse to throw away. It may be threadbare but it's comfortable and yours. The wise mentor understands that trying out new ways can be upsetting, even traumatic. It can make one afraid, anxious, and unsure. As Dr. Seuss suggests, "You will come to a place where the streets are not marked. Some windows are lighted but mostly they're darked. A place you could sprain both your elbow and chin. Do you dare stay out? Do you dare go in? How much can you lose? How much can you win?" Yes, change can be perilous, but that is not necessarily bad. Remember Cy Coleman's advice: "if you're going to last you can't make it fast." Change requires some upheaval. If we can ask our students to change, how can we stand by and ignore a teacher's need to change? As actor Kevin Spacey suggests, "If I am afraid, there is a good shot I'll take the part because I know it will stretch me to do better work." The dancer and choreographer Merce Cunningham, when asked why he no longer did his famous plastic bag routine, replied, "Because I was in it once." He's done it, and now it's time for renewal and new beginnings. Mentors understand that they must continually raise the bar for their protégés by asking what the point is of doing something they already know. Is this what you want to be doing a year from now, five years, twenty? They know they must encourage their teachers to avoid practices that are too easy. In a sense, the words of poet Anne Carson are the central core of an effective mentoring relationship. Carson puts it well: "You don't learn anything when you are still up on a window shelf, safe. The other way is to jump from what you know into an empty space and see where you end up. I think you only learn when you jump." Carson also suggests that " . . . the major task of a lifetime is to avoid boredom and trafficking in the inessentials of life such as lusting for retirement and spare time."[7] These, I believe, are the enemies of every competent teacher. But taking risks is scary, so we all need someone to hold our hand as we navigate through new territory.

4. Wise mentors are people who understand that teachers all arrive in the classroom with biases, premade judgments, and prejudices. Teachers are human. They arrive at the classroom door with the mental and emotional baggage from their background, training, and learned ways of looking at the world. Mentors understand that this is not something to be afraid of or keep hidden. The wise mentor knows to shine the spotlight on a teacher's dark side, recognizing and accepting it to set teachers free of self-imposed barriers that keep them from connecting with all students. Be human, have feelings you don't like and accept them, but don't isolate students because of color, gender, behavior, physical appearance, and so on. And don't spend all of your time with students who are more like you and are not threatening. The wise mentor makes teachers aware that even they do not like every one of their students. Many teachers, when asked the question, "Which students in your class threaten or unnerve you?" will often answer, "Not a one. I like and respect all my kids." They may believe this or be truly unaware of their own feelings, but in fact certain students threaten and unnerve teachers. Teachers silently hope that those students are absent, move, or transfer out of their classes. But effective mentoring helps teachers understand that their greatest potential for growth comes from accepting students who rebuff their good intentions and overtures. It is the teacher's job to figure these students out—to sweat, try new approaches, fail, be tough, be soft, do whatever it takes to win over these students.

With careful mentoring, teachers learn not to shirk off the responsibility for their lack of success with certain students. They learn to avoid an easy way out for their lack of success—blaming the parents, blaming society, asking the guidance counselor to transfer the student to another class, and so on. With effective mentoring, teachers learn to face their demons and fears to be more effective for all our students. In the process, the lessons they learn in terms of being more accepting of differences, of not attaching negative meaning to them, will not be lost on the students. Efforts by the teacher to be inclusive will be a major stimulus in helping students accept the variety of people they will encounter in the real world.

5. Wise mentors are people who understand that bad times, failure, or burnout can happen to every teacher, even the most successful ones. Sometimes being a star can kill the teacher professionally. Dr. Seuss suggests that many of us land in a "useless place" and experience difficulty trying to get out. The urge to settle down and get comfortable is always with us. Teachers may use the same lessons year after year and watch them turn yellow with age. They may allow themselves to become part of faculty-room conversation that focuses only on the negative—topics such as turbulent kids, tired teachers, pressures from parents, administrative lapses, lack of respect for teaching, and the overall lack of rewards. They may find themselves, as Ann Carson suggests, trafficking in the inessentials of life, lusting for retirement and spare time. The wise mentor understands that by laying fallow, teachers are allowing themselves to slide into sameness. Each day becomes a repeat of the one before, and teachers begin to count the days until June and the last day of school. Thoughts of September, a new beginning, remind them of just another year.

Failure and bad times come, often unexpectedly, to even the best and brightest teachers. These negative experiences—bad days, bad years—are not reserved for teachers who do little or teachers whose kids are out of control and breaking down the classroom walls. The wise mentor knows that even the most successful teachers fall victim to failure and burnout. These can be the star teachers, looked at throughout the school district, perhaps even nationally, as models to follow. They are certainly not the types of teachers the community would expect to run into trouble professionally.

Wise mentors also understand that becoming an expert can take the teacher away from the central focus: the kids in the classroom. If teachers write a book, present at conferences, spend more time away from the real world of the kids, they're not in the real game of school any more. They become known as the guy who got out—out of the classroom and on his way to fame and fortune. In the process, he may be losing his skills and the taste for classroom teaching. His fame and newfound accolades, are based on what he did before, not what he is doing now. His currency is past experience, who he was. He has begun to read and believe his reviews. He has landed in Dr. Seuss's "useless place" but at first doesn't realize it. It becomes easier to write and speak about teaching than to actually do it because it doesn't force him to take risks. The conference circuit—hotels, the buildup as he is introduced, the book signings, and cocktail parties after his speech—may make him soft. In politics they say, "The man is an empty suit." He finds that his craft, what he invented as a teacher, is being buried and forgotten under accumulated praise.

Wise mentors know that teachers can't be star conference presenters on the circuit and still be effective teachers. Being a star is antithetical to being a creative teacher. Stardom demands the validation, worship, acceptance, and accolades of the audience. In contrast, everyday teaching does not focus on the validation, worship, acceptance, and accolades of students and parents. The work of the teacher is to help his students value learning. It requires creating demands and expectations for students and helping them move on, well prepared. Students need teachers who push them to be better. It is often a battle, an ongoing confrontation. Students don't need teachers who are buddies or friends. Effective teachers need to satisfy their own need for validation themselves, not through their students. Once teachers become stars or experts, the tables get turned in the way they view their professional persona. Instead of having the focus of their work be on students looking to them for direction, they focus on looking to them for validation and praise. This is bad medicine for any teacher. Mentors tell teachers in this situation to be cautious when leaving their classroom on a regular basis to be a presenter. They may be leaving behind the skills and the joys that come with the everyday world of teaching.

6. Wise mentors understand and value loyalty and the privacy of their protégés. Effective mentoring requires a trusting and loyal relationship. When a teacher opens the classroom door and exposes his or her teaching style and classroom persona for critique, observation, and feedback, it's often a new and risky undertaking. Having a mentor observe every aspect of one's interaction with students and parents is, as any teacher knows, a little like walking a tightrope. Many questions will emerge, as they should. What will my mentor think about me after he sees the real me in action? Will he pick up on areas and subtle problems I have with some of my students? Will some of my

students embarrass me by acting out? How much of what he observes will become a formal part of my record? Having a mentor sounded like a good idea but now that it's a reality, I'm not so sure.

A major element in creating a safety net for anxious and uncertain teachers is for the mentor to remain very trusting and loyal. What goes on in the observations, feedback, and dialog between the mentor and teacher remains between them and not a part of any formal record. They will share any written assessments and then discard them. The real work of mentoring is in the observation, assessment, and setting achievable plans to learn what new skills the teacher needs. As such, all interactions between the mentor and teacher remain private, just between them.

In a sense, the casting of this loyalty and privacy net creates a new way of doing business in the schools and a way for teachers to get the renewal they need with dignity. Being listened to, getting feedback that is useful but kind, learning new skills even though there can be failure and setbacks involved, represents a welcome change in our schools. Trust and loyalty spark renewal and allow one to take risks. If the teacher fails there is support and a caring mentor to help, to grab the teacher so he or she doesn't fall through the cracks. This safety net represents a breath of fresh air blowing through the hallways, sweeping away the heaviness and isolation that comes with being independent as a teacher. Schools, after all, are notorious for spreading gossip and leaking private information about teachers who are having trouble. Gossip, rumors, and voyeurism feed into a negative school culture. Teachers learn early on to keep the focus on their colleagues and off themselves. They learn early on to keep their needs, questions, failures, and successes to themselves. To share openly how one feels, the problems one has with certain students, to ask a colleague for help, and to share one's successes are not acceptable in most schools. It's simply not done. To do so is to risk being labeled as needy, soft, at risk, or burning out. It is raising the red flag and asking for sarcastic rebuttals. Teachers also learn not to shine the spotlight on themselves and talk about their successes with students. The rule is, "Don't ask for help and don't promote yourself."

Imagine for a moment a teacher sitting in a crowded room and asking for help from colleagues. "Joe, you're a veteran teacher here. People respect you. I know you're free third period. Can you come into my class and give me some clues as to why these kids are acting out so much?" Imagine teachers saying out loud that they are uncomfortable with certain students and they would like to learn how to be more accepting and tolerant. Can you visualize a teacher talking about what a great lesson he had this morning and inviting colleagues to come in and observe his good work? In my experience, help is not forthcoming in the venue of the faculty room. It is not a priority. It is gossip, sports, and finger-pointing territory. Spare us your needs and accomplishments. This is the faculty room mantra.

Mentoring helps reshuffle the deck, so to speak, by allowing teachers to reveal themselves and ask for help. They can right behaviors that are destroying their classes. To change, they need protection, safety, a kind ear, credible feedback and advice, models for change, and ongoing support in the process. Schools are often quick to give students who are encountering difficulties this kind of support. Why not the same for teachers?

7. Wise mentors are people who understand that the personal and family problems of students can be very painful for teachers. A wise mentor doesn't shun or ignore the impact that personal problems have on a teacher. Students from every economic level come to school looking for a safe harbor, a refuge from turmoil at home. The most well-off students are sometimes more difficult to help because they are supposed to have found the good life in the right neighborhood. They hide their pain well. Sometimes help comes more swiftly to the poorer students because they show their needs—little money, poor clothing and nutrition, health problems, little parental support. They get the teachers' attention. Any keen observer of school life understands that teachers experience stress as a part of the struggles of students and the students' parents. This is true for teachers in every school—urban, suburban, and rural. Personal problems of students and their families know no geographical boundaries.

The number of personal problems they confront each day often takes beginning teachers off guard. Some are lucky; they have some training in how to react and get their students the proper help. Others, though, are ill prepared for this reality. They say, "It's not my job to help," or "I wasn't trained to deal with this." Some teachers literally push needy students aside with responses that imply that the students should get help elsewhere. They shut down their own emotional reactions to the pain they see the student experiencing. Unfortunately, this response often gets support from veteran teachers who, after many years in the classroom, still remain untrained addressing the personal problems of their students. These veterans advise teachers not to look too closely at their students, and to keep a safe distance. They suggest that if the teacher responds by connecting with kids in need, he or she will be in dangerous and unknown territory. These streets are unmarked, as Dr. Seuss suggests. And maybe these veteran teachers are right because, after all, they have no training in personal intervention and the institution does not expect that they get involved. In turn, they can't be blamed nor held responsible, can they? In the end, intervention is the responsibility of a few overwhelmed counselors and school psychologists who can never really address the needs of all the students. The result? Students' problems don't get addressed. Teachers look the other way or defer. It's a no-win situation. They know very well that the outdated system of a few counselors trying to help all kids doesn't work. Everyone loses: the needy kids, teachers who may want to help but are untrained to respond to specific needs, and counselors who know that they can't solve all the kids' problems alone.

Wise mentors understand these dynamics. They understand that teaching is a painful business and one can never be fully prepared for what the day brings. How does a teacher respond to the personal and nonacademic issues of his students—the tears from divorce, a swollen eye from a beating, soiled clothing from lack of care, steady absences from chronic and unattended health problems, and the look of fear of being unsafe in a child's eyes? The wise mentor knows these are issues to be addressed, not overlooked by claiming that teachers and administrators cannot do everything. He or she knows there is much teachers can do to help kids in need. Teaching teachers to intervene and support the personal needs of a student is something every mentor can learn. The key is showing teachers that the process of addressing the personal needs of troubled students provides them with a way to get those students back into the academic fold. Students who solve their personal problems have renewed energy to devote to learning.

8. Wise mentors understand that teachers may also have problematic personal relations outside school that impact their ability to be successful. Mentoring—observing, listening, helping teachers learn new skills, developing a trusting relationship—creates conditions that allow a teacher to talk about personal issues that may be affecting daily work. It is an unexpected and significant part of the mentoring process. Once a mentor creates a sense of trust and loyalty, it becomes apparent to teachers that anything, including their worst fears and problems, can be put on the table and discussed. It's a logical extension of the mentor and protégé's conversations. To be successful, teachers need personal lives that are intact and relatively stable. When teachers' personal lives are unbalanced their classroom performance is affected. They suffer and so do their students.

Should mentors listen to a teacher's problems that are external to the classroom? Of course. A mentor should address any issue that impacts on the performance of a teacher. Life's problems hit us all. Family problems, divorce, death, poor health, unruly children, alcohol and drug abuse, and career setbacks can weigh heavily on a teacher's mind. Often there are few outlets in the school for sharing these concerns. Silence is usually the keyword amongst coworkers, but beneath the surface a troubled teacher always gives off signs: increased sick days, isolation from colleagues, arriving late and leaving early, new, erratic classroom behavior, confrontations with students and supervisors, and addictions that he or she can no longer hide. A wise mentor who has refined his or her listening and empathy skills allows for time and opportunity to open doors to these issues. As a human being who has experienced the travails of life himself, he is not immune to these issues and, while not a therapist, he can hear concerns, offer sources of help, and be a monitor and confidant to observe the toll these events may be taking on the teacher and his students. Not every overture for help works. Getting help requires ongoing mentoring conversations that clearly allow the opportunity for personal issues to come to the surface. Sometimes teachers are ready to reveal and discuss a problem. They want help. Simple words work best, such as "Jim, I noticed that you've been very short, almost angry, with your kids today. It's not like you. You're usually so relaxed and having a ball. You mentioned you and your wife are splitting up.

Is there anything we can talk about?" A simple question may start your troubled teacher on the road to help. Helping teachers resolve personal issues as a way to improve teaching performance is a worthwhile investment for mentors.

Are there cautions to be addressed in this process? Of course. The primary function of mentoring is to improve teaching performance. Helping teachers resolve personal issues is a critical consideration but it should not dominate the conversations. Mentors are not therapists or counselors. If personal issues are the dominant theme, then the mentor must encourage outside help to assist the teacher, and himself, in the mentoring process.

9. Wise mentors understand that by its very nature a successful mentoring relationship will change over time. As a protégé grows in skill and knowledge, the mentoring relationship will change. The protégé will gradually acquire a teaching persona and stature of his or her own, and eventually be prepared to become a mentor for others. What is it like for a mentor to nurture a new teacher and then have to move out of the way so the talent of the protégé can shine? John Lahr aptly describes the process of what happens when a mentor is no longer needed in the same way in his description of the relationship between the playwright August Wilson and Lloyd Richards, head of the Yale Drama School. Richards says, "August was very receptive in the early days. He had a lot to learn and knew it. He was a big sponge, absorbing everything." Richards sent Wilson to the sound booth, to the paint shop, to the lighting designer. "As he learned structure . . . playwriting, really . . . he was also learning everything else," Richards said. But as Ben Mordecai, managing director of the Yale Repertory Theater, suggests, "As Wilson grew in confidence, craft and stature, it became increasingly difficult for him to play the protégé in the partnership. The two of them artistically began drifting apart, which was, I think, a natural thing. The collaboration wasn't happening at the level it had in earlier years." As Wilson saw it, "Lloyd slowed down." But it was just as true to say that Wilson grew up.[8]

The eventual maturing of the protégé into mentor should be a cherished goal. A successful mentor should be able to freely share wisdom and skills without selfishly remaining in charge, keeping the maturing teacher stuck in the protégé role. The mentor should know when it's time to step aside and let go. Giving the protégé freedom to move on and integrate the teachings of the mentor into his or her own persona is what it's all about. The mentor must recognize when it is time to welcome the protégé into the club as colleague.

Will teachers in mentoring relationships be ready to take on such a role? No, some will resist moving into a mentoring role even though they are ready. They are comfortable as the protégé. They need to be encouraged to be on their own. That is true of any mentoring relationship. August Wilson grew up in his relationship with Lloyd Richards and he had to move on. But we are not all Wilsons. Sometimes it seems easier to stay even though we know it is time to move on. A major theme in this book is that people tend to stay with what they know. Teachers stay with what has worked in the past. Protégés in the mentoring process tend to stay subservient, in awe of their mentors. Moving on means leaving behind what we know and are comfortable with—the aged, threadbare sweater. It is the only choice if we are to continue on the road to success.

Knowing when to end the mentor/protégé relationship is a two-way process. Mentors must be aware when the time has come to disengage. They know that to attempt to maintain the status quo of the relationship will diminish and undermine the power of the mature protégé who is ready to help others. Mentors also know that to remain as is will undermine their own need to move on and mentor others. The protégé, too, must be aware of and trust his or her own feelings of being ready to move on. To stay will keep the protégé in a lesser role, forsaking a mentoring role for himself. Disengaging is a difficult task and becomes even more difficult when the relationship has something worthwhile and life giving in it for both the mentor and the protégé. Knowing how to disengage is really what schooling is all about. Teachers have to disengage from students each June; when suddenly the school year is all over. Teachers build close relationships with students throughout the year and then all at once, they're gone, disappearing down the hall into a yellow school bus. They may see some of the students the following year, but the students will have moved on. Teachers can try to hold onto the relationship, and some do, or they can let go, accept the endings and committing themselves to new beginnings with new students in September. In the same way, the mentor and protégé must acknowledge the need for ending old relationships and beginning new ones, as well.

10. Wise mentors understand that not every teacher will embrace mentoring. They anticipate resistance and are not surprised when the first shot is fired across their bow. They must proceed slowly. In a sense, open, spoken resistance helps shape the leadership of a newly formed mentoring program. It gives the individuals involved a glimpse of who is opposed and what the issues are. It makes administrators aware of what teachers' perceptions are if they question whether mentoring is just another ill planned program to get more work out of teachers. It allows administrators to gauge the depth of teachers' resistance and suggests ways of going about convincing them of the benefits to them of a mentoring program. Other teachers may resist quietly, saying they support the project but still harboring a certain ambivalence. They leave themselves an open door to back out. Tacit resistance is problematic for leaders of a newly formed mentoring program because it is hard to judge where this kind of opposition stands. It is very important for mentors to engage not only those resisters who are openly opposed but also the silent resisters. Ignoring this group and failing to engage them in dialog early on can cost the program in the long run. Unanswered resistance doesn't go away; it looms over a program, always ready to raise questions of authenticity and credibility.

Why shouldn't leaders of a newly formed mentoring program be surprised by resistance? Teachers work in an environment with little novelty and change, often remaining in the same grade level and classroom for their entire careers. They work in an environment where the focus is often on the negative—which kids are misbehaving, which teachers are burning out, which parents are creating chaos, which administrators can't be trusted. It is typical school culture that would rather point fingers at teachers' kids who aren't making it rather than engaging in promoting the notion that all teachers need to be learners and involved in ongoing mentoring and support. When invitations come along for something new like mentoring, a mentor should not be surprised that many teachers will be, and probably should be, skeptical of any plan to "mentorize" them. They are used to the humdrum, gossip, and isolation of their daily lives. They will ask, "Why do you want to help me become a better teacher?" Many teachers have been sold on programs that were ultimately not in their best interests and benefited only outside experts. Many have a history of negative involvement with reform efforts. They have legitimate reasons to be distrustful and resistant. Wise mentors and their mentoring team understand and accept the responsibility of getting teachers to participate in the energizing process of mentoring. Their work is to convince teachers, one by one, that it is in their own best interest to become involved.

A part of this effort to overcome resistance is also to subtly speak to the dangers involved if the school and the teachers simply drift along without any ongoing opportunity for institutional and professional renewal such as mentoring. The mentor's message is that teachers do burn out without renewal opportunities. It can happen to any staff member. We are all vulnerable if we have no mechanism for self and institutional improvement. Institutional reform will emerge when teachers become better trained and more successful in their work.

But as Dr. Seuss suggests, "unslumping yourself is not easily done." Overcoming resistance to a mentoring program requires a clear plan. Mentors should include opportunities for teachers to openly voice their concerns, an acceptance and appreciation of these views, however negative and sometimes hurtful, a clear and proactive response as to why teachers should participate, a strong will, tough skin, and the hard work involved in continuing selling and guiding the program through periodic setbacks. Quiet persistence, keeping open the potential for change, and being available are the ingredients for success. Also, requiring participation in mentoring is not enough. Teachers must see this process as helpful and be willing to give themselves over to it professionally.

11. Wise mentors possess highly developed communication skills that can be used in a variety of interactions with protégés. Mentors know how to listen, be nonjudgmental, and provide useful feedback and modeling that can act as a guide for improvement. They know how to assess the classroom skills of their protégés, join with them in a dialog on how to improve their skills, and remain an active source of support as they inch along the road to becoming master teachers. Successful mentors know how to intervene, listen, be nonjudgmental,

give constructive and accurate feedback, confront failure-causing behaviors, support successful and failed efforts to change, be available
for counseling on educational and personal issues, and be a general
advocate for their protégés. They know how to offer hope and encouragement and, at times, critical assessment, for example, needed
feedback to address behaviors that may be destroying the teacher and
the class. They know how to say the right words to help teachers become aware of these behaviors and the work that needs to be done to
make corrections.

Why is caring and supportive feedback so important? It is hard for
teachers, or any worker, to improve in an atmosphere that is caustic.
A Gallup Organization study completed in 2000 shows that most
workers rate having a caring boss even higher than money or fringe
benefits. In interviews with two million employees at seven hundred
companies, the study found that how long employees stay with a
company and how productive they are there is determined by their relationship with their immediate supervisor.[9] Caring involves speaking the truth and giving feedback that is direct. Sometimes it becomes
apparent that a teacher needs to think about a career change or retirement. The wise mentor knows that the potential to improve one's skills
professionally is a necessary component of a job. Seymour Sarason
suggests:

> The ingredients of job satisfaction . . . are many and interacting, but
> there is one which tends to have devastating effects, and that is when
> one's work is no longer challenging, or interesting, or unpredictable;
> one knows from one day to the next, from one month to the next, what
> one will be doing and this stretches into an indefinite future. It matters
> little if what one does is valuable to others or even if others regard it as
> interesting and even fascinating. If one has mastered one's task, if that
> mastery does not lead to new challenges, if one's job no longer is *ex-
> perienced* as interesting, if one feels one has learned as much as one
> will in that job, one is in trouble and it compounds difficulties from any
> other sources. I am talking about not only so-called lower-level jobs
> but higher ones as well. I have seen too many professionals who are
> bored by their work to exempt them from those generalizations. Con-
> flicts within a setting around power, status, and money are in some

measure a consequence of the fact that people no longer find their jobs intrinsically interesting.[10]

Jean Ciavonne, a retired teacher from Colorado Springs, Colorado, describes how sometimes the enchantment related to teaching fades. She says, "For more than eighteen years, teaching was a wonderfully satisfying experience and I loved every minute of it, almost. How did I know when the enchantment disappeared? For me it was not a sudden revelation. Correcting papers began to seem like drudgery. After parent conferences I was not cherishing remarks from gracious parents. I didn't suddenly dislike children. It was just that the things that some of them did annoyed me more."[11] Mentoring veteran teachers almost always involves issues related to retirement and the decision to stay or to go. Like Ciavonne, teachers encounter a growing sense of something changing in their responses to children. The options of renewing or reinventing themselves or leaving altogether become a daily consideration. Questions such as these usually are not raised in the faculty room or administrator/teacher supervision meetings. Wise mentors need to be attuned to such questions and help veteran teachers talk out loud about the choices available, to say it's OK to have these thoughts and to ask, "How do you think you should proceed?"

The mentor's feedback takes many different forms. Some of it is very pragmatic. As John S. Holloway suggests, " . . . trained mentors help novice teachers plan lessons, assist them in gathering information about best practices, observe the new teachers' classes. The novice teacher reflects on their practice and applies what they have learned to future lessons."[12] The mentor advises and guides them on how to take care of the nitty-gritty aspects of classroom life that, if unattended to, will create mischief. Holloway also suggests that the ability of mentors to frame their discussions with protégés around the issues of teaching and learning is a vital part of the feedback and learning process. He reports on a 1999 study by Giebelhausa and Bowman of a large scale mentoring program, Pathwise—a formal induction program developed by the Educational Testing Service (ETS) for prospective teachers and their mentors. The purpose of the study was to learn whether a specific model for framing discussions on

teaching and learning would nurture and develop teachers' pedagog-
ical skills. Data analysis indicated that prospective teachers who were
assigned mentors trained in discussion demonstrated more complete
and effective planning, more effective classroom instruction, and a
higher level of reflection on practice.

Honest, accurate feedback calls upon mentors to create a climate
that encourages their protégés to talk about issues beyond the everyday details of classroom life. These might include issues related to career development, retirement, and one's personal life and well being,
issues that impact on the protégé's daily performance. There are different kinds of discussion, more personal discussions that have a
deeper meaning for the protégé and require an approach from the mentor framed by gentleness, acceptance, caring, and support. Caring, direct feedback is often necessary in helping protégés deal with emotional and health issues. The movie *Wit*—directed by Mike Nichols
and starring the actress Emma Thompson—gives us insight into how
mentors should and should not behave. This is a story about Vivian, a
literary scholar, and her last battle with cancer. The play begins with
Vivian's doctor staring into the camera in extreme close-up, blurting,
"You have cancer." More indignities quickly follow. In the hospital
Vivian encounters a young doctor who is callow and insensitive.
These are certainly not helpful mentors. Vivian also meets a nurse,
Susie, who has great compassion for her. Near the end of her struggle,
Vivian is visited by her aged mentor E. M. Ashford. Played by Eileen
Atkins, Ashford climbs into bed with Vivian, cradles her, and reads
from a children's book. Ms. Atkins' fragility and gentleness make the
scene shattering and heartbreaking.[13] Get the picture? Caring feedback
is not always in the words spoken. It is also in the compassion, the
eyes, shown by the Susie's of the world toward a person whose world
is suddenly falling apart, and in the spontaneous acts of people like
Ashford to make contact and be part of what the protégé is experiencing, even in death. Being fragile and gentle are skills to be remembered, honed, and used by every mentor when the time is right.

12. Mentors are people who know how to take care of themselves. They
know how to confront their own anxieties about the enormous responsibilities involved with mentoring colleagues, and in turn are
physically and emotionally up to the mentoring task. A major mes-

sage mentors impart to their protégés is teaching them that self-care is an important part of ongoing professional development. His message is, "You can't be a master teacher if you're not physically and emotionally prepared for the hard work teaching requires every day." Not being ready for the daily demands leaves teachers at risk and vulnerable to poor performance, ill-timed reactions, and burnout.

Mentors are people who know how to take care of themselves. They understand that it is difficult for educators to lead and be models when their own personal issues control and overshadow their efforts. They must be constantly vigilant, working to keep their personal life, health, and emotional well being under control. They know how to confront their own anxieties about the enormous responsibilities involved with mentoring colleagues, and in turn are physically and emotionally up to the mentoring task. A major message mentors impart to their protégé's is teaching them that self-care is an important part of ongoing professional development. Not being ready for the daily demands of teaching leaves teachers at risk and vulnerable to poor performance and burnout.

Effective mentors also understand they are not, and never will be, skilled in every area of mentoring. Some areas of interaction with protégés may test their communication skills. But they are aware of their humanness and, like their protégés in relationships with students, vulnerable to reactions that may surprise and even threaten them. For example, there will be teachers in the mentoring process to whom mentors have difficulty relating. Mentors, too, arrive at the mentoring door with the emotional baggage of their life experiences. While they are aware of their own biases and the people and issues they tend to avoid, mentors, like teachers with students, find communication with some protégés difficult. Knowing and accepting oneself, the positive and the dark side, doesn't eliminate the threatening feelings one can experience relating to others who are different and difficult to help. It requires ongoing discipline and focus. Mentors know that they can't help teachers relate to students who are different and difficult to help if they themselves are unable or unwilling to go through the same process with a protégé. Simply put, you have to walk the walk, not just talk the talk. Talking to protégés about how they should behave without having to do it themselves isn't fair, is it?

In order to maintain a high level of self-care and insight and awareness into interactions with protégés, it is important to have easy access
to credible feedback. That means having a mentoring team in place
made up of fellow administrators, teacher and counselor leaders, and
mentors themselves who serve as a support group for each other. People in leadership roles need easily accessible resources alongside
which they can compare their experiences. They need to continually
assess whether they are communicating effectively with their protégés
or allowing themselves to create barriers that will cause trouble within
their relationship. Mentors need to observe and take notice of each
other, be their brother's keeper, so to speak. When a mentor observes
or hears a fellow mentor becoming combative, they need to intervene
and help him or her sort things out. What are the issues causing the
conflict? Is there another direction to take? No, this is not therapy. It's
simply helping each other stay focused and on course.

13. Mentors have a keen understanding of aging and career development.
    Teachers often find themselves stuck in the one classroom/one school/
    one district career trap. Looking forward to a professional life in which
    one will remain in the same geographical place with little opportunity
    for novelty and change can weigh heavily on one's enthusiasm and
    zest for teaching. Unfortunately, the reality for many teachers is that
    this is the way they will live out their professional lives. Skilled men-
    tors understand that they need to be alert to teachers' comments about
    aging and lack of career change. Effective mentoring can be a posi-
    tive force in helping teachers redefine their careers without necessar-
    ily having to move into new job areas such as counseling or adminis-
    tration where their teaching talents might not be well suited. Helping
    teachers focus on what they are doing well, giving them praise and
    acknowledgement for their good work, helping them reassess their
    skills and select new areas for skill acquisition, and helping them
    mentor other teachers may in fact provide a much more exciting way
    of viewing their work than abandoning the classroom for what seems
    to be a new direction. Many administrators and counselors who have
    left the classroom, as they labor in intensive and pressured jobs, of-
    ten long to return to those days when they worked with students.
    Clearly, helping teachers learn how to mentor other teachers keeps
    them active in their own classrooms but also gives them a new status

in the school and community. It has a nice ring: A teacher of kids and a teacher of teachers.

Novel career change does exist. The Career in Teaching Program in the Cincinnati Public Schools is living proof that this kind of process is doable. As Susan Keiffer-Brown and Kathleen Ware suggest, teaching remains one of the few professions where novices have the same responsibility as twenty-five year veterans.[14] This situation poses problems on two fronts. Prospective and beginning teachers are overwhelmed by the challenges of working with students and experienced teachers have only one option if they want broader professional responsibilities and substantially higher salaries—to leave the classroom for administrative positions. The Cincinnati Career in Teaching Program addresses these problems in a systematic way. The Peer Assistance and Evaluation Program assigns all new hires to consulting teachers, advanced or accomplished teachers in the same subject or grade level who are released from classroom duties to work with up to fourteen teachers. Consulting teachers orient inductees to the district schools, assist them with curriculum and content development, and mentor their teaching skills. Experienced teachers who exhibit serious teaching deficiencies may also be assigned to the consulting teacher. Consulting teachers collaborate in planning lessons, team teach, and hold monthly groups on issues such as managing diverse classrooms, teaching toward the district's standards for learning, and creating multiple forms of student assessment. In this way, new teachers receive support from both the consulting teachers and colleagues. This approach points to the underlying philosophy of the program. Teachers in the district receive the support and mentoring necessary for professional improvement.

Holly M. Bartunek wisely suggests a model that offers mentors a useful resource in understanding the developmental needs of teachers. This model views a teacher's career as moving within a cycle that includes the following stages:

Pre-service
Induction
Competency building
Enthusiastic and growing

Career frustration
Stable and stagnant
Career wind-down
Career exit[15]

These stages are dynamically influenced by personal environmental factors such as family demands and organizational environmental factors such as societal expectations. This model can help remind effective mentors that novice, midcareer, and veteran teachers do indeed have different issues to confront. For example, a novice teacher needs safety, routine, and set boundaries. However, these same parameters may be the kiss of death for experienced midcareer teachers who need novelty, risk, and a career alternative such as mentoring to remain energized and committed. Being "stable and stagnant" has the smell of decay for them. Veteran teachers nearing retirement need a a mentoring process that encourages them to reflect on the help they gave to literally thousands of students and parents. They need to be reminded that their presence mattered a great deal to many people. Veteran teachers also need support to map out where they are headed next. A new career? A move to a new locale? They need gentle questioning concerning what's next. Poor retirement planning can leave newly retired teachers suddenly alone without the safety, routine, and set of boundaries they once knew. They need support in how to say goodbye, walk out the door, embrace their new space. Honoring and remembering retired teachers can help prepare them for a positive exit, help them not to look back

14. Mentors have finely honed political skills and can sell the mentoring program to others and convince them to get involved. Effective mentors must have good selling skills. They are, after all, selling a new product. They want teachers to open up their hearts and their minds to this proposal. In a sense, their mission is to go out among the people, door-to-door if you will, and like a politician, speak the words that make it easy for teachers to say, "I'll join." They have to clearly spell out what is in it for people. They have to use every forum and venue — faculty meetings, team meetings, coffee klatches, faculty room dialog, going to a local bar for a drink, phone calls to teachers at home, and the like — to communicate a core element of the program: the mentor-

ing process shouldn't be refined to one room in a school. It's a lot like running an election; in that mentors need to try to turn out as many positive votes and enthusiasm for the project as they can. Mentors have to believe in the program and believe that the staff really needs mentoring to help them be better teachers. Mentors have to believe that every teacher, even the most resistant and arrogant, wants a way out of being ineffective. The beauty of selling a program like mentoring is that it offers everyone a chance for a new beginning.

15. Mentors understand that sometimes mentoring relationships don't work out; perhaps both sides, the mentor and protégé, have both worked very hard to relate but in the end encounter barriers too difficult to overcome. They are relationships that might have worked out with more awareness, understanding, and intervention skills, but for some reason never successfully got off the ground. Maybe there was too much intimacy, contact, and reliance involved in the failed relationship. Too much of these characteristics on the part of the mentor, the protégé, or both can create a problem and prove to be a risk to the ultimate goal of mentoring—readying the protégé to be self reliant. Mentors—like teachers who seek spend too much time with their favorite students while ignoring the needs of other students—can easily find themselves too involved with protégés who court their favor and involvement. The reverse can be true, where the mentor unconsciously courts the favor and involvement of the protégé. In these situations, a relationship is established early that is comfortable, safe, and enjoyable. Risks often hide in these relationships that become too intimate because they can easily move from being relationships with professional boundaries to a more personal relationship in which the goals of a mentoring program are secondary to the friendship the mentor and mentee form. The mentoring team needs to reinforce the dangers involved in becoming too involved with protégés and they need to intervene when they observe a mentor going down that road. In some cases mentors will need to end the relationship and a protégé will have to be reassigned. Is this a common problem? No, but it can happen in any mentoring program. It's best to be prepared and immediately address the issue with training and ongoing monitoring.

The match between mentor and protégé brings together two people with different backgrounds, cultures, and ways of looking at life. At first, these relationships might seem like poor matches. Sometimes the mentor's personality and mentoring skills simply don't work in relation to the protégé. The mentor's intervention seems to raise resistance rather than create openings for positive communication. An honest assessment by a mentor aware of the problem would rightly focus on ways he or she has to learn new skills to save this floundering relationship. Not all mentors will have this level of awareness or be connected to a mentoring team that could help them think through new alternatives, and the mentoring relationship will end because the differences between mentor and protégé were never solved. Mentors are perhaps flawed as a result because they fear they are likely to repeat this negative performance with another protégé whose different culture and background could threaten the relationship.

As I suggest, these are mentoring relationships that don't have to fail. Education, awareness, new skill acquisition, and monitoring by colleagues can quickly turn these relationships into success stories. Failure to act and leaving these mentors to wrestle with their own problems will result in failed mentoring relationships that might have succeeded. We learn more about ourselves and improve our skills when we are at last able to connect with colleagues and students who come out of a different experience from ours. In the process we learn to understand them and accept them and become a more caring school community.

16. Mentors understand that the mentoring process involves huge professional and personal benefits. Effective mentoring works both ways. It helps teachers become more aware, trusting, effective, and valued by themselves and by colleagues. But the process also helps the mentor. Engaging teachers in one-on-one dialog about their work, offering useful suggestions, and supporting efforts to change can be very animating for mentors. It provides them with the opportunity to know teachers in an intimate and personal way that no supervisory or faculty meeting could offer. It also gives mentors the opportunity for teachers to know them—their skills, the way they try to improve and renew themselves, their professional and personal goals, and their own successes. It also provides mentors with the opportunity to get direct feedback from teachers on how they are doing as a mentor. Is the mentor an effective listener? Is he nonjudgmental? Is he able to

give positive feedback? Is he able to model effective teaching skills? Is he able to help teachers confront sensitive issues such as gender and race? Is he caring and supportive? In the mentoring process he too becomes a learner and opens himself to feedback from his protégés that will help him be more effective. It no doubt comes as a surprise to teachers that mentors also considers themselves learners and want feedback about their performance so they can improve and renew themselves, as well.

Too often in the supervision process the only people who are observed and get feedback are the teachers. There is no place or opportunity for administrators, department chairs, and teacher leaders who do supervision work to get feedback for themselves from teachers. Some may not want feedback; it is not the usual way of doing business. But it does cut them off from growth and real contact with the people they are presumably helping. Elizabeth McCay, assistant professor of educational leadership at Virginia Commonwealth University, suggests:

> Recent efforts in school reform have focused more attention on the professional development of teachers than on the learning needs of school leaders, especially principals who direct the process of change. The isolation that many principals feel often hinders their ability to learn. Feedback from colleagues within the district is often not objective. The staff may fear retribution. Principals need objective, safe . . . feedback. . . . Before principals can take on the dynamic challenges of school reform however, they must become active learners, willing to change their own thinking and practices as they lead others in implementing reform.[16]

In the mentoring process the deck of learning is reshuffled. Mentors, whether they be administrators, department chairs, teacher leaders, or counselor leaders, now become colearners with their protégés, echoing the promise that mentoring can indeed help every educator in the school setting be a continuous learner throughout his or her career. Everyone is in the game of renewal, an idea that, when accepted throughout the school, will lead to a personal, professional, and institutional breath of fresh air.

John S. Holloway describes research in which both mentors and their protégés responded favorably to the mentoring process. Neil Scott analyzed the effects of the Beginning Teacher Induction Program in New Brunswick, Canada, and found that ninety-six percent of beginning teachers and ninety-eight percent of experienced teacher/ mentors felt they benefited from the program. The experienced teachers were enthusiastic because they believed that mentoring allowed them to help others improve themselves, receive respect, develop collegiality, and profit from the novice teachers' fresh ideas and energy.

When mentors—whether they are administrators, teachers, or counselors—become colearners it creates an opportunity for career and personal rebirth. In becoming colearners with their protégés, they too jump off their isolated ledges into the excitement of personal and professional renewal.

17. Mentors understand how to help teachers find and define their best teaching selves. In a real sense, the role of mentors is to help their protégés find their best teaching selves, the professional persona that works best for them. It is a process that encourages the evolving teacher to look within himself, identifying strengths as well as areas that need improvement in order to find their own teaching voice. Mentors encourage teachers to observe colleagues and borrow techniques, but not to blindly become a clone. Building a teaching self modeled on the skills and performance of colleagues is risky. As Arthur Combs suggests:

> The good teacher is not one who behaves in a given way. He is an artist, skillful in facilitating effective growth in students. To accomplish this he must use methods appropriate to the complex circumstances he is involved in. His methods must fit the goals he seeks, the children he is working with, the philosophy he is guided by. . . . The good teacher is no carbon copy but possesses something intensely and personally his own.[17]

Donald Cruickshank addresses the need to have teachers find their best teaching selves. He cites Robert Travers, who suggests that teachers must be always ready to modify their role and search for material and sources within themselves through which the modified role can be achieved. Travers calls for a mentor or "role trainer" to help teachers gain insight into their role by encouraging them to be like actors and become totally immersed in their unique role rather than simply saying the correct words and performing the correct actions. He cautions against becoming a robot, a clone, and following the role modeled by a particular teacher. The critical question asked by the mentor is, "What do you, as a unique person, bring to our students, staff, and school, and how can we help you to shine this light?"[18]

18. Wise mentors understand that an important task of the mentor is helping protégés clarify the many roles they play in the classroom, school, and community. The mentor understands that teaching is not an easy job and is not one easily mastered without help. Teachers must play many roles and show many faces. Donald Cruickshank highlights some of these roles that have emerged from school reform proposals:

"A competent teacher" is a teacher who knows what good or effective K–12 practitioners do and they are able to demonstrate these abilities.

"A student of teaching" is a teacher who is reflective; that is, he or she gives careful consideration to the act of teaching.

"A community builder" is a teacher who is humane and who enhances the self-image of students and members of the community.

"An artist" is a teacher who knows who they are, what they are like, and how they can use their unique talent to enhance student learning.

"A concerned teacher" is more concerned with the needs of students and less concerned with his or her own needs.

"An actor" is a teacher who understands the role of effective classroom practitioners and has acquired the abilities to perform it well.

"A problem solver/decision maker" is a teacher able to resolve problems and make decisions in a way in which benefits accrue to all parties.

"An enlightened teacher" is well educated and concerned primarily with students becoming well educated.

"A culturally responsible teacher" is ready and able to work with diverse students in diverse communities.

"An inquiring teacher" directly engages in inquiry related to teaching and learning.

Cruickshank's data serves to remind us that becoming a competent teacher requires the acquisition of many different roles and skills. This process of acquiring roles and skills also requires motivation, encouragement, and ongoing opportunity to sustain and improve these skills throughout one's career. Clearly, most teachers cannot develop these roles and skills on their own or overnight. They need mentors to teach and support them.

19. Mentors understand that they must bring some joy, energy, humor, and lightness to the mentoring relationship. It is important for mentors to keep in mind one axiom about a good school: it's a fun place to be and people—students, teachers, parents, and even administrators—are having a good time. Maybe not every day; after all, crises and bad times do come to the best of schools. But overall there is a lot of laughter, celebration, and hanging out when the work of the day is accomplished. We see students, staff, and administrators being themselves, not aloof professionals clinging to their degrees and professional status. Mentors need to foster this kind of climate with their protégés. The work of teaching is serious and the consequences of our actions are vitally important. But taking ourselves too seriously, forgetting that it is fun to be around kids, and living totally by the rules can result in a big dose of teacher boredom. What student wants to go to class where everything is serious, where no laughs are allowed, where the day is all about getting ready for SATs, state tests, and finals?

An important aspect of the work of mentoring is teaching protégés to be balanced—not too serious, yet not too undisciplined. That means encouraging protégés not to have too many rules. A mentor's mantra—and consequently, the teacher's—is, "Leave room for play, for the unexpected, for the *Catch-22, M.A.S.H., One Flew over the Cuckoo's Nest* issues that take place in a school every day." One way to get this message across to protégés is for the mentors not to have too many rules themselves, both as a school leader and as a mentor. What is this kind of behavior like? Herman Edwards, coach of the New York Jets football team, put it well when he said:

> I don't believe in too many rules. I believe in high expectations and making those known individually. I expect people to handle themselves and if they don't then we have to talk. I believe in an open en-

vironment because it's good for the team and good for the game. I believe in having coaches who are teachers and who display energy. I believe that players are the system and that coaches can play a greater role in ensuring that players do not fail. I always want our players to understand that everything we do here will be designed toward them being able to use their talents. It's almost like if you go to a park and watch kids play. They only have a couple of plays that they drew up in the sand and they use their talents from there. Sure, we can make it as complicated as we like, but the key is to simplify and let the talent surface. Coach to their talent and strengths. We will do that here and off the field. . . . I believe in these words. . . . Be you. It's good enough.[19]

This is good advice for mentors and teachers. Keep it simple. Let the talent surface. Don't let students and teachers be caught up in complicated rules and overly high expectations. In Edwards' words, "Be you. It's good enough." Mentors need to be balanced in their training with teachers. They need to arrive at the mentoring sessions ready for interaction that is serious while at the same time being prepared for lightness and a few laughs. Focus on the nuts and bolts of improvement but leave room for a little self-deprecation and learning to laugh at our mistakes and ourselves. This is how teacher lore is created, with stories and tales from the classroom that teachers remember because they are so bizarre that they have to laugh at themselves or cry. Every teacher has some of these experiences. Wise mentors know laughter sometimes softens bad landings.

20. Mentors understand that their lack of knowledge about every subject and grade level does not reduce mentoring effectiveness. In the real world of mentoring, it will not be possible to match a protégé with a mentor who is completely knowledgeable about his subject matter or grade level issues. This lack of knowledge should not be a barrier to effective mentoring. What really counts is the mentor's understanding of classroom dynamics and effective teaching. Skilled mentors see clearly when a teacher is zeroed in on his lesson and students, and knows when students are into it—zoomed in on the teacher and his delivery. There is a sense of excitement, rhythm, and risk in the air, an atmosphere that says "we all want to be here and we're loving this moment." The sub-

ject matter or grade level becomes irrelevant. What matters is that learning is taking place for both the students and teacher.

On the other hand, mentors also see clearly when teachers are not zeroed in on the lesson and their students. Instead of excitement, rhythm, and risk in the air, the classroom becomes a disjointed, even unbalanced climate in which both the teacher and students are at odds, finding no middle ground or harmony. Teacher and student look for a way out, an early exit from the stress of the classroom. They are like symphony musicians who have never practiced together; their music doesn't connect. Here the subject matter becomes irrelevant; it remains elusive. The class never seems to get to the point where knowledge and learning take place. The classroom lacks safety, routine, respect, and boundaries. Many classroom management issues need to be addressed before the students become learners. It's like an abusive family acting out. Order and safety must be restored before any semblance of family life—caring, respect, and love—can emerge.

Yes, knowledge of subject matter is useful, but I believe that understanding what constitutes effective teaching is a higher priority, a priority that helps mentors support what is working and see it clearly. It is a priority that requires mentors to intervene when they observe what is not working, when they see an imbalance that needs to be corrected.

21. Wise mentors understand that they have to teach their protégés how to create ongoing sources of support—a social network—to enhance learning and renewal, and in their mentoring role create "mentoring hubs" where informal learning and exchange are ongoing and easily accessible. At some point, mentoring reaches a conclusion. The mentor and his protégé must part company and move on to other tasks. It is critical for the protégé to have established his own support and learning network: colleagues he likes to spend time with, talk about new ideas with, and seek expert advice from. Many teachers lack a supportive network. They spend time with students, in faculty rooms, and at meetings, but often lack informal, ongoing contact with colleagues who can be supportive. Laurence Prusack and Don Cohen, authors of *In Good Company,* make the case that successful businesses pay loving attention to commonplace conversations and everyday life. They suggest that telling and listening to stories, chatting, sharing a little gossip, are the main ways that people in organi-

zations come to trust and understand one another. Because successful businesses rely on a foundation of trust, commitment, and novelty, they have concluded that they possess an enormous but untapped asset in the wisdom accumulated by workers over decades of experience. The challenge is creating an organizational setting in which workers come together on a regular basis to exchange conversation and pick each other's brains. Prusack and Cohen point out that in 1998 Alcoa, the aluminum giant, made a physical investment in social capital by moving its headquarters from a thirty-one story tower to an eight-story building that featured open offices, glass-walled conference rooms and escalators instead of elevators. Each floor had a family style kitchen to encourage workers to mingle. Executives at Oticon, a maker of hearing aids, noted that people often paused to talk as they passed on the stairs, so Oticon rebuilt its office to create broad stairwell landings with coffee machines and places to sit.[20]

But as Malcolm Gladwell suggests, while innovation and the best ideas arise out of casual contact among different groups in the company, getting people in a workplace to bump into people from other departments is not as easy as it looks. Gladwell describes the work of a researcher at MIT named Thomas Allen who conducted a decade-long study of the way in which engineers communicated in research laboratories.[21] Allen found that the likelihood that any two people will communicate drops off dramatically as the distance between their desks increases. A worker is four times more likely to communicate with someone who sits six feet away than with someone who sits sixty feet away. People who sit seventy-five feet apart hardly talk at all. Allen also found that when people weren't talking to those in their immediate vicinity, many spent time talking to people outside their company. He concluded that it was actually easier to make the outside call than walk across the hallway.

There is a subtle but powerful message in this data that speaks to the difficulty isolated workers like teachers face in their desire to be life-long learners. If you constantly ask for advice or guidance from people, you may risk losing prestige. Colleagues might think the teacher is incompetent. The people teachers are asking for advice might get annoyed. Calling an outsider avoids these problems. Allen's engineers were far too willing to go outside the company to ask for advice and new ideas. I believe that is the case with many teachers. The wise mentor understands the need to help his protégés to identify where and from whom to get advice. After all, many schools, particularly secondary schools, have huge campuses, some with student populations of 2500 or more. Mentors need to query their protégés on whom they spend time with, whom they talk to about new ideas, and where they get their expert advice. In other words, mentors should ask teachers to describe their network for support and where they go to get this exchange. Describe how they overcome the barriers that keep teachers isolated and dependent on themselves or, as in Allen's case of engineers, an outside person who doesn't really understand their work setting. The positive results of successful mentoring can quickly dissipate without supportive networks in place.

Finally, mentors should work to create informal gatherings and forums where colleagues can easily come together to exchange ideas. I call these gathering "mentoring hubs" because they are an extension of the one-on-one mentoring process. What are these mentoring hubs like? Schools don't have the resources to build new settings like Alcoa did that encourage more face-to-face exchange. However, teachers can be invited to pre-school and after-school coffee klatches, lunchtime brown bag discussions, and school meetings featuring topics related to teacher renewal. The idea is to help teachers stay in close contact with each other in diverse environments, hubs that foster professional exchange and growth, places to try out new ideas with colleagues and ask each other, "What's stopping you?" To accomplish this task, mentors need to look at their schools in new ways, not just as a series of classrooms and offices, a physical space. They must create a personal vision of where, when, and how ongoing learning and renewal can take place, and gain the necessary support for such interactions. They must create places that have a professional feel where people of service—and that is what teachers are—can gather, places of opportunity that can open new doors, the antithesis of the professionally eroding conversations of the faculty room.

Creating hubs of learning in the school setting can be a simple undertaking on a small scale. As Emitai Etzioni suggests, in order to increase a sense of community and connectedness, "we need to provide people shared space to mingle. It does not require a grand social science study to note that when chairs are placed in empty spaces in many public buildings next to elevators, people are often found there 'visiting.' The same holds true for other places to sit, from park benches to lounges in public libraries."[22] In schools it means creating new ways for people to come together by turning an empty office or classroom into a lounge area with a new or used sofa, chairs, and a coffeepot, a teachers' place to launch new ideas.

In a real sense then, mentors are the pulse-takers of the school. They have direct links to the many teachers and formal and informal networks these teachers create. In the mentoring process, one-on-one meetings with teachers elicit a great deal of data about their work experience. Teachers raise issues such as lack of trust, boredom, being trapped, and a strong desire for novelty and stimulation. This data provides clues as to whether the school setting is meeting the needs of teachers. In other words, is the school setting providing conditions that allow teachers to experience growth, differentiation, and diversity throughout their careers? Mentors are well-positioned to translate this data into ongoing hubs of learning that provide opportunities for novelty, communication, and testing of new ideas, places where teachers go to get and give information in an environment that allows easy access and exchange.

22. Mentors have a sense of the history of the school and the good work that has gone on there. One of the most troubling aspects of modern school life is the lack of tribute and respect for former teachers. There are usually no pictures of teachers who have served in the school, no brief history of their contributions—where they served, subject or grade taught, extracurricular activities such as coaching, degrees awarded, not even a memorial wall listing their names. It is as if they vanished when they retired or left the school for another position. The same can be said of teachers currently serving in the school; they too lack visible recognition that they are part of the school community, yet without their presence the school community would be diminished.

Wise mentors understand the important role of honoring former teachers and highlighting the part each current teacher plays in making the school an exciting and caring setting. They understand that teachers want to feel they are making a significant contribution and want to be remembered for these contributions. With this in mind they use their mentoring role to establish visible connections between former and current teachers in the school, such as a memorial wall. When teachers walk through the hallways and see memorials to former teachers who labored on the front lines of the classrooms, they feel a sense of history, continuity, belonging to an ongoing community of teachers, and reassurance that they too will have an honored place when they move on. Mentors also help create a living memorial wall for current teachers and other members of the staff, a visible testament that it takes many different professionals and support staff to create a positive school community and an acknowledgement that each person counts, students included.

Matthew King speaks to the need for this kind of honoring and recognition system. He describes a project to erect a Wall of Recognition at Lincoln-Sudbury Regional High School in Sudbury, Massachusetts. The purpose is to "establish a tradition of recognizing and celebrating the lives of people who have made enduring contributions to Lincoln-Sudbury. This tradition should help students understand and value the lives of people whose commitment has made the school a special place. Those eligible will be faculty, administrators, staff, and school committee members who have provided vision, direction, and contributions to students, faculty and the life of the school." Among those selected was Harriet Rogers (director of the drama department and English teacher, 1965–1978) who created the Lincoln-Sudbury drama program. An Emmy winner, "she was no prima donna. Sneaker-clad and chewing gum, she coached hundreds of students in a thirteen-year string of outstanding productions." Also chosen was Paul Mitchell (history teacher 1957–1990, department chairman 1960–1979) who "lectured, led, and dazzled his students with the spectacular history of Russia. His course emphasized self-exploration as students kept journals and even graded themselves." Another choice was former Superintendent C. Newton Heath (superintendent 1957–1964), who guided the creation of Lincoln-Sudbury as a regional high school. "'Doc' interviewed every teacher, met with every committee, and knew every student. His confidence and determination created a nurturing atmosphere and his trust inspired loyalty."

King wisely notes that these kinds of programs help to build strong schools. As he suggests, "Schools that get results are places where adults work hard, focus on improvement, and believe they make a difference in the lives of their students. We also know that schools with strong, positive cultures are places where rituals and traditions celebrate innovation and commitment, where an informal network of heroes inspires colleagues and where a pervasive sense of shared purpose and an ethos of caring and concern exist."[23]

Honoring our past and present staff with recognition like the Lincoln-Sudbury Wall of Recognition sends a strong, positive message to students, parents, and staff, a message that says that something worthwhile has gone and is going on here—produced by people like drama teacher Harriet Rogers, history teacher Paul Mitchell, and superintendent C. Newton Heath—caring and concerned people whose efforts make a difference in the daily lives of school-community members.

I believe developing a mentoring process for teachers at every career stage is a vital ingredient in helping our schools succeed. Simply put, most teachers will not improve if left on their own. They need an easily accessible and recognizable method such as mentoring to help them improve their skills. This list of mentoring characteristics hopefully helps future mentors become more aware of the complexity of the mentoring role and the skills that are necessary to do the job well.

In addition, there are also more subtle aspects about becoming a mentor that need illumination. Becoming an effective mentor has a lot to do with belief. An effective mentor, above all, has to believe in teachers and their capacity to learn and relearn. It is the same as teachers believing that each of the kids in their classroom is capable of learning given the right intervention. Mentor must believe that what they have to offer teachers matters and is of use to them. They must also believe that most teachers want sound advice, useful feedback that makes sense, and the opportunity to learn new skills if they are at ease and safe with their mentor. Teachers want to be successful.

It is necessary to understand that offering help and support to teachers is not always an easy task. In order for teachers to receive help and be open to acquiring new skills, they have to trust their mentor and be able to expose both their strengths and weaknesses, along the way discovering areas to build on, areas that need reworking, or areas that require a new beginning. It is a process of opening themselves up and saying, "This is me." What skills are working and what is dragging me down? Teachers, even the most successful ones, run into walls and experience failure at different points in their careers. Even the kindest and most caring teachers can get into the game of blaming the kids, the parents, society, whatever else may be an easy scapegoat. In bad times, hostility and blame are never far away. It is not easy to honestly look in the mirror and consider the possibility that one's own skills are not up to the task at hand and take responsibility for the failure. Ironically, taking responsibility for what is not working in the classroom is often more difficult for the most successful teachers. Dealing with a failed classroom experience can be crippling for every teacher, but it is doubly hard for those teachers who have been elevated to "teacher of the year" or the like—the best and brightest, the ones we should all emulate, the career .500 hitters who are now batting .150.

The well-prepared mentor also understands that a major reason for teacher failure is boredom and the line of thinking that fools oneself into believing that he or she understands all there is to know about kids and teaching. Their work is over—paycheck, please! They get stale, stop learning, and begin playing the waiting game—waiting for their break, for 3:00 P.M. on Friday, for June, and for retirement. When teachers play the waiting game, they are vulnerable to new challenges and the winds of change, like a sailboat drifting without a rudder. Kids sense when teachers are playing the waiting game, sitting and watching the clock, taking too many sick days. They are no fools. They often act out, demanding a response from the waiting teacher who may have forgotten how to respond.

The world of professional sports is filled with examples of failure on the part of star players who stopped working on developing their skills, thinking they would remain stars all the same. Skills and talent, they mistakenly thought, were givens. They, too, played the waiting game—in basketball not asking for the ball at crunch time, in baseball not wanting to be the man hitting with the game on the line, in football not being the "go to" guy on fourth down. They are, as Woody Allen, says, reading their reviews. The same goes for many teachers; thinking they understand kids and teaching and that things will never change. It allows boredom and waiting to enter their professional lives and do their destructive work. Good teachers must rage against it.

They have to fight sophistication. They have to fight knowing because once they know something, it's hard to be open and creative.

At the same time, failure also has the potential to be a professional life-saving experience. It can present the opportunity for new growth and learning. But all of this cannot happen, I believe, without the intervention of a skilled and caring mentor who holds the belief that change is always possible, whether or not the teacher is going through a good time. A wise mentor might say to a faltering teacher, "Shift your weight. If you are willing, as a teacher, to put in the hard work to learn new skills, the sky is the limit. A part of the so-called hard work is giving up and letting go of what worked in the past and learning how to create a new teaching environment. You will no doubt be afraid and uneasy. Giving up tired skills, what used to work, for new and untested skills is risky. Should you? Shouldn't you? As Dr. Seuss suggests, "You'll play lonely games. . . . Games you can't win 'cause you'll play against you."

Teachers need, I believe, a wise and skilled partner to stay with them and support them on the journey. Can teachers reinvent themselves without intervention? There are miracles. Some teachers can hit bottom and, on their own, claw their way back up, acquiring new workable skills inch by inch. But most of them need a trusted mentor they can talk to and who has a nonjudgmental voice and heart that can help them get better. It reminds us of John Steinbeck's *East of Eden:* "Get your eyes set on where you are going and then look to your feet, lest ye stumble."[24]

The road to gaining and regaining effective teaching is filled with bumps and pitfalls. One of the biggest challenges of mentoring is creating conditions and pathways of success to overcome the isolation and sense of going it alone that almost every teacher experiences. Teachers seldom, if at all, get the opportunity to observe and engage in dialog with a master teacher at work. Unfortunately, the window through which most teachers come in contact with other teachers is often limited to discussion in the faculty room of those colleagues and students who are not making it. These discussions of the failure of colleagues and students serve to fuel the fire of teachers' discontent. These faculty-room conversations, reflecting a desperate need of teachers to make contact in their otherwise hurried and isolated days are usually not helpful. Rather, these conversations often focus on gossip and ridicule of colleagues, parents, and students, representing, as Ann Carson suggests, examples of professionals trafficking in the inessentials of life. Teachers settle for less and become less so as not to be alone and lonely in their everyday work.

The stories and examples of how successful teachers work hard to develop their talent, art, and skills are rarely shared or heard, and almost never observed in action. Schools have no forum or venue to go to watch successful teachers do their work. As a result, successful teachers usually go unheralded and underappreciated. The stories of how they got to the top of their game, how they stay there, how they refined their skills over time, and how they dealt with failure are all locked inside. No one asks to hear about their journey and their secrets to success, and so others do not learn from their experience.

Effective mentors understand this negative and isolating process and work to create conditions that bring the work and skills of effective teachers into the full light of day, where colleagues can observe and learn the skills that truly make for professional competence. Mentors understand that in isolation it is easy for teachers to go down wrong roads and, like their failing students, reach a dead end. It is far too easy to lose the passion and spirit that may have brought them into teaching, especially with a daily dose of negative faculty-room talk. As St. Exupery reminds us, "Old bureaucrat, my comrade, it's not you who are to blame. Nobody grasped you by the shoulder while there was till time. Now the clay of which you were shaped has dried and hardened, and naught in you will ever awaken the sleeping musician, poet, and the astronomer that inhabited you in the beginning."[25]

Finally, there are bumps and pitfalls for the mentors as well. They have to believe that their vision of investing in teachers' ongoing professional development is a doable undertaking. It is one thing to talk about change. We all get excited talking about change and reform, but the hard work, difficult decisions, and gut-wrenching reactions that are involved in change call for specific and knowledgeable action. Mentors may have to reshuffle their priorities to meet the current needs of teachers. They may have to give up traditional practices, assumptions, and conventional wisdom about what a mentor's workday should look like. They may have to view the mentoring of teachers as the top priority, finding the most efficient way to intervene and help teachers, and discarding practices that may look and feel good but do little to improve the overall effectiveness of the teaching staff. Mentors may have to mentor teachers in small and large groups as well as individually, and also train department heads and teacher leaders to be leaders and constituents, thereby enlarging the mentoring circle. Mentors may have to use so-called free periods for school-day mentoring opportunities. By doing so, mentors will create a new landscape in the school for viewing teachers as learners and positive contributors to the growth of their colleagues and their students.

In baseball terms, this vision of a mentoring process involves using the whole field. Good hitters don't just look for their pitch and become labeled as left field, right field, fastball, or curveball hitters. Rather, they look for any pitch that is hittable to every section of the ballpark. They are not predictable. They use the whole field and are hard to defend against. In teacher training terms, using the whole field means moving beyond the predictable staff development programs common to many schools, the hit-or-miss workshops and conferences often not based on the real needs of teachers and generously labeled as teacher training. Replace this out of date model with a full service menu of learning and mentoring opportunities, making training so easily accessible and attractive that teachers want to say yes, not no, and use home-based mentors, administrators, and teachers as leaders in the process. Schools must fight the notion that their own staff can't become prophets in their own land.

NOTES

1. John Lahr, "Making It Real . . . How Mike Nichols Recreated Comedy and Himself," *The New Yorker* (21 February 2000): 197.

2. Cy Coleman, "It's Not Where You Start," from the Broadway musical *Seesaw,* 1972.

3. Stephen Sondheim, "I'm Still Here," from *Follies.*

4. Alan Riding, "The Joy of a Comeback that Leaves the Past Behind," *New York Times,* 29 April 2001, AR3.

5. Alan Riding, "Looking at a France That's Seldom Seen," *New York Times,* 27 August 2000, AR17.

72   Chapter 3

6. Kevin Spacey and Jack Lemmon, "A Couple of Winners Talk Awards and Acting," *New York Times,* 12 March 2000, MT2.

7. Melanie Rehak, "Things Fall Together," *New York Times,* 26 March 2000, sec. 6, 36.

8. John Lahr, "Been Here and Gone . . . How August Wilson Brought a Century of Black American Culture to the Stage," *The New Yorker* (16 April 2000): 49–65.

9. Amy Zipkin, "In Tight Labor Market Bosses Find Value in Being Nice," *New York Times,* 31 May 2000, C1.

10. Seymour Sarason, *Creation of Settings* (San Francisco: Jossey Bass, 1972), 115.

11. Jean Ciavonne, "Dandelions, Pine-Cone Turkey, and Abraham Lincoln," *Kappan* 66(2) (October 1984): 142–43.

12. John S. Holloway, "The Benefits of Mentoring," *Educational Leadership* 58(8) (May 2001): 85–86.

13. Caryn James, "Mighty Thou Art: To A Compassionate Heart," *New York Times,* 23 March 2001, E1, p. 27.

14. Susan Kieffer-Brown and Kathleen Ware, "Growing Great Teachers in Cincinnati," *Educational Leadership* 58(8) (May 2001): 56–58.

15. Holly Bartunek, "Classroom Teacher as Teacher Educator," ERIC, 1989, http://www.ericsp.org/pages/digests/classroom_teacher_edu_89-7.html (4 April 2001).

16. Elizabeth McCay, "The Learning Needs of Principals," *Educational Leadership* 58(8) (May 2001): 75–76.

17. Arthur Combs, et al., *Helping Relationships: Basic Concepts for the Helping Profession* (Boston: Allyn & Bacon, 1971), 7–8.

18. Donald Cruickshank, et al., *Preparing America's Teachers* (Bloomington, IN: Phi Delta Kappa Foundation, 1996), 63–64, 87–88.

19. Thomas George, "Jets Discover Their Coach's Joyful Energy," *New York Times,* 17 May 2001, D5.

20. Fred Andrews, "Learning to Celebrate Water-Cooler Gossip," *New York Times,* 25 February 2001, BU6.

21. Malcolm Gladwell, "Designs for Working," *The New Yorker* (11 December 2000): 60.

22. Emitai Etzioni, *The Spirit of Community* (New York: Crown Publishers, 1993), 128.

23. Matthew King, "If These Walls Could Talk," *Educational Leadership* 58(5) (February 2001): 64–65.

24. John Steinbeck, *East of Eden* (New York: Viking Press, 1952), 345.

25. Antoine Saint Exupery, *Wind, Sand, and Stars* (New York: Reynolds & Hitchcock, 1939), 23.

4

How Administrators Can Assess
Their Mentoring Skills

How does a busy school administrator proceed to become an effective mentor? I believe mentors need to address the following issues before actually beginning the mentoring process. Failure to deal with each of these issues can lead to program failure. Here are the issues:

1. Assess personal mentoring skills: strengths and areas that need improvement and further training.
2. Avoid the pitfall that every master teacher and education leader can become an effective mentor.
3. Select a mentoring team.
4. Train a mentoring team.
   a. Utilize the mentoring training described in chapter 4 as a training guide for would-be mentors.
   b. Build an effective mentoring team by identifying possible mentoring conflicts.
   c. Analyze the change in role from administrator to trainer of mentors and a mentor.
   d. Plan, with the team, the parameters and nuts and bolts of the program, such as how to hold one-on-one mentoring meetings.
5. Sell the mentoring concept to the school, including administrators, teachers, and staff.
6. Identify and overcome resistance from everyone involved in the mentoring process.
7. Create antennae to identify and head off problems that will surely arise.

This chapter focuses on the first issue—how a mentor can assess his or her own mentoring skills. Chapter 5 addresses the remaining issues that can lead to program failure if left unattended

HOW TO ASSESS PERSONAL MENTORING SKILLS

Step #1: The Personal Experience Inventory

An important first step in assessing your mentoring skills is to reflect on the positive mentors you have encountered in your professional and personal life:

1. What mentors helped guide you in your personal and professional life? Was it a coach, a teacher, a counselor, a minister, a college professor, a principal, a parent, an older sibling?
2. What skills did these mentors have? Were they good listeners? Were they nonjudgmental? Encouraging? Capable of delivering criticism in a positive way that made sense? Were they intimate, knowable, and accessible? When you were involved with these mentors, did you feel comfortable and at home?
3. What words of encouragement and support did these mentors use when talking with you? What words worked best to help you? Did they say something like, "You're doing really well coaching this team. One of the best coaching jobs I've seen in my career. Still, I have one small suggestion that may help you. You seem kind of hard on your second base player. How about sitting down and giving her some positive strokes? She gets easily discouraged. Build her up. It may be just the thing to help the team go all the way to the championship. You are good at this kind of thing."?
4. Have you modeled your own professional life after these mentors? Many administrators and school leaders go into teaching because they have experienced positive mentors in their own school experience. Many teachers nourish the care and guidance mentors have given them. By becoming mentors themselves, it provides a way to pass on their own positive experience to other teachers and students.
5. Do you employ some of the same skills you learned from your mentors in your role as administrator and school leader? Are you a good

listener, non-judgmental, encouraging, able to deliver criticism in a positive way that makes sense, intimate, knowable, and accessible?

It is also important to recall those would-be mentors who had a negative impact on you. Many professionals set out with good intentions to mentor colleagues, but in fact lack the skills, caring, compassion, and the ability to work one-on-one in an intimate relationship. Consider the following points:

1. What mentors set out to help and guide you but were unable to deliver in this role? We all get exposed to coaches, teachers, counselors, college professors, principals, parents, and older siblings who were unable to connect with us in a positive way. Was it your lack of ability, personality, appearance, color, or background that somehow made them set you apart? Or was their lack of intimacy and comfort with you really their issue or problem, somehow making you feel left out?

2. What mentoring skills did they lack? Were they poor listeners, judgmental, not encouraging, critical, and not intimate, knowable, or accessible? When you were involved with these negative mentors, was something amiss or even threatening?

3. What word did these mentors use that convinced you that you were in an unhelpful relationship? Was the conversation something like this: "Jim, I wanted to speak to you about yesterday's game. As athletic director it's my job to solve coaching problems. I felt you used poor judgment in leaving Mark Jennings in the game too long. He couldn't find the plate by the seventh inning. Then you chose to let Dwight Scott hit with bases loaded. Why? He's been hitless in the last four games. Sometimes I get the feeling you're just not the man we need in this position. I don't see much good. You may be a great teacher but I don't know about your coaching skill."?

4. In developing your own professional persona, have you deliberately tried to avoid becoming like these negative mentors? Or have some of their negative behaviors and attitudes crept in silently and taken hold of your persona? As professionals, we enter the school setting priding ourselves on our ability to work effectively with every staff member and student. The reality of school life soon strikes with the

awareness that we are not as open and inclusive as we thought. We do have communication and relationship problems with certain teachers and students. It is relatively easy to overlook this dilemma or even to say it doesn't exist. Over time, we become negative mentors for these teachers and students. Has this same excluding, denying process become part of your personal persona? Have you become a negative mentor for some? Are you a victim of settling and not willing to change, to be inclusive?

5. What mentoring skills have you developed as an administrator and school leader to avoid the characteristics of the negative mentors in your life? Being an effective mentor takes ongoing discipline and work. It is easy to slip into a negative mentoring stance. Schools are hectic places in which relationships and communication are easily strained. It is a fine line between being helpful and being critical.

Mentors should take a personal inventory of the teachers they like to help and guide as an important part of assessing their own mentoring skills. Mentors need to identify which teachers they like and gravitate toward:

1. What are the characteristics of the teachers you tend to want to help and guide? Do you feel more comfortable with female than male teachers? Younger teachers? Highly effective teachers? Teachers who present at conferences and help put your school, and your career, on display?

2. What part do issues related to age, gender, color, personality, ethnicity, appearance, and subject or grade level play in determining whom you like to help and guide? Are you more comfortable helping teachers who have supported your vision and goals? Who teach in subject areas you have taught? Teachers who came into the school with you and have remained close friends throughout the many changes in the school setting?

3. What needs of yours are met through interactions with these favorite teachers? Are your needs for friendship, praise, affirmation, and support met by interacting with these teachers? We all come to our work setting with personal needs to be met. But is your overall efficiency and leadership style being diminished by focusing too much on teachers who are most like you?

It is also highly useful to assess the characteristics of teachers we tend to avoid and find difficult to help and guide:

1. What are the characteristics of teachers you tend to avoid and find difficult to guide? It is important to reflect on those people you avoid. It happens to all school leaders and teachers. We arrive at the school door with our own biases, judgments, and prejudices. That is only human. The work is to try to figure out our own avoidance process and work at building our tolerance and inclusion level.

2. What part do issues related to age, gender, color, ethnicity, personality, appearance, and grade level or subject play in determining what teachers you avoid helping and guiding? Do you have difficulty communicating with aging teachers who are resisting retirement? Those who teach subject areas and grades you are not familiar with? Teachers who are ineffective? Female teachers?

3. What kinds of inner conflicts arise when you become involved in helping and guiding teachers who you sense are out of step with your image of an effective teacher? Resistance both within you and the teachers you have trouble relating to is a condition. Neither party welcomes the interaction. You have much to gain in coming to terms with the real you and overcoming your own resistance to helping others. Like teachers who have learned to overcome their inner conflict and resistance to help students they have avoided, you can become a complete mentor. Acknowledge that you have a dark side that senses caution, threat, and the unknown aspects encountered with some teachers. You may feel that they are not on your side or that they are not worth the effort. In fact, they are worth the effort if you are to become the complete mentor. Mentoring only those you feel comfortable with is half the game; it's incomplete. It is important to become aware of your biases and acknowledge whom you push away.

The value of this inventory is that it helps administrators begin a conversation with themselves about the mentoring persona they develop based on their own professional and personal life experiences. The inventory also clarifies that an administrator's own life experiences may in fact push them in the direction of wanting to mentor certain teachers whom they feel comfortable with and avoiding others with whom they feel out of sync. It reminds them that they are human and that more work needs to be done so they avoid this mentoring pitfall. Like teachers with their students, administrators are expected to connect with all of their mentees and avoid selective intervention.

In assessing their mentoring skills, it is also useful for mentors to reflect on their vision for the mentoring program. How is the mentoring program going to fit in with other ongoing programs? Will it be a comfortable fit or is there the possibility of jarring and upsetting resistance? Mentors might reflect on these questions in order to make the mentoring program run smoothly:

1. What is your vision for the school?
2. To what extent have you been successful in realizing your vision?
3. What individuals and groups in the school and community have promoted your vision?
4. What kind of ongoing support have you given these individuals and groups?
5. What obstacles have arisen to block your vision?
6. What individuals and groups in the school and community have resisted your vision?
7. How have you handled these obstacles and setbacks in furthering your vision? Have you created communication barriers with these individuals and groups?
8. New programs such as the mentoring program have two important requirements, a recognizable place and function in the school setting and wide-based support. How do you plan to achieve this goal?
   a. How will you promote your vision for mentoring?
   b. Who will be involved in your mentoring team?
   c. Who will be your allies?
9. How will you win over your detractors?
   a. What kinds of problems can you expect?
   b. What kind of problem-control strategy will you have in place? Problems not addressed will only get worse.
10. The development of new programs can be risky at both professional and personal levels. The process usually requires an increase in emotional, intellectual, and physical energy. How do you rate your

emotional, intellectual, and physical energy, your will to win, and your political savvy? What impact will this new program have on your professional and personal life?

11. What new, different skills will be required in developing the mentoring program?

Step #2: Checklist for Understanding Mentoring Skills

In step 2, administrators take a hard look at their present mentoring skills and determine what areas need improvement. Not every would-be mentor will possess all of the characteristics identified in chapter 3. Skill acquisition is incremental and ongoing. This checklist helps administrators identify where they are, what skills are in line, and what work needs to be done. Like a teacher working with students, mentors should take the positive road first by identifying what they are doing well and then moving on to what needs fixing. This checklist is based on the mentoring characteristics I described in detail in chapter 3:

1. Do I understand the dynamics of teaching and the real world of the classroom or have I been so involved in administrative duties that I have lost touch with the feel and texture of the classroom?
2. Do I understand the notion that teaching is hard work and renewing oneself is not always easy or sought after?
3. Do I understand that improving one's skills calls for risks and new directions?
4. Do I understand that every teacher in my school will arrive at the classroom door with their own set of biases, prejudices, and judgments?
5. Do I understand that bad times, failure, and burnout can happen to every teacher, even the most successful ones?
6. Do I value the loyalty and privacy of the protégés involved in the mentoring program?
7. Do I understand that the personal and family problems of students can be very emotional and painful for teachers?
8. Do I understand that problematic personal relationships of teachers—family, marriage, illness, divorce, death, addiction—impact on the teachers' effectiveness and well-being?

9. Do I understand that mentoring relationships will change over time, often with newly skilled protégés gradually taking on a mentoring persona and stature of their own?

10. Do I understand that resistance to mentoring will take place? Not every teacher will embrace mentoring and they will have to be sold on the process.

11. Do I know how to listen, be nonjudgmental, and provide useful feedback and modeling that can act as a guide for teacher improvement?

12. Do I know how to administer self-care? How to be physically and emotionally fit and up to the mentoring task?

13. Do I have knowledge about the aging process in career development so I can more effectively guide teachers?

14. Do I have finely honed political skills so that I can effectively overcome resistance and sell the program?

15. Do I understand that there will be mentoring relationships that don't work and will require new arrangements?

16. Do I understand that there are huge personal and professional benefits for me in the mentoring process?

17. Do I know how to help my protégés find and define their best teaching selves?

18. Do I know how to help my protégés clarify the many complex roles they play in the classroom?

19. Do I know how to bring a sense of joy, energy, humor, and lightness to the mentoring relationship?

20. Do I understand that my lack of in-depth knowledge of every subject area and grade level need not reduce my effectiveness in mentoring teachers?

21. Do I know how to teach my protégés to create ongoing sources of support, learning hubs, ongoing opportunities for renewal?

22. Do I have a sense of history of my school setting, the good work that has gone on in the past by caring teachers, the creative responses to changing needs and times, and the good work that now goes on each day?

This self-assessment of the skills and understanding useful in effective mentoring should identify areas of strength and areas that need improvement. It should serve as an early sign for mentors who approach the task with good intentions but limited skills. Good intentions are not enough to help troubled and failing teachers. Skills matter and make the final difference.

We now move from an exploratory assessment and checklist into the everyday world of mentoring. The heat goes up and real issues begin to take center stage, often with no time for the mentor to think twice.

Step #3: Making Mentoring Skills Real: A Journey into Everyday School Life

Developing the skills to be able to listen effectively, be nonjudgmental, and capable of providing useful feedback requires the following skills:

1. Effective listening and observational skills
2. The ability to give constructive, nonjudgmental feedback
3. Ability to help teachers overcome self-erected barriers between themselves, students, and colleagues
4. Ability to confront teachers who seem headed in the wrong direction
5. Ability to praise and support teachers who are doing well or poorly
6. Ability to give teachers problem-solving techniques for the class-room
7. Intimate knowledge of the teaching staff

Mastering these skills is not easy. At first glance, they may seem like a laundry list to be memorized for a class called Mentoring 101. How do we imbue real meaning into these words? The rush of school life—the smell, fast pace, and never ending conflicts—needs to be added to get our blood rushing. It is useful for would-be mentors to ask themselves how they stack up as nonjudgmental listeners by reflecting on how this skill gets translated into mentoring relations in everyday school life. Let's fast forward out of Mentoring 101.

Do you have effective listening and observational skills?

Listening to the other and observing his or her nonverbal behaviors gives the mentor important clues for identifying those areas in which a teacher needs improvement. What is the teacher's tone of speech? Is it comfortable or does he appear under stress? What about his physical stance? Does he look at ease or is there tension in his movements? How about his appearance? Does he look composed and presentable or is he disheveled and loose at the ends? What are his fears and concerns?

Let's make these listening and observational skills more concrete. Here is a vignette describing a conversation between a mentor, Principal Brad Foley, and his protégé, social studies teacher Tom Murray. Their mentoring relationship has evolved over the school year. A strong sense of trust, loyalty, and friendship has developed between them. The mentoring conditions suggested in this book have been well established so that when a crisis emerges, Tom is in good hands.

Tom, as is the case with most teachers, begins the conversation by saying that things are fine. As the conversation unfolds, he begins talking about a near confrontation he had with a parent at a conference the previous evening. As he talks, his voice trembles and his hands shake.

Tom Murray: I don't know what happened. Mr. Moriarty, Jim's father, came at the end of the parent conference time. He had a 7:30 appointment but he didn't show up until 9:30. I was just on my way out after meeting with Mrs. Donato when he came down the hall. I could tell he had been drinking but I asked him in, anyway. As soon as he sat down he began swearing at me, saying things like, "You son of a bitch, you don't give my kid a chance." And on and on. After a while I had enough. I said I wasn't going take that kind of abuse. I told him that Jim and I were working on things and they were getting better. But he wouldn't stop. Finally I just got up and left. He followed me down the hall, still yelling and swearing. Just as we turned the corner at the office I caught a glimpse of Jim hiding in the corner. He was crying and upset. He said, "I'm sorry, Mr. Murray, I tried to talk him out of coming. But he's been drinking. He wouldn't let my mom come, pushed her around like he always does before we left the house. He doesn't even live at home any more. I'm so embarrassed. Please don't tell the other kids." I felt so bad for the kid and managed to tell him it was OK and I would keep it between us and we could talk tomorrow. Then his father literally pushed me aside and grabbed Jim and said, "Don't talk to that creep. All he does is fail you." By the time I got home I was shaking all over and couldn't calm down. That's when I called you. I didn't know whether to call the police, and I was concerned about Jim. Who knows what this guy is capable of? But I did meet with Jim this morning before school. He was outside smoking when I arrived so I asked him to come to my room. He seemed shaken, like me, but OK. I told him I had no idea how much stress he's been under since his parents' divorce and his father's violence. He just broke down and cried. I tried to comfort him as best I could. I'm wondering what to do next. I'm not a psychologist.

Brad Foley: Wow, what a night. No wonder you called me. I am so glad you did. It's no good to be alone with all that on your mind. Let me first applaud you for reaching out to Jim. I know you two have been at odds. Maybe this is the opportunity you've been looking for to start a real relationship with him. It sounds like he could use a positive role model like you. What to do? Simple things first. Why don't you meet with Jim after your third period class and ask if it's OK with him if you set up an appointment with the school counselor, Gregg Barosa. I've spoken to Gregg already about the incident with Jim's father. He has an opening seventh period. If Jim is willing to get into counseling, why don't you bring him to Gregg's office seventh period and sit in on the session? That would make it more comfortable for Jim. I'll ask Gregg to call Jim's mother after the session and set up an appointment with her as well. Jim should know that we are doing this so he's not in the dark. It sounds like she is going to need support, too. I hear she is out of work and her husband, or exhusband, is not making any alimony payments. As for Jim's father, I'll ask Gregg to think about calling him and trying to steer him into rehab or counseling, as well. Also, I know our team is meeting tomorrow. Be prepared to let the other teachers know what is happening. I want the entire team involved in making some concrete plans on how to help Jim. Again, maybe this is the opening we've been looking for. Good work, Tom. No one said teaching is easy. The job involves a little bit of everything, from being a father figure to parent educator to psychologist. I know they never prepared you for this but better now than later. You've just been baptized, Murray, in the real fire of school life and you've taken the hit and are using it to help one of your kids. That's being a professional. I'm proud of you. Someday you might be in my shoes and be doing the same thing for another teacher. You know, Eva Nelson, the social studies teacher, has had similar problems with Jim and his family. Maybe you could fill her in and give her some advice on your way home. Get some rest. Also, before I forget, what do you think about moving Jim's seat right up front near your desk? He would be away from his group and maybe now he's ready to become visible and part of the class. He's been invisible as a student since he came here three years ago. Let's milk this opportunity for everything we can. I know you didn't catch the Knicks-Miami basketball playoff last night but I think it's useful to think about announcer Bill Walton's comment, "Everyone gets opportunities but not everyone knows how to use them." Let's use this one.

Do you know how to give constructive and nonjudgmental feedback?

As you can see, Brad Foley listens carefully without interrupting to give advice. Tom, as he says, has been baptized in the fire of school life. Things can get hot and out of control. One never knows what to expect when a student or parent walks through the door. As most experienced mentors understand, many teachers do not anticipate the pain and failure they will see on the faces of kids and parents who experience life's hurts when they enter the profession. But kids bring their personal and nonacademic problems into the school each day and these impact on their school life and lack of success in many ways—tardiness, truancy, acting out, and, sadly, a loss of hopes and dreams. They are deadened at an early age unless rescued by caring and skilled teachers.

Bad things also happen to so-called good kids who are born into families with resources and opportunity. Well-off kids, not just kids living in poverty, get hit by life's hard times. The only difference is that well-off kids are not supposed to have problems. All those vitamins, preschool training, tutoring, and test-prep courses are supposed to make them problem free and Harvard bound. But they, surprisingly to some parents and educators, are human too and vulnerable to risks—the risk of being too good and too successful early on, more a productive machine than a kid. Being too good can rob them of learning the skills they need to make it in a hostile and competitive world. As in the dialog above, Jim Moriarty may prove to be the lucky student because he is about to get the help he needs. His problem is out in the open for everyone to see. Embarrassed he may be, but he is attended to. The silent, bright kids may not be so lucky. They don't cause problems. They show up on time, they do their homework, they join clubs. There are no noticeable holes in their achievements. To the untrained teacher's eye, they seem fine. Not as much attention needs to be given to them as to the Jim Moriarty's, we sometimes think. Linking goodness and success to being problem free is not always a good approach.

Teachers observing the hurt and scarred children in their classes wonder, as Duke Ellington wrote, "Why anyone would tear the seam from anyone's dream." Teachers learn over time, as Tom is doing, that teaching is more often than not a painful business. They are never fully prepared for what the school day brings, no matter how many degrees, education courses, and years of experience they have under their belts. "I thought I'd seen it all but this situation is a new one," is a familiar teacher lament.

Tom seemed to have handled the situation well, but not perfectly. He might have called the principal earlier or called the police. Mr. Moriarty could have caused real damage to Tom, Jim, or himself. Tom might also have called Child Protective Services—Brad will make sure he has that number—and reported the incident and communicated that Jim might be in danger. This is all material for Tom and Brad to work on together. But for now, Brad rightly affirms Tom's responses, suggests that this is an opportunity to really get involved and help Jim, and sets up a plan for ongoing help and intervention for the Moriartyfamily. It's a step-by-step plan that shows Tom how to proceed. Brad also wisely understands that it is important for mentors not to put too much on the teacher's plate, not give too much feedback and too many goals to be accomplished in the future. It's like working with anxious kids. You give them tasks and ideas that they can solve and handle so they can feel good about themselves; they must crawl before they can take baby steps.

Let's also keep in mind what Tom would have done if he did not have a solid, trusting, and caring relationship with Brad Foley. Would he have acted differently? Probably. Maybe he would not have called or involved Brad at all. He might have, like Jim, kept things to himself. Without their mentoring relationship, both Tom and Brad would have lost out on an opportunity to be helpful to and learn from one another. Consider how many times similar kinds of incidents occur in schools in which teachers don't have a Brad Foley to turn to. Jim Moriarty and his family did not lose out on an opportunity for needed intervention, using the crisis as a springboard for help. Having a mentoring relationship is like money in the bank for the Toms of the teaching world. It's there when they need it

Do you know how to help teachers overcome self-erected barriers?

Here again, Brad Foley shows us how to transform the way a teacher views his students. Until this crisis, Tom say Jim Moriarty as a threat and a nuisance, a kid he would like to see jettisoned from the school's rolls. But the confrontation with Jim's father and Jim's cry for help touched Tom's heart and changed things between them. Let's not forget Brad Foley's critical mentoring role in this process. If Brad Foley had taken a hard line administrative approach, he might have pushed for a legal rather than a human response. But Brad Foley didn't take the hard line. He didn't make the wall impenetrable with a zero-tolerance approach. He also didn't use the incident to promote a political, legalistic agenda for his administration. He didn't ask police to do his work for him. Rather, he reduced the barriers between Tom and Jim with a human, caring, family-centered approach. He understood that teachers are adults. They can handle adversity. They don't need an administrator who is a father figure telling them *exactly* what to do. They need an administrator who presents a caring, compassionate model that says, "Yes, we can help. Now go to it!"

Do you know how to confront teachers who seem to be headed in the wrong direction?

Not everyone listens. Let's suppose Tom Murray had reacted in another way to Mr. Moriarty's assault. Let's suppose that Tom arrives at school the next morning and makes a beeline for Brad Foley's office, demanding that Jim be removed from his class. Here is what he tells Brad Foley:

Tom Murray: I am just a teacher and not a counselor or social worker. Jim has major problems. Sure, I would like to help him but I am a married man with a child on the way. I can't take the chance of Mr. Moriarty coming back, maybe this time with a gun, and making big trouble for me. Jim has to be removed from my class and put in an environment in which he can get help. I know the district has an alternative school for troubled kids. Besides, if he left, it would be better for the other kids. Learning could go on again. I know he scares Janine and some of the other kids in the class. Janine's mother has come twice to complain about Jim. Listen, I feel bad but this is the last straw. I've done what I can. I'm no saver of souls. I am just a social studies teacher.

Brad Foley: Thanks for letting me know how you feel, Tom. It's been rough. And last night's incident was no plus. Those things can push you over the line. But Tom, hear me out. Sit down and have some coffee. Your adrenaline is running, as it should after that experience. I'll ask my secretary to get coverage for your first two classes. Let's talk. It's been a busy day and it's only 7:30. Tom, let's talk about your growth as a teacher first. When you first came here two years ago, I must admit you seemed a little shaky and unsure, especially with some of the tougher kids. But since we started the mentoring program this year, I've seen some good things happen with you and your kids. You are much more open, friendly, and at ease with them. You know their names, something about their backgrounds. Plus you're having some fun, which is great for both you and them.

I know your relationship with Jim has been strained. But let me stop right there, Tom. This is an opportunity for you to help a kid in real need. You don't have to get rid of him to save him or yourself. You are not that brittle or unskilled to handle the Jims of the world. Sure, you've had a frightening experience. But so what? You're not alone. We've all had them. Actually, I think you handled the situation with Mr. Moriarty and Jim very well,maybe not perfectly but I see no reason for you to throw up your hands and run for cover. You're not a wimp. I've heard you talk about your football days in high school and college. Linebacker, right? My guess is that you've been hit a lot harder in football than Mr. Moriarty could ever do. Let me tell you something. If you keep Jim and continue to work with him, that's going to be a victory for you. A win. It shows your toughness and tenacity. But if you get rid of Jim—and I will move him if you insist—I think you are giving up too early on both yourself and Jim. You're letting a potential victory turn into a defeat. You are saying that you can't handle kids like Jim. And do you know the message that the other kids will get? They will understand that you have run from a fight. You think you've seen some turbulent behavior? Wait until you see what the other kids do after Jim goes. I may be mistaken but I think they will be emboldened. Word travels fast, Tom. I want you to think seriously about this. You've got Jim in the palm of your hand right now. From what you've said, he believes you are in his corner. You aren't going to throw this kid into the alternative school where no one knows him and there are *really* troubled kids, are you? Go for your strength and power, Tom. Don't send the message to the kids and Jim that you are weak and not up to the battle. It's the wrong message at the wrong time. As they say in baseball, "I've got the right man at the plate at the right time." And you are the right man, Tom. Be a contender, not a thirty-year-old guy who is giving up. You know it's been a painful learning experience for me with other teachers. Once you give up on that first kid, it's easier to give up on the next one who will confront you. You know teachers like that and so do I. They've lost the will to do battle with kids. Don't you, Tom.

Do you know how to praise and support teachers?

Praise is not always abundant for teachers in schools. Students by far receive the most praise. Usually it is showered on students who achieve academically, in sports, in music, or in theater. Teachers administer a lot of quiet, unnoticed praise for kids who make small breakthroughs after many setbacks. But praise for teachers who do good deeds and good works is limited. Sure, there is some, like the teacher of the year awards by unions, PTA's and yearbook staffs, or being chosen for a summer workshop. But it's limited. Why is this so? The good works and good deeds of teachers go unnoticed because they are carried out in isolation in the classroom. Usually no one observes the efforts by teachers to praise and support kids. Yes, I know, "no one" is a heavy indictment, but I believe it is mostly true. Maybe a few parents will write letters of praise to the teacher or building principal, lauding the teacher's effort on behalf of their particular child. But most of the time, the good efforts and work of teachers occur in a vacuum, unnoticed and unappreciated. Self-promotion—blowing your own horn and calling attention to your achievements—doesn't come easily for teachers. Being underappreciated and taken for granted are, unfortunately, hallmarks of the teaching profession. The lucky ones have enough pride in themselves to appreciate what skills they bring to the classroom, or better yet, they have a few colleagues and family who say when they walk by, "There goes a real teacher."

Effective mentoring, as Brad Foley demonstrates, can dramatically change this situation. Brad is clear in his praise and support of Tom Murray. The praise is an effort to clearly define skills that are working for Tom and to increase his awareness that, like a good musician or athlete, these skills are helping make him a successful professional. There is a method and a message to Brad's praise of Tom. He doesn't let him duck out of helping Jim Moriarty and take what appears to be the easy way out. In fact, Brad knows that the easy way, farming Jim out to an alternative school, may be the tougher road because it helps make Tom easy prey for tough kids who need a tough but caring response. Brad's message to Tom is, "We are in this together. I won't cop out in tough times and I don't expect you to."

Do you know how to give teachers problem-solving techniques?

Fixing classroom problems is not rocket science. Sure, when teachers are in the midst of a classroom uproar, the answer and the way out of the dilemma are not easily at hand. Teachers do not readily see the solutions and the alternatives when they are failing and in retreat. Another voice and another brain to pick, a mentor with solid classroom experience, can quickly point out the problem areas and help develop a strategy to regroup. We know problems can create opportunity for change. The classroom after all, is a hectic and ever-changing environment. The lessons and kids teachers counted on one day backfire on them the next. Tough kids make teachers sweat and feel confused and out of sync. They lose their way trying to figure out responses that will work. There are kids who, as the saying goes, "have our number." They smell teachers' weaknesses and vulnerability and zero in for the kill. But the difficult kids who taunt teachers and lead them down wrong roads also may be the bearers of gifts. The bottom line is that teachers often learn the most about the process of teaching, and about themselves and their kids, from students who rebuff their efforts and become confrontational. Teachers have to work, sweat, try new approaches, fail, be soft, be tough, do what it takes—use the whole field—to win these kids over. It's good to remind ourselves, as Brad Foley reminds Tom Murray, that the classroom is not a civil, orderly, or nice place in spite of our efforts to make it so with the latest mediation, bully-proofing, and conflict resolution programs. Confrontation is always in the air or close at hand in a classroom.

It is easy for teachers to lose their way in trying to find solutions to classroom problems. They are too busy putting out fires and often lack the information and awareness they need. Sometimes very simple approaches can turn things around. It is not rocket science but just common sense when Brad Foley suggests that Tom move Jim's desk to the front of the room and get together with him to talk things out. For Brad, as a skilled observer, this situation is a no-brainer, as they say. Small moves can solve a big problem. As Brad demonstrates, his mentoring sessions with Tom are really problem-solving sessions. What's going on? How can we change things around? Let's plan a simple intervention and see if it works. Tom is not left alone to solve his problems. As Brad suggests, they are in this together. It is amazing what a little support and problem-solving experience can do for a floundering teacher. Cost effective? You bet! Ineffective teachers are costly. They often create ongoing problems with their students and parents, problems that have to be resolved by busy administrators and colleagues. Effective mentoring can help retrain failing teachers and provide them with the necessary skills to be successful with their students, parents, and colleagues. With effective mentoring, poorly skilled teachers can become valuable resources.

Do you know your teaching staff on an intimate basis?

Developing an effective mentoring relationship with teachers requires establishing a level of comfort and trust with them. That means knowing them by name, their backgrounds, their interests, their personal and family lives, their school relationships—how they fit in, whom they hang out with—their hobbies, hopes, goals, dreams, talents and strengths, areas that may need improvement, and of course, their fears. Knowing and understanding a teacher's fears can open a dialog for further training. Mentors must establish a relationship that has an easiness about it and one in which each party is readily accessible for help. An example of this accessibility might be a late-night phone call from a teacher like Tom, wanting to talk about a confrontation he had with a parent and asking what he should do.

Developing this kind of trusting mentoring relationship requires a lot of legwork and prepwork on the part of the administrator. It's much like the work an effective teacher must do to really understand each of his students or like a coach sizing up his players' assets and liabilities. The mentor has to go beyond the numbers rather than limit his understanding to facts: Tom Murray, seventh grade social studies teacher in his second year of teaching. A mentor has to go further to understand and know the whole teacher just as teachers try to understand and know the whole child. Mentors must find out what makes teachers tick emotionally. They must realize that comfort, ease, and trust between them and the teacher develop slowly, just as in any other intimate relationship. These qualities are built on a series of interactions that work out well. It will not be perfect. Issues and problems arise in building any relationship. One has to persist, which is easier when mentors know and understand the person thery are trying to help and of course, themselves. What makes *us*—mentors—tick emotionally? Where are our buttons that teachers can push, as kids do with teachers? What sets us off? In getting to know others, mentors soon find out that they had better understand and know themselves. Intervening, mentoring, helping, and being intimate all require more than a degree and good intentions. Mentoring is not therapy, but it does involve a process most therapists understand, that in helping others we learn about ourselves. This is an unexpected but valuable benefit of mentoring.

5

Selecting and Training the Mentoring Team

In chapter 5 we take the next steps in developing an effective mentoring program. Your self-training and reflection in chapter 4 has given you a better sense of your mentoring strengths and those areas that need improvement. Now it's time to select and train your mentoring team, with the caution that not every master teacher and education leader is well-suited for the mentoring role. Not everyone can make the transition from being an effective teacher to being an effective mentor. Different skills are required. Teaching is a tough profession. Let me remind the reader that a list of the issues administrators need to address before actually beginning the mentoring process is listed at the beginning of chapter 4. Let's move on to the second element of that list.

ISSUE #2: AVOIDING THE PITFALL THAT EVERY MASTER TEACHER CAN BE AN EFFECTIVE MENTOR WITHOUT TRAINING AND SUPPORT

One of the major arguments I make in this book is that would-be mentors need to be involved in some kind of readiness training so they can learn about the mentoring process and what is expected of them in this new role. The approach I use in this book is a self-training process for administrators who can then use their newly acquired skills to train a mentoring team. The team is then available to each other to offer support, solve problems, and create new approaches to problems when needed. This model program allows the administrator to be involved as a learner, trainer, and participant but not totally responsible for the program. It allows for continuous support and oversight by each team member. No one team leader is alone, open and vulnerable to unforeseen circumstances and ongoing resistance.

Why is training and ongoing support and guidance vital to any mentor and mentoring program? As I suggested before, being unprepared can easily lead to resistance and setbacks. Failure comes easily, while success is hard to reach. Let's put a face, a persona, on what can happen when a master teacher becomes a mentor for colleagues without acquiring mentoring skills such as political savvy, and without receiving the ongoing support I described in chapter 3. There I described Kentucky teacher Irmgard Williams as an example of the competent teachers we should be trying to develop and nurture. Clearly she has all the right stuff; while not perfect, she is clearly a recognized leader in her classroom, school, school district, and state.

But does being the consummate teacher prepare a teacher to retrain subpar teachers to be more effective? Williams understands how much her colleagues need affirmation and "something to show people we're proud of them." She also understands that they need guidance from teachers like her if they are going to improve. So when the call came for her to become a Kentucky Education Reform Act (KERA) fellow and take a leadership role in retraining teachers in her school and schools throughout the state, she was willing to take this new step in her career. She was an accomplished teacher at the time, but clearly there were questions she and KERA officials should have considered before she took on this new role.

> In spite of her own success as a teacher, did she possess the right characteristics to become a successful mentor?
> Did KERA have profiles of a model mentor and the skills that were required for success in that role?
> Would KERA provide training for Williams that would teach her how to intervene with peers who need mentoring to become more effective teachers?
> Would the training provide her with methods of overcoming the resistance of peers to being retrained, especially by a colleague?
> Would the training role provide release time from her classroom in order to coach fellow teachers?

Would her building administrator support this new role, now and over
time?

How would she handle the roles of being a classroom teacher and
trainer of peers at the same time? How would she and her students
handle this new role?

How would she handle the jealousy of peers who would be envious of
her new role and special place in the state's education hierarchy?

The central questions for Williams and KERA should have been: "Is
Williams ready and set to take on this new role as trainer? Are we doing
everything we can to prepare Williams and ensure that this is a successful
experience for her? Or are we setting up this teacher-turned-mentor for
failure by not providing her with the necessary training and support to do
the job?" Williams may be a tough-minded teacher and able to handle
anything in the classroom, but was she tough enough, skilled enough, for
this new role? Here is what happened.

Williams, with all of her talents and ability to work hard, develop skills,
and change over the course of her career, typifies the simultaneous problem and opportunity involved in retraining teachers at the school level.
The problem is, "How do administrators get other teachers to be more like
Williams?" The opportunity is that Williams herself is a superb resource.
How do administrators showcase her talents as a successful, competent
teacher so that fellow teachers can observe and learn from her and others
like her? What happened to Williams when, as part of KERA, she began
to serve as a model and guide for other teachers? Williams's experience
provide us with some important guidelines on how we should proceed in
training teachers to be mentors.

The following are some of the highlights and effects of KERA:

KERA was an effort by the state of Kentucky to rebuild an entire school
system from scratch.

KERA placed great emphasis on teachers in the classroom. KERA
stressed that teachers are directly responsible for making the reforms
work and must improve their practice.

State legislators increased the number of paid days available for staff
training from four to nine and initially allowed school districts to ab-
sorb some of the extra days by replacing up to five of the required

175 instructional days with paid staff training. Legislators also boosted spending on staff training from one dollar per student to $23 per student per year.

The state held teachers accountable for making reform succeed and, ultimately, teachers could lose their jobs if their students didn't reach state goals on tests given to a different group of students in selected grades each year.

While teachers were trying to learn how to do their jobs differently, they also had to field questions from parents, listen to complaints from colleagues, and deflect criticism from observers who claimed the teachers were not working hard enough.

For many of Kentucky's 38,000 teachers the cost of change was too high. They found themselves caught between the desire to do a better job and the impulse to stick with what they knew. A record number of Kentucky teachers retired in 1993 and 1994.

When KERA came along, Williams embraced its challenges. There was no limit to what she personally was willing to do. She became the leader of a team of teachers at South Heights, a KERA fellow, and trained other teachers in Henderson County. But by 1995, the fifth year of reform, she was feeling more depleted than fulfilled. She believed strongly in what she was doing and wanted badly for the reforms to succeed. But she feared that hard working teachers would stop trying to improve if people didn't acknowledge their efforts. When a record number of teachers retired in 1993 and 1994, Williams was concerned about the spirits of those who stayed on the job.

What Williams hadn't counted on were the demands that KERA placed on teachers as a group. The expectation was that teachers would work together to rise to a higher level *collectively*. But the state did not provide direction for accomplishing this goal. The new emphasis on collective responsibility forced Williams into an uncomfortable role. For most of her life she had been content to stay in the background. She didn't like to draw attention to herself; she believed that others should mind their own business. Although she knew she was personally accountable for her own actions, she never considered it her place to judge anyone else. Now the state seemed to be suggesting that she should.

When she opened the door of her classroom after years of isolation to take on this new mentoring role, Williams couldn't help but notice the difference between herself and some other colleagues. They seemed to recognize the disparities, too, and often approached her for advice about teaching. When she became leader of one of the primary teams, the questions multiplied. Williams always seemed to know what to do. Yet rarely did her guidance lead to improvements in other teachers' classrooms. Her colleagues had a tough time transferring her techniques and Williams did not have the luxury of mentoring them on the spot. The lack of progress among her colleagues troubled her. She preferred to influence others by example, not by dictating to them. They were professionals, too. But despite her gentle reminders, some teachers hadn't heeded her message that they needed to make major changes in their methods, and fast. KERA expected all students to learn at high levels, but they would never succeed if teachers didn't give them the skills they needed.

What could Williams do about other teachers? What should she do? She was already busy trying to address her own students' needs. Wasn't that enough? Certainly, education reform required more of teachers, but did it mean that they must expect more from each other? Were they obligated to confront incompetence, even if it meant challenging a friend from across the hall? "How can you tell another teacher how to teach?" Williams wondered. It is a question that many people in Kentucky and around the nation are beginning to ask, as well. Can you tell another teacher how to teach? Williams's case shows that you probably can't. She clearly cares about her colleagues and wants to help them get better. But it is difficult for her to move out of her role as classroom teacher, a role she developed over twenty-seven years of teaching, and into the role of teacher/mentor and the political arena. Over time, her role as mentor seemed to become less rewarding than teaching her children. She feels depleted, unrewarded, and confused about her role and how to proceed. It appears she didn't have much support or guidance from KERA. She seemed on her own to wrestle with transferring long-held beliefs, values and practices—they had worked for her for twenty-seven years—to her new role.

There are several aspects of the new role that Williams finds troubling:

Assuming that teachers would work together to achieve to a higher level of performance.
Thinking that assessing the level of competency of fellow teachers and identifying areas they need to improve is "judging." For most of her

professional life she has been content to stay in the background. Although she made certain she was personally accountable for her own actions, she never considered it her place to judge anyone else.

Not seeing any major results in using the training model in which teachers observe and the master teacher practices. Williams always seemed to know what to do when other teachers approached her for advice about teaching. Yet rarely did her guidance of other teachers lead to improvement in their classrooms.

Not having time to coach her fellow teachers. Her colleagues had a tough time transferring her techniques and Williams didn't have the luxury of mentoring them on the spot. The lack of progress among her colleagues troubled her.

She preferred to influence other teachers by example not by dictating to them. Her colleagues were professionals, too. But despite her gentle reminders, some teachers hadn't heeded the message that they needed to make major changes in instruction, fast.

How can you tell another teacher how to teach? Certainly, education reform required more of teachers, but did it mean they must expect more from each other? Were they obligated to confront incompetence even if it meant challenging a friend from across the hall?

Can we tell another teacher how to teach? Probably not. But in sound education reform we can *show* another teacher how to teach. We do know how to proceed to reach this goal. There is a profound difference among *telling, influencing by example* (as Williams did) and *demonstrating,* that is, showing and teaching how to improve. Telling and influencing by example will not reach the large body of teachers who need intervention. They need demonstrating—someone showing and teaching them how to improve. Mentors need to give teachers the skills they need to confront incompetence in their subpar colleagues. Mentors and teachers need not so much to challenge a friend across the hall as to intervene when a friend across the hall is floundering and needs to acquire a new set of teaching skills that work—to be our brother's keeper.

We need to learn from KERA and the Williams case what not to do, or else we will end up with the same results—disgruntled teachers, unfilled expectations, and the energy of reformers being spent unsuccessfully trying to get resisters on board. This case study of Williams's role as mentor of peers provides us with some important clues as to how we need to proceed to train future mentors so they will surely succeed. We should remind ourselves that enthusiasm and the willingness to mentor fellow teachers are admirable but not enough to get the job done. What is required is a new set of mentoring skills, similar to the ones I have described in chapter 3, that will get the Irmgard Williams of the future ready for the mentoring task.

Irmgard Williams is a courageous teacher who was willing to go out on a limb and do what she could to help other teachers. It appears she had precious little time and support to get the job done. She mentored by telling and example. What else could she do? It appears she had no release time for coaching her peers. Although she was troubled by incompetent teachers, she didn't want to intrude, judge, and interfere with their professional lives. She had always been content to keep to herself in the background. That was the education world she knew and felt comfortable and safe in. She was, I believe, given too steep a challenge. She was asked to do too much with too little training and resources.

Implicit in the KERA training role was a subtle mandate to change her style, to move out of the background and initiate contact with fellow teachers who were less than able. She found it hard to develop a new style that to her appeared confrontational and intrusive. She saw it as being judgmental, not something she aspired to. She was asked to initiate mentoring with fellow teachers without being given release time to coach and provide follow-up support. Enthusiasm and willingness were her calling cards in the classroom but they were not enough to carry her in the area of education reform.

Successful teachers like Williams can mentor their peers but those in leadership positions need to make sure they have the training, resources, and support to get the job done. Who knows what Williams might have accomplished with release time from class for training and coaching, mentors who could have guided her through her confusion around fuzzy issues such as the difference between judging and intervening, and coaching in how to move out of the background and begin to showcase her talents? Chances are she would not have felt depleted and bereft of affirmation for her work. She might have helped some other teacher become a more competent teacher along the way.

We must remember that Irmgard Williams is not alone in her effort to translate a highly successful career as a teacher into a teaching-mentoring

role. Let's examine another mentoring episode, as described by Abby
Goodnough.[1] New first grade teacher Donna Moffett and her mentor
Marie Buchanan work at PS (public school) 92 in Brooklyn. The school
uses a highly organized approach to teaching, sometimes even expecting
its staff to work according to a minute-by-minute script. Frustrated by
these constraints, Ms. Moffett tries to squeeze in lessons of her own
choosing: stories about New York City, for example, or writing assignments about "the funniest thing your mother ever did." But on this day,
Marie Buchanan, a veteran teacher at the school and Ms. Moffett's offi-
cial mentor, had come to observe the school's approach. Smiling stiffly,
Ms. Moffett opened the textbook to Section 1, "Pets are Special Animals."

When she got to the line about a boy mischievously drawing on a table,
she playfully noted that the boy was "just like some students in here." Ms.
Buchanan frowned. "You don't have to say that," she admonished. When
Ms. Moffett turned to a page that suggested an art project related to the
story and started passing out construction paper, Ms. Buchanan chided her
again. "You're not going to have time to complete that. You'll have to
prepare for these lessons and closely follow the teachers' guide," Ms.
Buchanan told her afterwards. "We're going to do the same thing tomorrow and you're not going to wing it."

Despite her frequent criticisms of Ms. Moffett, Ms. Buchanan, her mentor, says she has learned a lot since September. Asked for examples, she
said that Ms. Moffett has improved her classroom bulletin boards by putting
up only the best work instead of work by every student and become a better disciplinarian by not frolicking with the students as much as in the fall.

Ms. Moffett, who was among 350 people with no teaching experience
recruited last fall to work in the most troubled school in New York City,
entered her new profession brimming with idealism and determined to put
a unique style stamp on her classroom. But like others recruited to work
in those schools, she has struggled to be creative within highly specific
guidelines set by the city and state.

Abby Goodnough's story of the education of Donna Moffett drew some
critical responses in the letters to the editor section of the *New York Times*.[2]
While some letters lamented the rigid curriculum Ms. Moffett had to adhere
to in teaching to improve test scores, some of the criticism was directed at
mentor Buchanan for encouraging Ms. Moffett to put only the best work on
the bulletin boards instead of work by all the students. I would add that Ms.

Buchanan's verbal feedback during her observation of Ms. Moffett's class probably didn't do much for her self-esteem and confidence level, critical elements for all teachers but more so for first year novices with no prior teacher training. Put yourself in Ms. Moffett's place. You're in front of your class trying to bring an example in a story close to home. In the midst of the lesson you say playfully, and innocently it seems, that the boy in the story is "just like some students in here." This a comment made by a teacher who cares for her students but knows her students are not perfect. They too can be mischievous like the boy in the story who draws on the table. But your mentor interrupts and says, "You don't have to say that." Bang! The attention shifts from you as teacher and your students. The lesson and the point you are trying to make probably evaporate. Your students witness a superior openly challenging what you say. This is not the stuff that builds trust and respect between the students and Ms. Moffett and certainly not the stuff that builds trust and respect between Ms. Moffett and her mentor. But the verbal feedback doesn't end here. Or should we call them interruptions? As you proceed to begin an art project, Ms. Buchanan, as reported, says, "You're not going to have time to complete that." As the class and the observation wind down, Ms. Buchanan jumps in again and says, "We're going to do this again tomorrow and you're not going to wing it."

Many would say, myself included, that seemingly critical feedback delivered to a novice teacher and witnessed by her class leaves much to be desired. Why weren't Ms. Buchanan's observations shared in a private, one-on-one conference? Why was there—at least as the *New York Times* article portrays it—little positive feedback for Ms. Moffett to build on? This is not an indictment of Ms. Buchanan herself a respected and veteran teacher. Rather, it is an indictment of a mentoring process that appears to ignore any of the characteristics of a wise mentor such as those I have addressed. Was Ms. Buchanan's feedback helpful and useable? Is she making an effort to build up Ms. Moffett's confidence, worth, and belief in herself and her judgments? Is she as mentor developing trust, loyalty, and a sense of privacy with Ms. Moffett? Is she judging Ms. Moffett's practice in a negative way rather than accepting her style of teaching? Does she know how to bring a sense of joy, energy, humor, and lightness to the mentoring relationship? The mentoring role here seems to be more one of a supervisor, a person who oversees, directs, and manages. This is not our definition of a mentor: a wise, loyal advisor, friend, teacher, and coach.

In a sense, Irmgard Williams and Donna Moffett—at opposite ends of the spectrum in teaching experience—may share a similar fate. Ms. Williams gives up part of her highly successful classroom experience to mentor colleagues. The experience does not go well and she runs into barriers. It is difficult for her to move out of her teaching role that she developed over twenty-seven years and into the role of mentor in the political arena. She feels depleted, unrewarded, and confused about her new mentoring role. Ms. Moffett comes into teaching brimming with idealism and determined to put a unique stamp on her classroom, but she too runs into barriers in trying to be creative within highly specific guidelines set by the city and state. As she says, "I feel like I am beaten down and I have to keep getting up over and over again."

Perhaps mentor Marie Buchanan is also a victim of her mentoring role of trying to help novice teachers adhere to a rigid curriculum with highly specific guidelines set by the city and state, a curriculum where creativity is often discouraged. She is, after all, at the flashpoint where there is growing political pressure to improve reading and math achievement in long-struggling schools. PS 92 has been classified by New York State as failing for more than a decade. There appears to be great pressure to increase scores on the standardized reading and math tests in the third grade. Ms. Moffett's adherence to the rigid curriculum is a must, or as school officials suggest, a blessing for novice teachers like Ms. Moffett who had only a month of training. Given these conditions and the political pressures from the board of education, city hall, and the state education department, maybe Ms. Buchanan's overt and direct responses made to Ms. Moffett make sense to her in the setting in which she mentors. There is pressure on everyone to raise test scores. Harold O. Levy, the New York City Chancellor, is quoted in the article as saying, "You [teachers] are the cutting edge, the shock troops, the people who are going to make things happen." Maybe Ms. Buchanan doesn't have time for positive feedback, building confidence, and one-on-one conferencing. As Ms. Buchanan suggests, "I just can't let her take off on her own and do things that aren't educationally sound. It's detrimental to the students and in the long run it's detrimental to her."

Teaching in urban schools is difficult at best. Teachers come and go. As cited earlier, in urban school districts, close to fifty percent of newcomers flee the profession during the first five years of teaching. As the

National Center for Education Statistics's "Condition of Education 1998 Report" suggests, teachers in high poverty urban districts are more likely to be underqualified.[3]

The mentoring role can have many pitfalls for mentors themselves. Not everyone is cut out for the work. Many times the conditions for mentoring lack support. The case of Irmgard Williams and KERA should remind us that hard-earned experience as a classroom teacher and the desire to help colleagues may not be enough to be successful at the task. Mentors need training, ongoing support, and time to do the job well. And as exemplified by Marie Buchanan, sometimes mentoring may become a political tool, trying to get novice teachers to adopt a teaching style determined by education leaders and bureaucrats outside the school setting.

Because of a lack of training and support and politicizing the mentoring role, many teachers like Donna Moffett may find themselves hindered in finding their own teaching style and their best teaching self. Marie Buchanan suggests that Donna Moffett is "going to be a master teacher one day." But how is that going to happen in the context she works within and the ever-present demands to raise test scores? As the article reports, her expectations for the job were different from the demands of the district, as summarized in an essay she included with her application to become a teacher through an alternative route program, New York City Teaching Fellows. "I want to manage a classroom where children experience the thrill of wonder, joy of creativity, and the rewards of working hard. My objective is to convey to children in the formative years the sheer pleasure of learning."

The work of would-be mentors is to keep Donna Moffett's vision of teaching close to their hearts. Her words and vision are a precious gift to be nurtured, her classroom a place we would all want our own children to be part of. Developing our own voice and persona as mentors should include not only the skills but also the philosophy to support such a vision for all children. Mentors' work is to make this happen. We need to learn how to sell the notion of what effective mentoring is and how to bring it about. We also need to understand the political pressures that may try to lead us to mentor only for test improvement, and learn how to turn these pressures aside. We need to be about creating school settings in which effective mentoring is possible, places in which people like Irmgard Williams and Marie Buchanan, highly successful teachers, have the right kind of training and support to model and communicate their unique teaching style and experience. We need mentors who can advise their protégés how to be master teachers, people who have been there, learned through trial and error, and still remain at the top of their games, creative and caring.

ISSUE #3: SELECTING A MENTORING TEAM

Administrators can't expect to accomplish the task of mentoring each teacher in the building by themselves, particularly if they are an administrator of a large secondary school, many of which have student populations of 2500 students and more. They will need a team made up of other educational leaders in the school, a team that represents a cross-section of staff such as an assistant principal, department chairperson, teacher leader, and counselor leader. Mentors need to look for people who have the following important attributes:

They are known as trusted, loyal leaders.

They are respected by various groups—veteran teachers to newcomers —in the school. They haven't built walls and isolated certain groups.

They are highly skilled in more basic mentoring skills such as listening, leading one-on-one discussion groups, providing nonjudgmental feedback, and delivering criticism in a positive framework.

They have political and selling skills that can be vital to promoting the mentoring program. They know how to work the room and get people to make a commitment.

They share your mentoring vision that teachers at every developmental stage in their careers need support and renewal opportunities.

They share your belief that teachers need opportunity for career alternatives such as becoming mentors themselves.

They are committed to your definition of a mentor: a wise and loyal advisor, friend, teacher, and coach. They are not interested in a "supervisory" mentor role in which they would oversee, direct, and manage teachers' work.

They are emotionally tough and physically up to the mentoring task. Some teachers will resist mentoring. Mentors will be attacked at both the professional and personal levels. Names will be called and rumors will spread. "What is he after now with this mentor role? A new job in administration?"

Feelings of jealousy go with the territory. Schools, after all, are fertile places for jealousy, envy, and even retaliation toward anyone who tries to get out from the four walls of the classroom. The lack of novelty and change in teaching can fuel anger and resentment toward any colleague who tries to be different, start a new program, or take on a new role. New programs, new roles, and new arrangements often cause threat and unease. People like the status quo even if it's not working. They know it, like the thread worn sweater that should be yard-saled but remains snugly in the bottom drawer. When the status quo changes some teachers will fight back. Mentors need a tough skin and fire in their belly to continue. And they need to be in good physical shape to take the punishment of resistance.

Not everyone can make the transition from being an effective teacher to being an effective mentor. Different skills are required. Will every mentor possess all the right attributes? No, of course not. But these are the attributes of a mentor that you are looking for. The key is selecting people who have the potential to grow into these important aspects of the mentoring role. Your modeling and training of these would-be mentors should enhance their skills and in the process make them more effective education leaders.

ISSUE #4: TRAINING A MENTORING TEAM

Training mentors places administrators in a new and exciting role. You are moving from managing curriculum and budgets to a training role. The training process should be very similar to your own self-training model described in chapter 4. Here is a five-step plan of approach:

1. Guide your trainees through the personal experience inventory (see page 74) and encourage them to reflect on the following points.
   a. The positive mentors in their personal and professional lives.
   b. The negative mentors in their personal and professional lives.

    c. The characteristics of teachers they tend to gravitate toward and help.

    d. The characteristics of teachers they tend to avoid and not help.

2. Suggest that they explore their vision for the school and past efforts, successes, and failures that would help or hinder the creation of this vision (see page 78).

3. Have them compare their skills to the mentoring skills and understanding checklist taking a hard look at their current mentoring skills and what skills need improvement (refer to page 79).

4. Next, mentees should undergo training to be a team member and assessment of their overall team strengths and non-strengths. This is a critical part of the training program. Skill acquisition is *the* critical element in the preparation of mentors. But skill acquisition doesn't get far without the ability of the mentoring team to function as a cohesive, democratic unit. Here is one approach you can use to build your team before they go into action.

    a. Have each member identify their mentoring strengths and skills and what resources they bring to the team.

    b. Use this data to identify the overall strengths and skills of the team.

    c. Have each member identify his or her mentoring skills that are not strong and need improvement.

    d. Have each member reflect on his or her communication skills and ability to interact with others. Teaming with others can be difficult. Fellow team members can differ in terms of philosophy, values, and educational vision. It is critical for would-be mentors to identify which team members they feel more comfortable with and those with whom they feel some dissonance. It is good preparation for getting ready to mentor teachers who may be different and, as such, more difficult for mentors to connect with. Also, it identifies early on potential conflict and communication problems, serving as an important reminder to the team that differentness need not lead to conflict and distrust.

    e. Have each would-be mentor reflect on his or her individual role in group planning: how does he assess his ability to be heard, offer ideas, listen, and promote effective group decision-making?

    f. Have each team member reflect on how he or she plans to support and empower each team member and the entire team. Teams are like families. They can be an effective mechanism to help all members be all they can be. Team members can be available to listen to other members' concerns about not being able to mentor a certain teacher or be available to hear about a major breakthrough in helping a resisting teacher become more effective. But teams, like all families, can work the other way and stifle individual and group success. Self-interest can and will take over if the goals shift from collegiality to individual stardom. Mentors, like newly acclaimed star teachers, can quickly become famous, coveted as conference speakers and presenters and may begin talking more about the process of mentoring and doing it less.

g. Have each team member reflect on how he intends to go about seeking out the assistance of the team when he runs into problems in the mentoring process. Here are some examples of mentoring conflicts that have a good chance of occurring.

   i. Remember that not every teacher will want to be mentored. Some will resist quietly ("Oh, I'm sorry I missed our mentoring conference again. I've been so busy with my kids I just forgot."). Teachers who fit into this category are hard to pin down. Mentors are in a position based on collegiality requiring quiet persistence, a not-letting-you-off-the-hook attitude delivered with force, and kindness. However, would-be mentors are not in a supervisory role.

   ii. Others will resist more overtly ("Look, Brad, I know your intentions are good. But I've got five years and three months before I retire. I'm out of here. Sure we can meet and you can observe my class, but don't expect any enthusiasm from me. You have a job to do but it's over for me."). For some mentors this kind of quick shot is hard to take. It may shake their confidence. Yet knowing exactly where you stand in a mentoring relationship does cause you to reassess and mount a new approach. Overt resistance may be viewed as a gift.

   iii. Some protégés will want more out of a mentoring relationship. Effective mentoring is an intimate and caring relationship. Some teachers, because of their own loneliness and separateness, may seek a deeper relationship beyond mentoring, a deeper friendship, intimacy, even a romantic relationship.

This is not an unusual or unforeseen part of any helping relationship. Professionals in the helping professions—mental health counselors, psychologists, medical doctors—often find they have to set clear boundaries of what the relationship is about and what it is not. Maintaining professionalism is critical to the mentoring relationship. One-on-one conferencing is held in the school, not in a social setting. While issues brought up in conferencing may involve personal concerns, they should not dominate the discussion.

iv. Some mentors may want more out of a relationship. Being human, mentors may find themselves at risk in some mentoring relationships, finding themselves seeking more in a relationship—a deeper friendship or connection. They need to be able to talk to team members about their feelings. Mentors also need to be sensitive to their own needs and behaviors that may signal a red light and seek out the advice of a teammate. Team members can be helpful in observing a mentoring relationship that may be crossing the line from a professional to a more personal, even romantic, relationship. Too much intimacy can be a warning sign. Having a clear definition of professional boundaries helps.

5. Discuss your changing relationships with the team and theirs with you. As administrator, you are the boss, so to speak. Yes, you operate democratically and collegiality is a hallmark of your administration. But still you are a supervisor who oversees and manages people. Here, as a trainer of mentors and a mentor yourself, your role changes dramatically. You are now operating more as a peer and colleague. This can be unsettling for you. The trappings of your administrator role are not necessary or even wanted in this new role. You are there based on one prerequisite—skill. Skill as a trainer and mentor. It takes getting used to, and it may take some getting used to for your mentoring team. To them, you've been in charge until now. You still are, but this new role as trainer, mentor, and team member is different. In fact, one of the team may emerge, based on skill and successful experience, as the leader of the mentoring program. How much freedom and equality do you allow? These issues need to be addressed with your team by asking the following questions.

    a. How do they perceive your new role as trainer of mentors and a mentor?

    b. Do they plan to interact with you as a peer and colleague rather than as an administrator?

    c. How will these interactions be different? What has changed?

    d. Suppose they observe you having a problem as a mentor. Do they plan to give you the necessary feedback to improve? Can you count on them to be trusted critics?

6. Plan, with the team, the parameters and nuts and bolts of the mentoring program. Now you are moving into an action plan. Here are some practical issues you and your team need to deal with.

    a. Clarify the three major parts of your intervention. The following activities should provide the cornerstone of the mentoring process.

       i. Classroom observation of the protégés.

      ii. One-on-one follow-up conferencing.

     iii. Team meetings to review interventions, resolve problems, offer support, provide ongoing training, and create ongoing hubs of learning such as workshops on effective discipline.

    b. Identify time allotments for mentors. Mentors now have a full-time position. They will need release time for mentoring and tools to keep a close check on how they are balancing the role as mentor with their other position. It is easy to spend too much time on mentoring and neglect other duties. This can create problems and cause other educators to question the program. Encourage your mentors, and yourself, not to neglect regular duties and leave work for others to pick up. Things need to function as smoothly as they did before the mentoring program was introduced. There are issues that can arise for teachers, counselors, department chairs, assistant principals, and principals who become mentors.

       i. Teacher as mentor. The optimum arrangement is for the teacher to have a permanent substitute, a person known to the students and ready for the daily tasks required. Hiring a substitute who is ill-prepared will create problems for the program and the students. Hiring a number of subs to fill the teacher slot can also cause chaos for the program and the students because the classroom would not have enough consistency and normalcy. Parents also have to understand and support this new role of the teacher. Left out of the loop, they can, rightfully so, cause great resistance.

ii. Counselor as mentor. The optimum arrangement is for the counselor to have a reduced load, which does not mean dumping some of his or her counselees on other counselors—a surefire way to incite resistance. As with the teacher as mentor, the best approach is to hire a permanent sub.

iii. Department chairperson as mentor. Department chairs usually have a teaching duty in addition to their supervisory role. They may be the best-positioned members of the team to do mentoring as they already have available a block of time in their schedule. The key here is moving from an overseeing and managing role to a mentoring role. This dual role can cause conflict if not thought through. Department chairs are expected to perform such duties as book orders, budgets, testing arrangements and so on. These tasks are not part of the mentoring process. Department chairs will have to leave their management tasks at the door when they begin mentoring or mischief and confusion—for them and their protégés—can arise.

iv. Assistant principals as mentors. This can be a difficult role. Usually assistant principals are in a reactive and negative role—on the front lines, handling crisis and discipline situations. It is. It may be tough to try to fit mentoring into such a chaotic schedule. Yet having some mentoring opportunities may prove to be a big boost for these educators. Helping and guiding protégés can open up a positive career alternative for creative educators mired in problem-solving roles. Assistant principals too need novelty, change, and opportunity for renewal. Their daily work can be draining and have few positive moments. Again, it is a matter of trying to achieve the right mix, still maintaining their work schedule but creating time for mentoring.

v. Principals as mentors. Again, there is no easy arrangement for principals to become mentors. It will require determination, commitment, and discipline. They have to want this new role and create the conditions for it to happen. Many teachers, cen-

tral office, and middle management personnel will want to retain the status quo and keep the principal in the office. But principals, too, need novelty and change. Much of their daily work
involves solving problems and dealing with the negative side of
school life—students acting out, angry parents, problematic
teachers, and so on. This is an opportunity for the principal to
take on a training and teaching role. It is no secret that administration jobs are hard to fill. Forty percent of all U.S. principals
will probably retire within the decade.[4] A 1998 survey by the
Educational Research Service found that many schools are having difficulty filling administrative positions that opened up because of resignations, promotions, and retirement.[5] This should
come as no surprise to working administrators. Who wants a
job that focuses mainly on solving problems? Becoming a mentor can change a principal's work in drastic ways. It creates an
opportunity to help and guide teachers, train new mentors, and
learn new skills. The mentoring role gets principals out of the
office, temporarily away from the business, marketing, law en-
forcement, and political aspects of the role. It is a rewarding
part of the daily schedule when principals can focus on real instructional leadership and address the problems of ill-trained
teachers, and teachers and students will have more positive
contact with them. Their needs for novelty, change, learning,
and positive relationships may be answered in mentoring and it
might give them new energy to deal with the more mundane
and isolating part of their regular principal duties.

7. Along with the full mentoring team, plan how to sell the program to
the teaching staff. Good ideas and good intentions don't make a new
program successful. It is very important for the team to understand
that they have to go out among the teaching staff and get people to
get involved in the program. Memos, written reports, and speeches
at faculty meetings may be useful, but the real work is one-on-one
involvement with teachers that will help them see that the program
has something in it for them, something worthwhile, useful and yes,
even fun. How is this accomplished? Here are some suggestions.

   a. Make time available to query each teacher in the building personally before the team formulates any start date for the program.

Teachers need to understand what's in it for them and how the program will impact them and their students.

b. Assign each mentor a list of teachers with whom to have informative meetings. Every mentor should have certain teachers with whom to communicate intial ideas. Allow teachers to air resistance and negative comments. Acceptance is the key word.

c. Have mentors prepare a list of positive aspects of the program (e.g., the possibility of becoming a mentor in the future) and how teachers will benefit.

d. Enlist teacher leaders to serve on an advisory board for the project that will meet periodically with the mentoring team. Get teachers involved.

8. With the team, discuss how to identify and overcome resistance to the program. The team will need time to discuss resistance to the program and how they will handle it. Any change has its critics, and the burden swaying these resistors is on the mentoring team. It is their idea, so if they want to make it fly, they must show everyone why it is an excellent idea. If they can't, they will have to bury the failed mentoring program in the school's graveyard replete with failed programs. Overlooking resistance and mistaking a lack of comments for support are secret killers of any new program. How does the team proceed to let resistance emerge so that it is identifiable, welcomed, and confronted in a positive way? Here is one approach.

a. Have the team list the teachers who they think will welcome and support the program. This is the allies list, a critical constituency. These are the people mentors will need to cultivate and encourage to speak up in support of the mentoring program. The team needs to make sure that this group is given ongoing attention. Don't assume that because they are initially in favor of mentoring their support will continue once the project gets into the reality stage. The team needs to continuously shore up these allies.

b. Have the team list teachers who they think will oppose or even try to divert the mentoring program. These are the naysayers capable of blowing up the project, another critical constituency in a different way. They are critical in the sense that if their concerns are not heard and responded to, they are not going to go away. They are going to come back and haunt the project, continuously raising questions about its efficacy. Resisters can be cruel. How can their concerns be heard without giving them a platform to destroy the project? Large-scale meetings to review the project can be taken over by resisters with their own agenda. Well-intentioned teachers can easily be swayed to abandon their support of the project when they are faced with disagreeing with their peers. Your best approach is for team members to sit down one-on-one with each critic, hear them out, and try to get them on board at some level. One meeting may not be enough; it may take several meetings to establish a level of trust. Can every resister be turned around? Probably not. The goal is to incrementally reduce the number of resisters, one by one, so that only a small group remains, no longer in a position to torpedo the project. It is important that the team not isolate or make enemies of this group. Keep communication lines open and keep working with them. Times change and when the project runs into foul weather, the team doesn't want these resisters to begin their assault again.

9. Have the team reflect on how they can remain sensitive to problems and how to create a safety antenna.

   a. It is important for the team to reflect on how they plan to address problems that may destroy or alter the mentoring process in the future. Often, we assume that what is working well will continue to work that way, without adjustments or setbacks. Time can bring many changes, however, as new projects evolve, grow, and change. The original leaders of the project may move on to new positions or turn over the reins to new mentors. Although a mentoring team may not be conscious of it, change is always taking place within the project and everyone involved. With change, there is always the possibility of extinction. How does a mentoring team identify problems and make the necessary adjustments? Problems are signals that something is amiss, and as such they can be seen as friendly reminders, shaking our complacency and alerting us that adjustment is necessary. Here are some ways the team can remain sensitive and be proactive problem solvers.

      i. Anticipate changes in the teaching staff. Staff changes can rearrange the teaching staff in dramatic ways. Teaching staff are often graying, ready for many veteran teachers will retire over the next ten years. There will be an influx of novice teachers, some without preparation. The impact may result in increased demand for mentoring.

ii. Be vigilant. Don't become set in your ways. Complacency is always nearby in any successful project. It is the quiet enemy, lurking, waiting for the opportunity to take over. The team will probably get tired. The initial push for a new program requires a great deal of emotional, physical, and intellectual energy. There comes a time when we want to rest and turn on the automatic pilot. That's when complacency rears its head in unusual ways. If the program becomes very successful, participants begin spending time presenting at conferences and away from the real world of kids and mentoring. The mentors become stars and instead of the focus being on mentoring teachers, it is now on accommodating visiting educators, researchers, and self-promotion. What took years to build falls apart quickly when no one takes care of business, and the great goals of the project slip away. The team needs to be vigilant to such a process and understand that it can happen to them. Be wary of success and self-promotion.

iii. Anticipate changes in support. Administrators come and go. Budgets get reduced. Supporters retire or withdraw to other interests. It is important for the team to continually reassess their level of support. What was initially strong support can easily change with the arrival of a new superintendent or principal with different agendas. The resources for release time for mentors can easily be wiped out in a failed budget. Being political, the program needs to try to develop a variety of resources that can keep the project afloat during bad and changing times. The team might connect with a university or the state education department to fund the mentoring program as a professional development lab. Knowing and understanding local politics and the funding and program opportunities available from external sources are critical tasks for an alert mentoring team.

At this point, you have assessed your own mentoring skills, done some reflection and self-training on how to improve your skills, and trained your mentoring team. Now you are ready to take a more comprehensive look at mentoring relationships.

NOTES

1. Abby Goodnough, "Teaching By the Book, No Asides Allowed," *New York Times,* 23 May 2000, A1, B7.

2. Letters to the Editor, "The Education of Donna Moffett," *New York Times,* 29 May 2001, A14.

3. NEA Quality Fact Sheet, "Ready or Not: A National Teacher Shortage Looms," NEA, 2001, http://www.nea.org/teaching/shortage.html (19 April 2001).

4. Vincent L. Ferrandino and Gerald N. Tirozzi, "Our Time Has Come," NAESP Online (National Association of Elementary School Principals), http://www.naesp.org/ misc/edweek_article_2–23-00.htm (23 February 2000).

5. Education Research Service, "Is There a Shortage of Qualified Candidates for Opening in the Principalship? An Exploratory Study," NAESP Online, http://www.naesp.org/misc/shortage.htm (23 February 2000).

6

The Mentoring Team in Action

Taking Steps toward Building a Whole-School Mentoring Process

In this chapter I present a series of vignettes that focus on different team members' unique mentoring roles. Hopefully, these vignettes will reinforce the mentoring skills you and your team will need to be effective and point out the subtle differences involved in differing, unique mentoring roles. These vignettes are based on real mentors I have seen in action in my capacity as Director of the Bay Shore Public Schools–Stony Brook University Teacher Center, an innovative school-day training program facilitated by classroom teachers, and Director of Teacher Training at the Louis Armstrong Intermediate School, a project jointly sponsored by Queens College, the United States Department of Education, and the New York City Board of Education. I have seen these mentors make a difference in the lives of teachers and spark renewal.

Are there mentors like this in every school? Probably not. But I believe many schools have administrators, teachers, counselors, department chairs, and assistant principals who have the potential to fill a mentoring role. The key is recognizing that the skills educators use in helping kids—nonjudgmental listening, positive feedback, affirmation, positive role modeling—can also be applied to help teachers renew themselves. It's no mystery but it does take a redoing of the way help is delivered to teachers. It is not a "you should be" or "you shouldn't be" message but rather a message based on accepting and recognizing where teachers are and helping them make the changes that are required for success. Will every effort to renew and guide teachers be successful? Of course not. But we can lay the foundation so teachers don't fall through the cracks. We can invite them into a process of renewal and gently, or sometimes forcefully, inch them forward to being master teachers. To do otherwise is to abandon our work of helping make every teacher the best teacher our kids can have.

This chapter also highlights the kinds of issues that might be discussed at team meetings with mentors, bringing to the team issues and themes that teachers are dealing with in the school. This is not a process that invades the privacy of the mentor-protégé relationship but is a compiling of the areas in which teachers need support and further training. A need expressed by many protégés is that they need to acquire better discipline skills. This data can then be translated into hubs of learning such as teacher-led workshops and networking with needed university resources. In a sense, the issues and themes raised by protégés become the curriculum for ongoing learning, a vehicle to respond to the immediate and long term needs of teachers. Finally, while these vignettes focus on secondary educators, the basic core of the intervention, follow-up support, and creating of ongoing learning hubs can easily be applied to the elementary level, as well.

THE PRINCIPAL AS MENTOR

This vignette focuses on the role of the principal as mentor. Here we see in action some specific mentoring characteristics I identified in chapter 3:

Mentors understand the dynamics of teaching and the real world of the classroom.

Mentors understand that every teacher will arrive at the classroom door with his or her own set of biases, judgments, and prejudices.

Mentors understand that the personal and family problems of students can be very emotional and painful for caring teachers.

Mentors understand that there are huge professional and personal benefits in the mentoring process.

Mentors know how to help their protégé find and define his best teaching self.

Mentors know how to teach their protégés to become involved in ongoing sources of support, learning hubs, and opportunities to enhance renewal.

Mentors understand that the mentoring relationship will change over time, often with the newly skilled protégé gradually taking on a mentoring persona and stature of his own.

This vignette further expands the mentoring role of Brad Foley and his protégé, social studies teacher Tom Murray, described in chapter 4. One of the key figures in Tom Murray's search to become a more effective teacher is a student who is acting out, Jim Moriarty. Jim first challenges Tom but as their relationship evolves he begins to see Tom as a caring and helpful mentor. Brad Foley uses Tom's conflict with Jim as a catalyst in getting Tom to learn new skills. Hopefully this vignette will help pinpoint Brad's mentoring skills and in the process demonstrate how Tom integrates these same skills into his own teaching persona to help Jim Moriarty become a successful role model and leader.

Our First View of Tom's Class

Picture a social studies classroom in a junior high school. The bell rings. Students come into the classroom. Some arrive in groups, pushing and laughing: they are the in-crowd. Others walk in alone: the loners who are part of the out-crowd. The teacher, Mr. Murray, stands behind his desk. He asks for quiet. "Take out your textbooks and notebooks. Our topic today is the Depression years in America. Also take out your homework and pass it forward. Moriarty, I don't expect a repeat of your behavior yesterday. You've got two strikes against you. Your next move is out the door. Got it? I've spoken to the administrator about you. Am I being clear? Let's begin. Janine, what's your answer to question one?"

An unskilled mentor's view of this class sees order and control. But he misses the opportunity to help Tom Murray become a more effective teacher. Tom is lucky he doesn't have this administrator as his mentor. An administrator unskilled in mentoring observing this class would say this is a standard junior high school classroom. Students walk in and get settled down. The teacher gives directions, throws in some needed reprimands to student Jim Moriarty, and proceeds with the lesson. Things are under control and the lesson is proceeding. Janine, one of the brightest students in the class, will set a positive tone with her usual insightful and correct answer. Even though Tom Murray is a beginning teacher, he has things under control. We need more Murrays in our profession.

Fortunately, Tom has Dr. Brad Foley, a skilled mentor, as his administrator. Foley quickly identifies the problem areas that Tom needs to address. A skilled administrator as a mentor observing the class sees and hears much more. He notes that the teacher is not at the door to greet his students. He remains behind his desk. He also notes that Tom doesn't greet any of the students by name or get involved in welcoming conversations: "We missed you yesterday. I heard your dad's been sick. Is everything all right? Let me know if I can help out" or "Hey, you played great yesterday. Is the soccer team really in the playoffs? When is the next game? I'll be there." Nor does Tom make any effort to involve the loners with invitations to get involved: "Frank, the social studies club is meeting today. How about joining us in Room 317 after school? I think you could be a big help to us with your interest in history. Your report on World War I was great."

Dr. Foley observes that Tom Murray remains behind his desk throughout the class. He doesn't move around the room and make contact with students who are clearly not involved in his presentation. It's as if he is talking and interacting with only a small percentage of the students, those who seem bright and constantly raise their hands to answer questions. Out of the twenty-eight students in the class, Dr. Foley notes that only ten are participating on a regular basis. The remaining eighteen students, mostly boys, are sitting quietly, many with their heads down, or whispering and acting out. Many are minorities. Among them is Rachael, a new student from Puerto Rico, and Christian, who just moved from Texas with his mother after his parents divorced. Jim Moriarty is desperately trying to get Tom Murray's attention with his laughter and joking. Dr. Foley notes that he needs to ask Tom why he calls Jim by his last name and seems to let him remain isolated and uninvolved. He seems afraid of Jim and threatened by his behavior.

Finally Dr. Foley notes that Tom Murray's focus on only a small percentage of his students has another element to it. He often focuses on girls who are known as high achievers in the school. He seems to feel safe and unthreatened with this group, a class within a class. Dr. Foley wonders if Tom is aware of this dynamic. It's only October and the class is clearly divided into those with the answers and those who choose to opt out of participation. The class is also divided along gender and racial lines. As Dr. Foley notes, "Things seem quiet but as the year progresses these issues may become more combustible if they are not addressed and resolved by Tom. He may not sense he is in trouble but he is. I plan to address these issues with Tom at our next mentoring session." After class Dr. Foley asks Tom if they can meet third period. He says, "Let's meet in our new conference room, Tom. It's more comfortable than my office. I think we are off to a good start but there is work to be done on both our parts. See you then. I'll bring the coffee. Two sugars, right, Tom?"

Dr. Foley uses his mentoring skills to help Tom become aware of areas where he needs to become more effective. As promised, Dr. Foley arrives at the mentoring session with coffee. He understands that Tom is a relatively new teacher, in his second year, and he is apprehensive about his first mentoring session. So is Dr. Foley. The mentoring program is new this year and Foley has had to delegate more of his responsibilities to his assistants. Being out of the office, away from the rush of daily crises, is a new world for him. But he believes he can have his biggest impact helping each of his teachers raise their level of competence. His boss, superintendent Mary Lewis, is behind him as long as "you keep the lid on the school. Not everyone is going to understand but if the mentoring program works out, maybe the other administrators will come on board. I'll give you two years." In a way both Tom Murray and Brad Foley are in the same boat. Both are starting anew.

Brad Foley sets the stage for the mentoring session by inquiring about Tom's personal life and interests. Brad knows that Tom is interested in sports and is a Civil War buff. He also knows that Tom is recently married and has a baby on the way. His wife, Mary, is a pediatric nurse at the local hospital. Tom is a New Yorker who migrated to the Midwest to go to college and stayed because, as he says, " I like the slower pace." They talk quietly and in the conversation Brad lets Tom know that while he is still finding his way through the new mentoring program, he is enjoying the face-to-face interactions with teachers. He is having much more contact with real teaching situations and is learning a lot about classroom dynamics and how good his teaching staff is. No, they are not perfect. There is work to be done if they are all going to grow professionally. His paperwork and problems are still there when he gets back to the office but it's been worth it. The first few minutes of the mentoring session are designed to create a sense of ease and safety for both the teacher and the mentor. No, Tom and Brad are not friends, but so far they are trusting of each other and believe that they will be able to learn from each other.

Once the coffee is gone and the opening conversation has established a sense of ease and trust, Brad begins his work as mentor. First he offers Tom some praise: "Tom, your classroom control is excellent and you are ready to go when the students come into class. The lesson proceeds fine. All in all it's good stuff. But," he adds, "I have some questions for you that may help us pinpoint some areas that you might want to consider as you work toward being more effective with every student in the class. And let me emphasize the words *every student* because I think you are making good contact with some students but more can be involved with some simple steps on your part."

First, I notice that you're standing behind your desk when the students come in. Have you thought about standing at the door or in the hallway and greeting each student with a hello and sharing something personal with them, such as you missed them when they were absent or you saw them play a great soccer game?

Second, I notice some kids, like Larry Donato, come into class pretty much alone. You probably know that Larry's parents recently split up and he is having a rough time. Have you thought of ways to get him involved? I've observed that he does pretty much the same thing in every class, just sits by himself. I've asked your team leader, Frank Munson, to bring his name up at our next meeting. We need to get him off his duff and into some ego-building activities. How about the Social Studies Club? I know he loves the Civil War. The same goes for the new kids, Rachael and Christian. This is a huge move for them. Imagine coming from Puerto Rico and Texas? This is the well-to-do suburbs. I don't think we really understand what they are going through. Maybe for our next meeting you can think of some things we can do to help them get settled. Hank Mobley, the gym teacher, tells me they are both good athletes.

Another area that I notice, and I know it is a difficult one, is that you are really interacting with only ten or so students. They seem to be very bright kids, like Janine, and pretty much dominate the class. I know myself, when I was a teacher, I often went with the kids who had the answers and kept things moving. In fact, I was hesitant to ask the other kids because I knew they either didn't have the answer or would take forever to say what they had to say. I was afraid of losing the momentum, of the silence. I was im-

patient, rushing. That was not good for me or for the kids. And to be honest, some of the other kids, like Jim Moriarty, who sat in back of the class
and carried on, made me shake. I didn't know how to get across to them and
get them involved. So what did I do? I went with letting the quick and well
prepared kids answer. It was easier. It took me a while to figure out how to
get the other kids involved. But you know, the answer was simple. I had to
spend time with them, get to know them, not address them, as you do with
Jim Moriarty, by their last names. And believe me, I did the same thing as
you. I had to come to believe that every kid wants to be involved, be successful, fit in, be someone special. You know, it comes down to this. It's up
to us as teachers to find the way. That's why they pay us the big bucks,
right? How about inviting Jim in for a conference and having lunch on a
regular basis? He's a very good drummer, by the way. He plays in a rock-
band and hangs out at the mall. No, he's not much into school but he has
something to offer. It's something to think about.

And finally, I think that, while things are going well now, you may be setting yourself up for some trouble as the year goes along. Here is one area that
could get to be a real thorn in your side. It's not something to be threatened
by or to be avoided. We can work on these issues together. I notice that most
of the interaction in your class is with the girls. Most of the ten students participating actively are girls. Most of the eighteen others are boys or minorities. I am not saying there is any maliciousness here; you may not even be
aware of it. But the good news is that it is an area that you can address now
that I am making you aware of it. Be consciously aware of this dynamic and
try not to be afraid of it. It's there. It's an area in which you need to develop
some new skills. In order to get better at the teaching process, we all have to
look at the dark side, those kids and issues we tend to avoid. Let's put it another way. I know you are a New York Yankees fan. David Cone did not get
to win twenty-five games a year throwing only fastballs. He has had arm in-
juries; he has had to adjust, change, learn new approaches, develop a change-
up, throw sidearm sometimes. That's also true for you. Tom Murray needs
more pitches, if you will, to be a more effective teacher. You have to open
up your vision and see the whole field. That means involving yourself with
the whole class. Make sure you are connecting with each student, each day,
in every way possible. As I said, we can work together on these things. I am
learning new things about this job and so are you, so we're both in the same
boat. By the way, I've invited one of my associates at Spring College in for
a coffee klatch to talk to teachers about how we can all better understand mi-
nority students. His name is Frank Able; he's a talented and helpful guy. He
is coming over next Monday at 7:30, before school. How about joining us?

I am thinking that down the road maybe you and some other teachers could team up with Frank to run a workshop on how to overcome the barriers of working with some students who come from different backgrounds and cultures. It's food for thought.

Brad Foley then asks Tom to try out some new behaviors. He gives Tom the following list of suggestions to work on during the coming week:

1. Change your behavior at the beginning of the class. Be more welcoming and inviting as the students enter the classroom. Let them know you are glad they are there. Make a big deal of saying hello and making meaningful small talk. Think of yourself as the maitre d'.
2. Get to know your students more intimately—what they like, what they do for fun, their personal issues.
3. Invite students like Jim Moriarty in for a lunchtime conversation. Break down some of the barriers that exist.
4. Be assertive about asking everyone in the classroom questions. Move around the room. Get them involved. Try not to go for the right answer every time. That will help the Janines in the class be aware of others who struggle to get it right and take some of the pressure off her.
5. Use Janine and her able classmates to help tutor the other students. Instead of lecturing, break the class into small groups and bring different parts of the class together to work on projects. Use the bright kids as mentors.
6. Remember the resources we have that you can tap into, such as Frank Able from Spring College.
7. Begin thinking of yourself as a resource, a mentor, for fellow teachers by becoming involved in workshops on issues that you are trying to work through.

Now it is Brad Foley's time to ask for feedback. He is direct and he asks Tom to rate his performance in this mentoring session. Tom, of course, is hesitant. Brad accepts this behavior. It is a new area for both of them. But Brad persists by saying that in order for him to be a more effective mentor, he needs to know how he is coming across. Is he helping, supporting, pointing out the necessary work that both he and Tom have to do to help

Tom be a more effective teacher, or are his comments too intrusive, aggressive, or off the mark? Tom's answer says it all.

I am so glad that we talked. I was very apprehensive about this mentoring program. I knew you would be coming into my class on a regular basis and we would be having these one-on-one sessions. I didn't know you very well. You were always in the office and busy my first year here. I know a lot of the other teachers, even the most experienced ones, were apprehensive too. And our union rep told us to be very careful about what we said, although he said you were very pro-teacher. But this seems to be working out well for me. I like your casual approach, the coffee, and our easy talk in the beginning of the session. I am surprised you knew so much about my personal life. It made me feel good. As for your observations, I think they are right on target. I've always tried to keep myself a little distant from the kids, not get too involved with them by sticking to my subject area. My graduate school professors stressed that getting too close to them can lead to losing control. I remember them saying, 'Don't be friends with your students. Be an authority figure and things will go your way.' But I think that's not been good. I've isolated myself and I am surely not enjoying the kids. Even Jim Moriarty—I was just like him as a kid. But I made him an enemy, an outsider. As for the girls/boys/minorities thing, I frankly wasn't aware of that but now that you bring it up, I can see it could be a time bomb. I've been pretty tight just trying to get the right answers out and have the kids be ready for the state tests. Plus I've been worried about my wife having the baby. She's been having problems. I guess things will be all right. I don't want to burden you with my personal problems. Your ideas for inviting the kids for lunch and breaking kids into groups sound good. Maybe the next time you could help me set up the groups and sort of coteach with me so I get the hang of it. I've never worked in groups before but I see that it could help the kids who are not so involved.

You made me think about a lot of things today that will help me improve as a teacher. I like your easy conversation and your making critical observations that seem very helpful and doable. I never felt you were putting me down or demeaning my work. You are a good listener. You're not afraid to say what needs to be said. You give good, workable suggestions and you are not in a hurry. My last principal, in Indiana, was in and out in a flash. All I got from his visit was a written checklist that contained mostly plusses on work. Not one word was spoken. It didn't help me learn much. I don't know how to describe our relationship. It's different. It's both personal and professional. You are opening up to me about your work and asking, imagine that, my advice. I never had a principal do that before. And thanks for the information on Frank Able. It would be great to discuss some of these things with colleagues. These topics, you know, don't come up in the faculty room. Are you really serious about my being involved in offering a workshop with Able and other teachers? That would be great stuff. Wait until I tell my union rep about this meeting. He'll be knocked out. Teachers giving feedback to administrators on their performance? Wow!

This story suggests the positive power and possibilities for both the teacher and administrator involved in an effective mentoring relationship. It also clearly describes the loss of opportunity for Tom to grow professionally if his mentoring is carried out by an unskilled mentor who sees only issues to control. Fortunately, Tom now has the data necessary to begin to acquire new skills and behaviors and he has the support and the guidance of a good mentor in Brad Foley. Most important to our work is identifying the skills that Brad Foley brings to the table, skills noticeably lacking in our first mentor's observations. Here is a list of the skills Brad Foley brings to the mentoring sessions:

1. He has informed himself about the personal life and interests of his teachers.
2. He is not a threatening figure. He creates the conditions in which a two-way helping conversation can take place and grow. There is safety and ease in his intervention.
3. He understands classroom dynamics and knows what works and what doesn't. He has been there as a teacher and is not afraid to share his mistakes.
4. He is a good listener and observer.
5. He is aware of the barriers that both teachers and students put up to remain uninvolved and isolated.
6. He is nonjudgmental in his view of Tom's classroom performance. His focus is solely on the skills and new practices Tom has to learn to be more effective.
7. He is not interested in blaming or being the guy with all the answers to Tom's problems. He is not blaming Tom for the behavior of some of his students. Rather, he is saying, "Let's address it with a set of new skills and interventions before it clouds your other areas of successful teaching."
8. He knows how to praise, reward, and shore up good teaching practices.

9. He knows how to give teachers classroom problem-solving techniques that can help them avoid practices that produce failure.
10. He introduces his teachers to school and community resources. He knows he can't do all the mentoring by himself. He is always on the lookout for credible resources both in the school and in the community who can share the leadership.
11. He encourages teachers to view themselves as potential mentors for colleagues and students by becoming involved as workshop leaders. Again, this is another way to build his mentoring constituency and expand his leadership team.
12. He encourages teachers to use successful students as mentors to help other students.
13. He is having some fun and enjoying his staff. He is not locked in an office reacting to the phobias of poorly trained teachers; he is doing something about it.
14. Brad Foley has a vision of where he wants to go. His plan is to involve all his teachers in the mentoring process but he doesn't plan to stop there. He wants the Jim Moriarty's and the Janines involved as a team, putting together the brightest and the neediest, to be mentors for other students. Brad understands that's how kids learn tolerance and acceptance of each other, by being involved in projects that build community, awareness, and trust.

I believe Brad Foley's skills are attainable by every administrator who sets out to be an effective mentor. It is sound, effective communication and coaching skill. It is my belief that every administrator would like to be like Brad Foley and every teacher in our schools would like and need his intervention. It is my belief and experience that every teacher wants to get better at his or her craft and be more effective. Like students and administrators, teachers don't want to fail or to be viewed as less than competent. Teachers who are failing their job know it and often their plight and story are known by everyone else in the school and sadly become a topic for faculty room and PTA talk. Administrators who are skilled mentors can intervene and change the lives of failing teachers and in the process bring life, energy, and hope back to the students in the classroom and set an example for other teachers, wherever in their careers they may be. They can learn that things can change and new skills can be acquired, but it does take hope, work, commitment, and practice on the part of the teacher and also the mentor involved. As Tom Stoppard, the playwright, suggests, happiness and change involve equilibrium, shifting one's weight. It often means giving up outmoded skills, jumping from the ledge, and creating new classroom dynamics based on the present.

Finally, early intervention to help teachers like Tom Murray identify and learn new skills is surely a clear-cut way to save tax payer money by cutting down job-induced illnesses and sick days related to lack of success, and improving skills so students can have the academic gains they may have missed with a failing teacher. It is also a clear-cut way to save and improve the lives of professionals who, without intervention, deteriorate over time because nothing seems to work right in their classrooms.

THE TEACHER AS MENTOR

This vignette focuses on the role of the teacher as mentor. Here we see some specific mentoring characteristics I identified in chapter 3:

Mentors understand that a teacher's personal problems, such as divorce or a growing addiction, impact on the teacher's effectiveness and well-being.

Mentors know how to listen, be nonjudgmental, and provide useful feedback and modeling.

Mentors have knowledge about aging and barriers to career development.

Mentors understand that renewing oneself is hard work; it's often not simple or even sought after.

Mentors know how to take care of themselves and be physically and emotionally up to the mentoring task.

Mentors value the loyalty and privacy of the protégé.

Mentors know how to bring a sense of joy, energy, humor, and lightness to the mentoring relationship.

This vignette describes a relationship between mentor and teacher Frank Bronkowski and his protégé, math teacher Ellen Turner. Frank, a veteran twenty-year English teacher is in his first year as a mentor. He has been a very successful teacher and coach. Coming to the school fresh out of college, he quickly established himself as a class act, an effective class-room teacher who is great with kids, a colleague others seek out for advice, and a teacher committed to working with kids after school as a basketball coach and faculty advisor. He also continued his own learning experience, acquiring a master's degree plus. He now serves as adjunct professor in a local university's education department and recently coauthored a book on how teachers can help teens solve personal problems.

Frank was clearly an easy choice for the mentoring program. Still, the mentoring position is a new and challenging one for him. He has two periods each day for mentoring. While he has a gifted permanent sub, he continues to oversee her work, teach two classes himself, coach, and participate in weekly mentoring team meetings. He thanks God that he has a stable, caring home life that offers him support. And he is in excellent physical shape, running five miles a day.

Ellen, his protégé, has had a rockier career. She is in her thirtieth year of teaching, coming to the school fresh out of a master's program in 1972. For the first twenty-five years she was a school leader, teaching the more difficult math classes, administering the tutoring center after school, and working on a Ph.D. But for the past five years she has seemed to withdraw from all activities except her classroom teaching; she has given up on her long-sought Ph.D. and turned the tutoring service over to younger teachers. Consequently, her teaching has suffered. Her department chair assigns only the most basic classes. She has started to miss school, calling in sick at least once every few weeks. The administration is considering requiring her to bring a doctor's note to verify her so-called illnesses. She doesn't look well and rumors say she is drinking heavily and is seen at a local liquor store each evening.

What happened to this once energetic, gifted teacher? The faculty room gossip says she's turned into a nightmare teacher, poorly prepared and unable to be an effective disciplinarian. Gossip also suggests that she has home problems. For the past three years she has been involved in a hostile divorce. Close friends say her marriage has been on the rocks for years. She increasingly isolates herself, arriving at school at the last possible moment, eating lunch in her room, and as one administrator puts it, "She is out of the parking lot before the buses leave." The school's administration and some of her colleagues are very concerned for her well being but they seem unable to help her, somehow not able to find the right words. It is sometimes easier for teachers to help troubled kids than colleagues. There are other teachers who are not so kind. They mock her behavior in the faculty room and even have placed bets on how long she will be able to survive. Some teachers are not so kind when they see a colleague in trouble. Does it create uneasiness in them, an uneasiness that suggests that this could happen to them someday? To them it is better to make a mockery of it, to make the failing teacher the victim, rather than internalize their own fears and vulnerability.

Does the mentoring program offer some hope for Ellen? Clearly, Frank has a big challenge trying to help Ellen get back on the right track and fight for her professional and perhaps her personal life. She seems to have given up. But how should a mentor give someone life? How does a teacher break through the depression and wake up to the reality that she is failing and failing fast? We all know teachers like Ellen who are in flight; they are not strangers to us. Yet, like Frank, we ask ourselves, "How do I help?" Like Frank, we are not counselors or therapists. Teachers are not certified as helpers. But that doesn't have to matter. Everyone has helping skills. We know how to listen, be nonjudgmental, and provide feedback that can help shake and shape our colleagues in need. We can be helpful in our own unique way if we are willing to take the risks to intervene and be a loyal friend. We understand that problematic personal relationships of colleagues impact the teacher's effectiveness and well-being. And we understand, because we have been there ourselves. Maybe the words a mentor uses to connect with someone like Ellen are not terribly significant. Maybe what is important is the effort, a willingness to try and in trying to be willing to accept the rebuffs and refusals. In trying, we learn by doing and hopefully find the right words that will have meaning to someone like Ellen.

Mentors need to remember that there are few instant successes in connecting with teachers headed for trouble. The red light of danger may be on but they don't see it or they choose not to see it. It is the job of mentors like Frank Bronkowski to have them see the warning lights and advise and direct them to sources of help. Let's see how Frank proceeds.

Frank is a master teacher and he has been trained as a mentor. He knows the drill. But being well trained and knowing the drill doesn't always prepare him for mentoring real people with real problems. Frank's first task in helping Ellen is to understand what is wrong and right in her classroom. Once he has this data he can make an accurate assessment and plan for intervention. Ellen's is a classroom that was once alive with an energetic, caring teacher and students at ease, knowing they were in a safe place but yet challenged. There were no negative criticisms, no accusations, no screaming; it was a class students looked forward to each day. But now, as Frank is to see, it is a classroom in despair, a teacher screaming and name-calling, a classroom inhabited only by students who have no way out, no parent to rescue them by complaining to the principal or counselor and demanding another teacher. It is a classroom in which the teacher—Ellen Turner, who almost has a Ph.D.—and her students have no way out. The only escape is for the teacher to call in sick and the students to cut class. Who will care if they do?

A View of Ellen's Class

Picture a classroom in despair: the bulletin board holds pictures yellowed with age describing events long past; a blank chalk board looks strangely unused for a ninth grade consumer math class; desks are spread out around the back of the room with no order, no rows, pushed as far away from the teacher's desk as possible. Ellen's desk seems isolated, not part of the classroom at all. The students slowly drift into class, many of them late, minutes after the final bell. Although the class enrollment is twenty-two students, only fourteen are present. Ellen, sitting at her desk, seems to ignore what is going on, waiting for the kids to sit down. Five minutes into the class she takes attendance. When she calls out the names of absent students, the response of other students is often, "She cut." Sometimes the students deliver quick, insulting remarks such as, "I don't know why I'm here. This class sucks." Or, "How come Fred got transferred to Ms. Eglin's class? Probably his parents got him out. I wish my parents would do that. I agree with Sandra. This class sucks. We're not learning anything." Ellen is unresponsive to the insults and challenges to her authority. She doesn't even seem to mind that her mentor, Frank, is observing this fiasco. It's almost as if she is saying, "Who cares what these kids do or what I do? I certainly don't any more. These kids are the bottom of the barrel. Teaching consumer math is the lowest of the low. I can't get much lower." She passes out a worksheet and says, "Do problems one through six in class and finish the rest for homework. If you fail to turn in the worksheet tomorrow it's an automatic failure." One student named Mike interrupts: "What if you're not here? You're always out on Fridays. You sure get sick a lot. It's a wonder they still pay you." Ellen, seeming oblivious, returns to her desk. The students quickly begin fooling around, throwing papers out the window. They look at Frank in a somewhat embarrassed way as if to say, "We know we shouldn't be doing this but Ms. Turner doesn't care so why should we?" Minutes before the bell the students get up and leave. Ellen doesn't challenge them, telling them to stay in their seats until the bell. Frank thinks it's a miracle that the students hadn't acted out even more. Ellen established no control or boundaries, and demonstrated no preparation or interest. Was Ellen really that oblivious to all the chaos in her classroom? Clearly she knows the difference between good and bad teaching. She was an effective teacher at one time. Frank wondered how she had arrived at this point. What happened to her pride? Her skills? Her craft? How did she develop such a tolerance for pain?

An unskilled mentor's view of this class rightfully sees disorder and chaos. But he misses the opportunity to help Ellen Turner become a more effective teacher. Ellen is lucky she doesn't have someone unskilled as her mentor; she might be out the door. An unskilled mentor might say, "Some way has to be found to get rid of Ms. Turner. Medical leave, whatever. Let's find a way and quickly. This lady is in trouble and we are not a clinic or rehab. We don't have the time or resources to coddle her. Let's call her in and encourage her to resign or apply for medical leave. I don't care that she was once a great teacher. The past doesn't matter. She's killing the kids. I know the union will go along with us."

Fortunately, Ellen has Frank Bronkowski as her mentor. Frank has a plan to help. He knows that there has to be a good reason for this decline in Ellen's performance. He feels that the best approach is to go to Ellen in the one-on-one conference with what he has observed as problems and get her to react. He'll do it gently, of course, but will accept no avoidance of issues. He thinks, "Let's stop treating her as a patient. Let's forget about her divorce, isolation, even the drinking—if that rumor is true—and focus on classroom issues." He will leave Ellen plenty of room to bring up personal issues that may be draining her enthusiasm and energy, but the first step is to identify the classroom problem areas she needs to address. Ellen is no dummy; she knows good teaching. He will remind her what that is and what it would take for her to get back there. Frank begins to wonder who is isolating whom. Has the school been isolating her, avoiding her? Was her seeming incompetence a cry for help? Frank sees opportunity here. He does not allow his students to become isolated and uncared for and Ellen will get the same treatment from him.

It is not hard for Frank to identify the problem areas that Ellen needs to work on. He lists his reflections on the problems and how he might address them in the conference:

1. Get some life into the classroom. Fix the bulletin boards. Bring in some flowers or pictures of your daughters and grandchildren.
2. Let your students know something personal about you, not your personal problems but something you're involved in. Do they know you started the tutoring program here? Many of your students get the help they need there. Think about going back to work there. It would be an ideal spot to help your students.
3. Find out something personal about your students. Sandra has just completed a great season with the soccer team. Mike has been doing some good stuff with the peer-counseling program. His dad passed away last summer and he is working with a group of elementary kids who have lost a parent. You have some interesting students. Many of them don't have much parental support but they're survivors, like you.
4. Let the students know you want them in class on time and they are not allowed to leave early. First appeal to their good judgment. Say it looks bad for you and them if they are in the hall after the bell. If that doesn't work, give out detentions. Be tough. They'll respond.
5. Get rid of the worksheets and do some real teaching. You're putting the kids and yourself to sleep with the worksheets. You don't seem to care so why should they? You've been there. Use what you know.
6. Rearrange the desks so there is an emphasis on discussion. Give each student an assigned seat. No more back of the room isolation for them or you.
7. Create an atmosphere of self-respect and caring. Stop letting the students take pot shots at you. Stop the insults. Tell them you won't tolerate it any more. In turn you will respect them and treat them the same way. It will take a while because you've let it go on.

8. Get out of your room and start mingling with the staff. You've isolated yourself. I know some of our colleagues can be cruel and they criticize others to keep the heat off themselves. But keeping to yourself doesn't help you and it sparks unkind and malicious rumors. If you make yourself known people will talk less behind your back. Show your face.

9. What I am saying is to take back your classroom and your self-respect. We are going to work on this together. I know rebuilding pride isn't easy. You're going to have to make some changes but that's OK. I'll be there as a loyal friend. What goes on between you and me stays here. I'll be loyal and respect your trust in me—if you'll give it to me. This will help me learn as a mentor. And who knows? Maybe this is a way for you to become a mentor someday. You're not the only struggling teacher in the building. You know that.

One-on-one conferencing following classroom observation is the heart and soul of the mentoring process. What kinds of conditions does Frank have to create? Consider the following suggestions:

If possible the meetings should be held in an attractive and comfortable environment, in an atmosphere of safety, trust, and professional respect. Protégés need to feel welcomed and affirmed and have a sense that this is a good place to be. Simple things can help humanize the mentoring setting: a pot of coffee, snacks, flowers on the table, comfortable seats. It should be a setting that encourages conversation. Ironically, these kinds of setting are rarely found in schools. The environments in which we work often lack comfortable, professional spaces that allow for privacy, as educators often place all of their emphasis on the students and their needs. Professional comfort zones that can enhance conversation and professional dialog hardly exist. What we schools have is faculty rooms, often unkempt, with outdated, yard-sale furniture brought in by teachers. Teachers settle for the minimum, as if they as educators aren't worthy of better conditions. This is a glaring example of teachers' inability to take care of themselves professionally, to demand more. Effective mentoring requires different, comfortable settings. Mentors need to create these kinds of comfort zones and learning hubs if they want their protégés to reflect on their teaching issues. Trying to carry on mentoring conversations in the anomie of the faculty room doesn't foster a feeling of privacy and safety.

In addition to creating an attractive setting, Frank needs to be ready to greet Ellen, raise critical issues, encourage her to respond, and develop an informal contract on how they will proceed as a team. Consider the following suggestions:

Bring some joy, energy, humor, and lightness to the meeting. Frank should greet Ellen with some positive feedback even if it's hard to find. His physical stance should be welcoming. He should smile, appear relaxed, and seem to be looking forward to the meeting.

Frank is good at asking questions that lead to reflection on Ellen's teaching process. He uses expressions like, "What is your take on what is happening? Here is what I see. Have you ever thought about . . . ? Here is how we might proceed. How does that sit with you?"

Frank gives homework assignments to both Ellen and himself. He might ask Ellen to write a reflection on how she views her teaching style, the positives and negatives, and how she views what work has to be done to improve. Frank suggests that he will do the same, take a look at his own teaching style. He also suggests to Ellen that she do a daily reflection on her teaching day, a reflection she can share with Frank if she chooses.

Using these hints Frank does not arrive at the meeting clueless. He has set the right conditions, he knows the right words to use to encourage communication, and he has a plan to help Ellen based on his classroom observations. This is how their conversation goes.

Frank: Hi, Ellen. Thanks for coming. Coffee? I got some great donuts at Hilda's bakery. Try one. Look, I am glad we could get together. As you know, this mentoring role is new for me. I want to be helpful if I can but I am not an expert by any means. I know every teacher has to be involved in the program but I want to keep this as simple and low-key as we can. With that in mind, let me say that what we talk about and work on together stays between us. Brad Foley made it clear that this is not a supervisory situation. I am here to help . . . period. Maybe we could begin by my asking you how you view the program.

Ellen: Frankly, it's not something I want to be involved in. I've got other things to do. I also haven't been feeling too well lately so this is another burden. I am here because I have to be. I can't afford to jeopardize my job, especially right now. Frank, I like and respect you. You are a person I know I can trust, not like some other people in the building. But don't expect too much from me.

Frank: Sounds fair to me. I appreciate your honesty. Let me ask you how you think things are going in your classes. I've observed you three times and I've got some suggestions. But first I'd like to get your take on things.

Ellen: Whew, that's a tough one, particularly since I just told you that I'm not into this mentoring thing. Well, you're no fool, Frank. You see what's going on. I've just sort of caved in. I'm there. That's about it. Kind of weary of it all, I guess. And you're too nice a guy to bring it up but it's all over school that Rob and I have finally split up. Twenty-two years and the last few hell on wheels. I am just worn out. But money is tight and I can't afford to leave. Everyone's upset—me, my kids, my grandkids. I've got to sell my house and get an apartment. Jesus, I've lived there for twenty years. It's all I have and now that's gone too. But no one here seems to care. It's a mess and I'm a mess. You see it, the kids see it. I used to teach calculus and now they've stuck me with consumer math. I've become a nothing. Am I a burnout? I don't know. What a comedown.

Frank: I'm glad you're sharing this with me. Yes, it does look like you're struggling in the classroom and at home. It's a tough time. I'm glad I'm going to be around to support you. Part of mentoring is getting to talk about real life problems that may be affecting your teaching. And you are experiencing some tough ones. But, as you say, you also seem to be experiencing feelings that you've landed in a bad spot, dropped from calculus to consumer math, and your home problems may indeed be making you weary, burned out maybe. I'm not a counselor or a therapist but it's easy to figure out why you're struggling in the classroom. There's not much joy around right now.

Ellen: You've seen it. I'm just letting things go in my classroom and that's not really helping me. It's making things worse, really. You can't imagine how ashamed I am when I go home each day. It's so painful to see me as I am now. My poor performance only adds to my woes. I think if I enjoyed teaching and the kids once again, I would be a lot happier, but I can't seem to get started in that direction. I've got no one to talk to, except maybe you. I don't know. I'm open to any suggestions. This is killing me.

Frank: I think you're right. Working on some ways to improve your teaching may be the way to go. It may give you some uplifting success and increase your feeling of self-worth, which I sense has taken a beating. My sense is that it will probably take a while for your home issues to work out. Getting some counseling might help but I'm sure you've thought of that. It might take some of the burden off your shoulders. Having someone to talk to does help. But I think there are some things you can work on right now to begin to get back to your best teaching self. You've been there. You know what good teaching is. I have some suggestions that might help you. Let me share them with you and see if you agree. Am I on target? Some of the suggestions are quite simple and I don't think you have to make a lot of major changes. Try brightening up your classroom with pictures and flowers. It'll help you and the kids. Let the kids know you have been having a tough time—you don't have to get into the details—and you're trying to change things. Think about rejoining the tutoring service or some other activity so you can get out and see people. The peer-counseling program is looking for facilitators to help lead a divorce group. It may be just what you, and kids experiencing divorce, need. You're there; you know how hard it is. Get to know your students on a more personal level. Ask about their lives outside of school. Who knows? Some of them may be experiencing a divorce, too. Also, set some rules and boundaries in the classroom. Expect the students to arrive and leave on time. Get a little angry and demand respect. You don't need to be talked down to. You may be weary but that doesn't mean you have to take crap, excuse my English. Rearrange the desks for discussion. Get back to questioning. Using worksheets, in my opinion, is not adding zest or creativity. Think about how else you can reach these kids. You're a pro. You've been there. Get that bright and experienced mind of yours going. Think about getting out of your room for lunch. Stop letting people think you're troubled. Don't let them label you. The more you're out talking with others, the better it will be for you. Sure, you're having a rough time, but so are a lot of other teachers and administrators. Life hits us all. Also think about writing a reflection on your teaching every day. It might help you focus on what's going on and how you're doing. And finally, think about counseling. It might help shore things up as you make changes. It might also help you find the words to talk about what's going on with your kids, grandkids and colleagues. Finally, I wrote these things out for you. If you want to take them with you, great. It's a list of things we might both work on. What do you think?

Ellen: You're right. A lot of these things are very simple but it does feel like too much to do all at once. Maybe I could just start with the room. I've got some great pictures of my kids and grandkids. Funny, I don't think I've ever shared anything about them with my class. I also have a great garden with lots of flowers. Gardening is a passion and hobby with me. It makes me feel at peace. I'll bring some flowers in, maybe even try to tell my students about my garden and what it means to me. Maybe I'll even make a lesson out of it, the profitability in professional gardening. Look, Frank, this has been very helpful. I dreaded coming here. Even thought about calling in sick. But thank God I am here. Let me take the list and see what I can do before we meet again. I appreciate your concern for me and your offer to help. You really listened to me, got me to think, and your suggestions make sense. It's the first time in a long time that I've felt a little energy and hope that things can change. I just got through reading an article last night called "The Kindness of Friends." You certainly are one. Thanks.

Perfect ending? Who knows? Time will tell. But for this day, this moment, Ellen has some hope that things can improve. She has a little energy and a pulse. Without the well thought out and skilled intervention of Frank, chances are that things would have only gotten worse for Ellen. But now she has a trusted, loyal friend and some concrete issues to work on. She is not left to deal with her demons alone. And Frank has the positive feedback he needs to reinforce his self-worth and mentoring skills. He sees that his effective questioning can result in reflections that make his protégé more aware of her teaching self, the good and the bad, and the work that needs to be done. Where does someone like Ellen go if her school does not support mentoring? Some lucky ones find angels and saviors, or they save themselves. But most slip away, some silently—"She just called in and said she wasn't coming back. I knew she had problems but this is so sudden. Who do we have to fill her spot?" Others, though, exit their school with a bang: "I knew it was going to happen. I could see it coming, that one day she was going to lose it. It was that seventh period class with all the difficult kids. She just exploded, started screaming and cursing and then she ran out of the building Everyone—the kids, the teachers, the aides—was watching. Her ex-husband called last night and said she wasn't coming back. I wish we could have done something but we're no miracle workers."

THE DEPARTMENT CHAIR AS MENTOR

While both Tom Murray and Ellen Turner had personal issues, the focus of mentoring support was on improving classroom performance: different teachers with different issues but the same goal. Every teacher needs help at some stage. In Ellen's case help came fast. She just had to be asked how things were going. She knew things were falling apart and she was ready when Frank arrived to help. Both vignettes describe an important part of an effective teacher's work—setting clear boundaries. Tom is a new teacher searching for and creating, with Brad Foley's help, a set of rules to govern what student behavior should be like in his classroom. He is also creating a teaching persona that defines his role. He will be available to help students like Jim Moriarty but he avoids taking on a parenting role. He realizes that he can't take Jim home with him and give him the care and love he needs, but he can, within the classroom limits, be a mentor and advisor for him.

Setting clear and reasonable boundaries is also an important goal for Ellen. Somewhere along the way she has lost the ability for, and maybe interest in, making very clear what is acceptable for her students. And she has lost the ability and interest in setting clear boundaries for her personal and professional behavior. She arrives at school at the bell, leaves early, calls in sick regularly and allows her classroom environment to deteriorate. She has also lost important personal boundaries, her marriage and soon her home. But with Frank's intervention, she has a guide and a plan to restore order.

Sometimes important issues about setting boundaries occur outside the classroom. Some involve quiet, little-spoken-about relationships between teachers and their students, the kinds of issues that "aren't supposed to happen here." These are certainly not simple issues that can be easily addressed, as in the case of relationships that cross over the teacher-student boundary into friendship or even romantic involvement. Sometimes teachers involved in helping their students work through painful personal experiences take on Messiah, savior, friend, or parenting role, spending more time with certain students, sometimes evening meetings outside of school. These teachers, some inexperienced in setting boundaries, don't heed the red light of caution and cross over their professional boundaries. Their behavior is often observed by colleagues and administrators who fail to intervene. They can't seem to find the right way to help, the right words of caution, the right skills to bring sense to the situation. In this vignette we focus on such a teacher, Shawn Mallory, and his mentor, department chair Randy Edwards. The difference here is that Randy Edwards does try to intervene and advise Shawn Mallory to be careful. He realizes that Shawn is a novice teacher. Shawn may think he knows what teaching is all about but he has many lessons to learn. He is well-liked by his students, even adored some might say. As a new teacher he has brought excitement and zest to his department and the aging school faculty. He's loving his job, but he may be headed for trouble. Being too involved with needy teens can be risky business, for them and for the teacher. Highly successful careers can easily be detoured when boundaries get blurred. Interventions don't always work. With the current rash of school violence, aren't we all looking for teachers who care for at-risk students and reach out to them? Aren't our schools calling for more teachers to be mentors and advisors, to see that their teaching role should now include helping students solve nonacademic personal problems as well as academic problems? Doesn't helping students resolve personal problems free them to be better academically? Before we search out teachers to be mentors and advocates for students, we need to have a support system in place, such as mentoring, that can give off an early warning sign when a teacher's own personal feelings and need for re-lationships spill over into an intimate relationship with a needy teen. Our emphasis will be on reflecting on some specific mentoring characteristics I identified in chapter 3:

Mentors know how to help their protégés clarify the many complex roles they play in the classroom.

Mentors understand that the personal and family problems of students can be very emotional and painful for teachers.

Mentors have finely honed political skills, skills that may be put to good use in protecting their protégés from external and internal threats.

This mentoring relationship involves the health and physical education department chair, Randy Edwards, and first year teacher, Shawn Mallory. Randy followed and found his dream. He was a local boy who graduated in the top of his class and starred in three sports—football, basketball, and baseball—deciding early on to be a coach and physical education teacher. He was awarded a scholarship to Springfield College, where he was named All-East Coast in both football and basketball. He returned to the district where he became an innovative teacher and coach, a new kind of physical education teacher who moved a stale program. Randy introduced a number of new programs to address the health and well-being needs of students, such as a weight training room, Project Adventure, peer support for athletes, and workshops on eating disorders and substance abuse problems. He also developed a wellness program for staff and parents. At least half the staff made use of the training room and participated in faculty workshops to address health and aging issues. When the department chair slot opened up he was the front runner. He vowed to continue building a model health and physical education program by bringing in teachers who represented new thinking in the field. Shawn Mallory was his first hire. Randy was a natural selection for the mentoring program. His interest and expertise in wellness added an important resource to the team.

Randy also brought an additional resource to the team. He had developed a network with a local university's education department and medical school. He periodically brought in experts to offer a wide range of wellness programs to students, staff, and parents. In turn he served as an adjunct professor at the university wellness lab. As part of his training he participated in a workshop on preventing sexual abuse by teachers. It was his first introduction to the topic, one he had never given much attention to. Sure, he remembered a male teacher he had in high school who had been fired for having a relationship with a senior girl. It was a big story for a few days but eventually faded, with many community leaders saying that it was an aberration. Things like that didn't happen in their community. And they were right. There were rumors sometimes about some teachers getting too involved with a student, mostly a male teacher with a female student, but occasionally a female teacher with a male student. There were even rumors about same-sex relationships. But they remained rumors.

As Randy immersed himself in his mentoring role, observing his teachers in both their classrooms and coaching roles, he began to become more aware of how his teachers handled close, personal relationships with their students. He also remembered some of the data and suggestions about teacher-student sexual relationships that he had learned in his workshops:

> There were 110 documented cases of sexual abuse between staff members and students in New York City schools between 1991 and 1995. Most of the cases concerned some kind of willing involvement by smitten students.

In a 1991 survey of former students at a North Carolina high school, thirteen percent of the graduates reported they had engaged in sex with a teacher during their high school years.

Many teachers lack training and supervision in how to carry on close and intimate relationships with students. If their own personal needs for love and affirmation become thwarted, they may unwittingly seek to meet these needs through a close involvement with a needy student, a student looking for a caring, loving adult, a confidante, whom he or she sees on a regular basis.

Inexperienced teachers are often more at risk to teacher-student sexual abuse because they don't understand how to create clear boundaries with needy students. Initially flattered by a student's interest and response to their caring, novice teachers may not see the hazards and risks ahead.

School administrators and colleagues need to recognize the danger signals when they observe them in other teachers' interactions with students, and they need to know how to intervene.

Teacher-student sexual abuse knows no geographical boundaries; it can happen in any school. It is not just an urban phenomenon.

Teacher-student sexual abuse is not unlike sexual abuse in other professions. Intimate helping relationships can go awry if the professional involved lets his or her own personal needs take over. Every professional involved in an intimate relationship needs ongoing supervision and mentoring.

Professional training programs and having a professional degree are sometimes insufficient preparation for real world helping issues.[1]

In mentoring teachers, it is important to observe how they interact with their students on a personal level. Yes, schools want teachers to be involved in helping students who are at risk and lack a significant adult in their lives. Schools need teachers who are responsive, caring, and who are positive role models for needy students. But mentors need to be alert when they observe teachers becoming too involved. There are hazards and risks and when mentors observe such behaviors, they need to act. Sometimes their intervention will be rebuffed but it is still best to take the risk. Turning our backs on problem-creating situations or saying that it's not our job can leave protégés at risk. Like teachers with their students, mentors need to be able to address the nonacademic aspects of their protégés' professional lives and not focus only on the classroom issues. That is an important part of a mentor's work, but not all.

Randy has wrestled with how he is going to address a sensitive issue with Shawn. Shawn is his first hire and in a few short months he has turned into a dynamo, teaching two ninth grade health classes, two physical education classes, and team teaching a class on tobacco addictions. He has made a quick, positive impact. The students, staff, and parents give him high marks. He is also coaching the girls' volleyball and soccer teams. He seems to be everywhere—eating lunch with students, walking the hallways, greeting kids (he seems to know everyone), arriving early to supervise the weight training room. He's young and seems to have boundless energy, the kind of teacher every school needs to provide a shot of adrenaline. He's a prize that needs to be cherished, but he also should be taught a lesson about the complex life of school. As Randy understands, Shawn is inexperienced and vulnerable. In spite of his boundless energy and enthusiasm, he will make mistakes, maybe more than other more cautious first year teachers because he is willing to take on many projects.

The sensitive issue Randy is struggling with is Shawn's seeming overinvolvement with a ninth grade student, Aileen Lopez. He has noticed that Shawn has been having lunch with Aileen in the school cafeteria on a regular basis. He has also observed Shawn giving Aileen a ride to school on some mornings. Aileen is also on Shawn's soccer team and he seems particularly supportive of her efforts. On one level Randy is hesitant to say anything. Maybe all Shawn is doing is trying to help a student who is having troubles. Aileen is new to the district, having moved from an urban school in Philadelphia. Evidently her parents are divorced and she is living with a grandmother. Her younger siblings are living with other relatives in various parts of the country. She is in a new school with little family support. But she seems bright, eager to learn, and is a good athlete. But the other students haven't welcomed her. She's very attractive and adultlike. It's as if the other students don't know how to react to her. She seems much older than her age of fourteen, as if she belongs in high school or college. Maybe Shawn is just trying to provide a safe place for her until she learns how to fit in.

On another level Randy has some concerns. Shawn is young, only twenty-four. And the female students think he is, as they say, a hunk. He gets a lot of eyeballing and contact from them. You know teachers like Shawn in your schools, more student than professional teacher, still wet behind the ears. While he may be trying to help and support Aileen, he is drawing attention to himself by eating lunch with her on a regular basis and driving her to school. It may be perfectly innocent behavior, but some of the staff are beginning to talk. A few have come to Randy and voiced concern, not so much that something is going on between Shawn and Aileen but that it doesn't look good. It will hurt his chances of getting tenure. Should Randy let things be, hoping Shawn will resolve things himself, or should he speak to the issue and maybe sound a warning and show Shawn how to set some boundaries?

Randy: Hey, Shawn. Good to see you. Coffee? Oh sorry, forgot, you're a no-caffeine guy. Got some juice, though. Donut? Oh, wrong again. No sugar, right? Hey, here's a health bar. I keep them for you health nuts. Seriously, how are the classes and the coaching going? From what I observe, you're really moving and grooving. Kids, staff, and parents all seem to think you're doing a great job. And I do too. I haven't heard one criticism. It's very unusual for a young teacher to have such an impact. I guess I know how to hire the right people.

Shawn: Thanks, Mr. Edwards. I mean Randy. I keep thinking I should call you sir or Mr. Yeah, it's been great. The kids and the staff have been great, and so have you. I didn't know what to expect, really. I've been fortunately successful all my life but I wasn't sure how this experience was going to be. My student teaching was in a very conservative school and my mentor there was really out of touch. All he really did was turn the classes over to me and go out for a smoke. But it helped make me independent and rely on myself. I couldn't do some of the things I do here, like Project Adventure, but I survived. The kids there didn't have any of the programs you developed. Looking back I feel like they were being robbed of things that could really help them, like the tobacco workshop. The students here are lucky and I'm just glad to be here. I'm up every morning and ready to go and the day goes by so fast. I can't believe it's February already!

Randy: That's great, Shawn. Your happiness and enthusiasm show. You've brought a great gift, yourself, to us—to me, the staff, the kids, and parents. It's much appreciated. I want to do what I can to cherish and support you and your gifts. You have all the makings of a master teacher. But there is one area I think we need to talk about. It has nothing to do with your teaching performance. You're aces there. And maybe it's not really a problem at all. I just feel we need to get each other's input on the situation and figure out how we should proceed. As your department chair and mentor, I am, after all, somewhat responsible for your well-being, learning and career advancement. I need to address any issues that may get in the way of this process. Does that make sense to you?

Shawn: Sure. I know you're in my corner. I never imagined that you'd be in my classes and at my games so often. I appreciate your interest in me so much. I know you're not out to hurt me. What's going on?

Randy: Again, this may not be a problem, but I've noticed you spending a lot of time with Aileen Lopez. I know she is new and has some personal issues to resolve, and I know she doesn't easily fit in with the other students. Ivy Harrison, the school counselor, shared some of that with me. She's counseling Aileen on a regular basis. What concerns me is this. You may be creating the wrong impression by eating lunch with Aileen on a regular basis and giving her rides to school. And, my take, you seem to be giving her more attention than needed in soccer. Now, this may not be true, but the wrong impression I'm talking about goes like this. Schools are political places. You're new and you may not grasp that yet. You have no ulterior motives but some staff members do and they may draw attention, negative attention, to your seeming over-involvement with Aileen. Rumors can start and rumors can be vicious. Things can be said that may threaten your career, your tenure, even though you're the best new teacher we've had in years. You have to be sensitive to the picture you're giving other people. Sure, help Aileen, but don't give the impression that somehow there is a friendship, or worse, a romantic relationship, developing between you. That's not fair to you and not fair to her.

Secondly, we are all human. Teachers, in trying to help students, become emotionally involved with them. It's part of the deal. We get to know them, their lives, their struggles. We feel their pain. Sometimes we want to do more, become their savior, confidante, even take them home so they can have a good meal or a decent night's sleep. It's part of being a concerned and caring teacher. Sometimes our personal desire to help can go too far. I am not saying that this is happening with you and Aileen. But sometimes teachers can become too intimate—become friends, or even lovers—with students. It happens. And it can happen to any teacher in this building. That's why some teachers avoid becoming involved in personal relationships with students. They are academic teachers only—they teach their subject and go home. You know why? Because deep inside they're unsure of themselves in intimate relationships with students. It's safer for them to keep their distance. Their stance is, "Don't tell me about yourself. I don't have to care about you if I don't know your story."

But if you are a caring and concerned teacher, which you are, you have to learn how to set limits and boundaries. We can't be the student's parent or make all the wrongs right. We can care, listen, give advice, be there when we can, but we have to draw a line. That's something you're learning and in a way this situation is a gift because it provides a wake-up call about school life and creating boundaries. Let me be specific here. I want to hear your response to my query. But here are some specific suggestions regarding Aileen. Stop having lunch with her on a regular basis. Some staff, students and, inevitably, parents will pick up on this. Some may start unkind rumors. Don't expose yourself or Aileen to this threat. Stop driving her to school. Again, some people will misread your good intentions and assign less than admirable intentions to you. Put a stop to the rumors before they start. Support her in soccer but be aware that you may be giving her too much attention. The other kids and parents aren't dumb; they see it. Don't let it become an issue in your coaching and teaching.

I am not saying end your involvement with Aileen. She clearly wants your support. Withdrawing that isn't useful for her. What I am saying is make the support and the lines clear. Be involved with her in class and in soccer. Be there for her. She will seek you out when she understands that's where the focus of your relationship is. But no phone calls, no rides home. Bluntly, don't be naïve about school life. It can be cruel and hurtful, not just for kids but for teachers as well. For some teachers, schools are dull places with little novelty and excitement. They live their professional lives on rumors and finger-pointing. Learn that lesson. You can be the greatest teacher in the world every day but if you're drunk at faculty parties or womanizing with colleagues, that's the image that gets talked about. Don't make yourself at risk and vulnerable.

Let me handle the politics. Learn from me how to do it. I'll try to silence any negative references to this situation that may be raised by staff. I don't believe in letting rumors go unanswered. I've learned from experience. My record as first-year football coach was two and seven and we barely won those two games. I came on board after a championship season replacing Earl Allen as coach. Allen was a legend here. A lot of rumors started after that season. Getting rid of me seemed a given but I went to the athletic director and superintendent and made my case. They gave me cover, three years to turn things around. I'll give you all the cover you need. I'm a local boy and I know how things work. You're in good hands.

Finally, don't worry. This will pass. In fact, as I said, this is a valuable experience for both of us. It's a lesson for you that there's more to learn about school life than teaching. It's good that we're going through this together. I am learning, too!

What do you think about my observations and suggestions? I've hit you fairly hard, maybe unfairly. But I need to say these things if I'm going to be true to my mentoring role and our relationship.

Shawn: Wow. You caught me by surprise with this one. You're right about Aileen. She lives around the corner from my place. Plus she's in my health and P.E. classes and on the soccer team. I met her at the deli one Saturday morning and we began to talk. She's pretty much alone here. Her grandmother is eighty-five and quite ill. She has a lot of worries about her family. Her dad went back to Mexico and her mother is living with some guy in Philadelphia who has a drug problem. I guess her mother does, too. And her two younger brothers are living in L.A. with an aunt and her sister is up in Boston with another relative. She's literally on her own. I guess some of the other students haven't been too kind to her, using racial slurs. It's been tough for her but she's eager to do well and make a place here. So I've tried to spend a lot of my time listening to and guiding her. No, there's no sexual stuff. Maybe friendship. But I never thought of that until now. It seemed normal, like I was trying to help a kid in trouble. I didn't realize that the spotlight would be on me as a beginning teacher but I guess it is. Jesus, what do people think? You're right about other things. I find myself spending more time than needed with her at soccer, even giving her a ride home. Whew! Never thought about this stuff. As for your suggestions, I think I'd better listen to them. I mean, I wasn't doing anything wrong but as you say, the picture isn't good. Thanks for noticing.

Perfect ending? Who knows? But both Randy and Shawn learned a valuable lesson. Randy gets to affirm his mentoring skills and judgment. He acts, as Shawn suggests, as a guardian angel, warning and protecting his novice from two kinds of threats: threats from the institution that may derail his career, and threats that lie within himself that may propel him unwittingly into a more intimate relationship with a needy student. *Mr. Holland's Opus* presents an image of how close a teacher, an experienced one, can get to becoming overly involved with a needy student.[2] It becomes very difficult for the play director, Richard Dreyfus, to break off a fast-moving relationship with his needy student, who sings:

> There's a somebody I'm longing to see.
> I hope that he turns out to be

Someone who'll watch over me.
I'm just a little lamb who's lost in the woods.
I know I could always be good
To someone who'll watch over me.
Won't you tell him please to put on some speed,
Follow my lead. Oh, how I need
Someone to watch over me.

As Mr. Holland's character vividly presents, acting to head off a possibly disastrous relationship isn't always easy. Rowena, the talented and attractive student star, mesmerizes Mr. Holland. He finds himself spending a great deal of time with her and enjoying it. He has relationship problems with his wife and is on unsure ground with his deaf son. It seems easier for him to be the center of Rowena's interest than deal with the festering problems at home. As the story unfolds, Rowena begs Mr. Holland to come to New York with her and share a new life. Although she is only a teenager, she knows what she wants. Unfortunately Mr. Holland doesn't have a trusted mentor like Randy to talk to and help him sort out the complex feelings and decisions involved in this relationship with Rowena. He has to do it on his own. This kind of relationship can happen in any secondary school to caring, but unwitting teachers like Shawn. Intimate one-on-one relationships between caring teachers and needy students can lead to a surrogate parenthood or romantic relationship without intervention from wise, experienced mentors like Randy.

THE ASSISTANT PRINCIPAL AS MENTOR

One of the major themes in this book is the acknowledgement that bad times, failure, and burnout can happen to every teacher, even the most successful ones. It may be more difficult for star teachers to be aware that they are losing positive contact with their students and colleagues. It's not supposed to happen to them. These are the teachers who have won the teacher of the year awards and held elected office in local, state, and national professional associations, such as the National Middle School Association and the Association for Supervision and Development and Phi Delta Kappa. They regularly make keynote speeches at conferences, lead staff development workshops, and serve on select state and national government committees on issues such as education reform. They are known throughout their school, district, state, and even nation as prime examples of professionalism and creative teaching. They are always in demand from an education, parent, or citizen group, receiving a steady stream of phone calls asking them to be keynote speaker at a conference. They are the go-to experts that the media zeroes in on when an issues arises, such as student violence at Columbine High School. They are interviewed by the press and on television and radio.

In a sense, these teachers create another "expert" persona in addition to their teaching persona. And in a real sense they have created another role that may increasingly take them away from their primary role, that of classroom teacher. On the fast track to stardom, their primary focus moves from the classroom to the speaking circuit. In the process, their teaching world, and the teaching world of their students, begins to change. The boundaries get rearranged. At first, this new "star" role is met with support and enthusiasm by district superintendents, principals, school board members, and community leaders. The newly acclaimed teacher begins to draw rave reviews. It helps put the district and school leaders on the map. They have to be doing something right if they are cultivating such fine teachers. It helps pass budgets, raise morale, and move the educational climate away from a focus on problems to one of success. It's a win-win situation, or so it seems, for everyone.

Things often change, however, as the star teacher begins to miss more and more class time. A vacuum sets in and a sense of loss develops. The boundaries are different for students, parents, and colleagues. Students, faced with a succession of subs, grow disgruntled. Kids develop a close relationship with an effective and caring teacher. When that is taken away from them, they notice. Like children in a family affected by divorce, they develop a sense of loss or even betrayal. Parents, too, sense a loss and betrayal. Although initially proud of the star teacher's success, they grow weary of the parade of subs and lack of continuity. They vow that next year's teacher will be classroom-based with a main focus on working with the class. Fellow teachers also begin to react to a star teacher, as well. Statements are heard in the faculty room: "Is she ever here? I bet she's angling for a state education department or college professor job. Even when she's here she's always running out of her classroom to take a phone call. The secretary is sick of running up and covering her class. I wouldn't do it. I hear she's getting paid $500 a shot for her presentations and still collects her paycheck here. What gall. I hope the administration sets her straight soon."

This movement into a star role isn't viewed by the teacher as a bad experience, failure, or a situation capable of burning them out. It feels good. It's exciting, novel, and a source of new energy. But it is also a treacherous, seductive role, one that lures teachers away from their teaching role by the possibility of life in the spotlight. It can result in teachers giving less and less attention to their teaching role and eventually bring about failure as a classroom teacher. Some teachers naively, even foolishly, assume things will stay the same in their classrooms, that they can return at any time and things will be as they were—the students, the parents, their colleagues. But they have changed and so has their classroom. The speaking circuit becomes a fool's gold situation for them, giving teachers novelty, change, and a sense that they have become a "somebody." Numbers of teachers attend their presentations and cling to their words. They feel a rush they never felt as a classroom teacher. Is it unrealistic to think that they can be successful in this dual role they have created? Can teachers be both star presenters and effective classroom teachers?

When a star teacher returns to her regular teaching duties, she begins to sense that she has drifted away from her school, students, and colleagues. She essentially becomes a visitor, and the old parameters no longer exist. She pulls into the same parking space, but that's all the permanence that remains. When she walks into the building, she senses being viewed as "someone who used to work here." Relationships have changed and she suddenly finds that while she may be succeeding as a presenter, she is failing as a classroom teacher. She finds she cannot successfully manage both roles, and one has to go. Do star teachers stay or move on? Do they try to recapture their lives as successful teachers or move on to being consultants or presenters? If they decide to stay, are they willing to give up being "somebody" and accept being "just a teacher"?

This vignette focuses on how mentoring can help a star teacher resolve the question of whether to stay or move on, how to reestablish boundaries or form new ones. As Dr. Seuss suggests, this teacher has come to a place "where the streets are not marked." She must make a decision but the way is not clear. The emphasis here will be on the mentoring characteristics I identified in chapter 3, characteristics that can help awareness and clarity:

Mentors understand that bad times, failures, and burnout can happen to every teacher, even the most successful ones.

Mentors understand that resistance to mentoring will take place.

Mentors know how to help their protégés find and define their best teaching selves.

Mentors know how to help their protégés clarify the many complex roles they play in the classroom.

Mentors understand that their lack of in-depth knowledge of every subject and grade level does not reduce their efficacy in mentoring teachers.

This is the situation that assistant principal Linda Alvarez and teacher Myra Fryman find themselves in. Linda has been assistant principal of the school for three years. Prior to that, she taught eighth-grade Spanish and started the English as a Second Language program. She is very involved with the growing number of Latino and other immigrant students and chair of the school's diversity committee. She has championed a district-wide effort to provide staff development workshops for teachers in the area of diversity and inclusion. Her parents were immigrants from Cuba to America. Schooled in Catholic schools in Miami and at the University of Miami, she is a strong believer in discipline. She expects students and teachers to take care of business. Her philosophy of education, and life, is written on a poster behind her desk: "Be a responsible and responsive member of this school community. Don't make a mess that others have to clean up." She was a natural choice for the mentoring program because of her energy, clear focus, expertise in diversity and inclusion issues, and her no-nonsense approach to leadership.

As prepared as Linda Alvarez is, she wasn't ready for some aspects of the mentoring program. Her experience with Myra Fryman would prove to be a novel learning experience. Myra Fryman is one of the best, if not the best, teachers in the school. Her science students routinely finish in the top five in science contests. She is sought out by prominent parents who want their students to be in her classes. Her room is called "Fryman's University" by the students because of its many resources—computers, lab equipment, and research tools—acquired by Myra with grants from universities, government agencies, foundations, and other sources. Her school has more resources than any other school in the state and even some local colleges. She is a go-getter, and an excellent grant writer and salesperson. She knows where the money is and she goes after it. With grants, her budget is over $100,000 for the past five years, exclusive of district funding. It is her money to manage; she has an oversight board but she steers the money to create new programs of her choosing such as a summer science camp and a mentoring program with Harvard University.

She has created an empire for herself in the district. The superintendent and school board regularly brought visitors to the school to show off Myra's lab. She was famous within the district and state and even on the national level, where she served as a consultant and head of the Teacher Education Committee for the National Center for Disease Control and Prevention. She is also on the governing board of the National Science Teachers Association and chairs the science section for the new national testing standards. A picture of her receiving the national Teacher of the Year award from President Clinton in 1995 hung over her desk. Her achievements created a situation where she was literally her own boss. Some colleagues said she is beyond supervision and certainly, no one controls her. She seems to come and go as she pleases, in a world of her own. The often-heard comment in the faculty room is, "Whatever Myra wants, Myra gets."

Things began to change for Myra when Brad Foley became principal and brought Linda Alvarez on board as assistant principal. It wasn't a dramatic change, but something was in the air. In the previous administration, Myra came and went as she pleased. She regularly took part in presenting at local, state, and national conferences, and she was often away training other science teachers. She really had several different jobs—science teacher, grant writer, teacher trainer, and conference presenter. The previous administration was eager to support Myra's multi-role situation. They basked in her national success when visiting educators from throughout the country made visits to their school, and a new secretary had to be hired to help Myra manage her grant process and greet the growing number of visitors. "Fryman's University" was an organization of its own and unconnected to the school except for the classroom component.

At first, both Brad Foley and Linda Alvarez were surprised by how often Myra was out of the building. Her requests for subs seemed out-of-bounds. In the first year of Brad and Linda's tenure, Myra missed thirty days of school, fulfilling commitments she had made with the approval of the previous administration. When Brad promoted the mentoring program, he asked Linda to serve as a mentor for Myra, and in that role to look for an opportunity to address Myra's growing absence and the impact it was having on her students. Although many parents wanted their children in Myra's classes, there was growing discontent that she wasn't present to provide necessary continuity. For the first time, some students had asked to transfer to other classes. Even Myra was shaken. Cracks were beginning to appear in her star-teacher armor. Early on, Linda recognized that these issues would be a major focus in her mentoring role with Myra, but Linda wasn't naïve. Myra was tough and she had political backing. She wasn't about to allow herself to be mentored. Linda felt that to leave Myra on her own, increasingly removed from her students and the school community, would not be fair to Myra or her students. Things had to be brought under control and Myra would need some boundaries, like all other teachers.

Myra was surprised when Linda began to observe her classes and invite her in for follow-up mentoring sessions. She knew that Brad had started the program and was requiring every teacher to participate, but she thought that with her busy schedule, Brad would let her pass. Brad indicated that this would not be the case. Every teacher would have to participate, including Myra. How would it look to the other teachers if Myra were not included? No, Linda would be her mentor, do class observations, and meet with Myra for follow-up conferencing. Several issues emerged from these sessions.

Myra: You know, Linda, I really don't have time for this today. I'm waiting on a call from a professor at the University of Michigan who wants to bring a team of educators here in January. I also have the summer science camp curriculum to review and two ninth-grade research classes this afternoon. Can't we say we met and skip this one? Besides, you know I'm a good teacher. You see the rapport I have with my kids. I don't mean this as a criticism but you're not a science person. What do you really know about my subject? How can you mentor me? Wouldn't your time be better spent with a new teacher or one of those burned out teachers? You know who I mean. Really, this is a farce.

Linda: Thanks, Myra, for coming in today. I know you are busy and yes, I can see where you might question how much I can be of help. But I want you to know that I want to be a resource for you and I do have some issues we need to discuss. It's not about your teaching, per se. When you're in front of your class you are, as you say, a great teacher, one of the best I've seen. I feel it's a privilege to be working alongside of such a gifted person. You blow my mind with some of the ways you involve your kids. The issues I am referring to go beyond the classroom.

Myra: Linda, I really don't like being part of this mentoring program. You know I am an effective teacher, and you know I'm very busy promoting our science program and projects. Do I really have to be involved in mentoring? Can't you talk to Brad and arrange some sort of gracious way out for me? You know the science fair is coming up in two months. Plus my top science kids are involved in the Westinghouse Scholarship program. They are going to need a lot of help from me.

Linda: I know you're busy and very involved in many projects. Brad and I appreciate all you do to promote our science program. But every teacher is required to take part in the mentoring program. There can't be any exceptions. If we give you a pass there will be a group of teachers knocking on our door for the same exemption. I know I am asking you to be involved in a process that take some time and getting used to. I know it's not easy for you. My sense is it's hard for you to sit and talk. You're always moving and doing something, but I am asking you to slow down a bit and listen to what I have to say. How you use it is up to you. It's what I call necessary feedback. It can, I believe, help you to redefine your best teaching self.

Myra: Look, it has been a long time since I've been in any supervision or mentoring situation. I've operated on my own for twenty years. John Owens, the principal prior to Brad, never came into my room. Every year he wrote the same glowing evaluation report for me. We had a deal. He let me promote the science program and left me alone. You have to understand this is a big change for me and I sense this project could lead to changes in the way I do my job.

Linda: Whatever the case, Myra, I am concerned that you are missing a great deal of class time. You were out of the building more than thirty days last year. That's a lot of missed time for your kids. And it's not time out for illness; it's being involved in all of your presentations and speeches. Your kids, it seems, are missing you because of all of this involvement outside of school. The reason they wanted to be in your classes was the expectation that you would be there for them, maybe not every single day but most of the time. Parents expect that as well. It's only fair. It must be hard on you trying to juggle all of the extra roles—grant writing, teacher training, presenting at conferences. How can you manage to be successful in all those roles? Something has to give and from what I am seeing the kids are on the losing end. A lot of your energy is being spent on activities and projects that are unrelated to them. You're expending a lot of energy welcoming visitors from all over the country and the world. I'm not saying this is bad but it takes away from your interaction with your students. You become a host, not a teacher. It seems like all of this should be difficult for you because teaching has been such a passion for you and you get such joy and satisfaction from it. Here is the main question I have, a fastball right at you. Why are you giving up teaching, something you love so much and derive so much pleasure from, and focusing on the other projects that, while they build self-esteem, don't seem to be as fulfilling? You talk about being a leader on the national scene but what about your classroom? Are your continued absences fair to you and your students?

Myra: Look, what I am doing is not just for me. It's for you, the administration, my colleagues, for the district, for the community. I'm putting myself and this school on the map. We are known and recognized throughout the country because of my work. It's not something to sneeze at. I've worked my tail off. You think being a presenter at conferences is a picnic? I come home drained. Sure, it feels good while I'm part of it but when these things end, I'm beat. Hotels, airports, restaurant food—I get sick of it after a while. At first it's a high—my picture in the paper, being on TV, getting the teacher of the year award, and having lunch with Bill Clinton. But it wears on me after a while—too many handshakes, Chardonnays, too much politicking. In some ways I am sick of it and the question you're asking me is right on target, I hate to admit. Sometimes I think I'm running on empty. One more meeting, one more visiting team from God knows where, one more flight to Washington, one more delay because of bad weather. I come home dirty, sweating, tired, like I've been through the mill. And you're right, I'd rather challenge you, set you back on your heels, than sit and listen and talk. It scares me. If I stop running, I think I might collapse. With the kids I feel guilty; I know that when I'm not here it's not the same. They miss me and what I can give them. When I'm in and out it upsets all the continuity, for them and for me. It's no good, a lose-lose situation. I know some of the students and their parents are upset with me for being out so much. This is the first time I've had kids ask for a transfer. It's insulting, even hurtful. But I guess I can't blame them. Sometimes I think about throwing in the towel and getting a job at a university. But that's not for me. I honestly don't know where to begin to make things right. Got some ideas?

Linda: I am so glad you were able to talk about things and I appreciate you listening to my observations. These are things we can work on. I think that first you have to decide what you want. You can't do everything or be everything to everybody. You need to do what works best for you, what makes you happy. Clearly going on this way isn't going to work. It's too draining. Maybe in a sense you've achieved your goal already. You've put the school, and yourself, on the national map. You are somebody and you've helped the school to be somebody too. But maybe enough is enough. Not to be funny, but being in the spotlight too long can burn you. The conferences and presentations, hotels, airports and travel—those are not the real world, are they? Sometimes they're places people go to run away, steal some time away from the daily struggles. Usually you're speaking to the converted anyway. Maybe you've done all that. Maybe returning to work only with the kids will get you off the star track and back to being a great teacher. You seem to find great joy in that. Why take away something you love and replace it with something that drains you? Other people can take over the grants and projects, or they can just be put on hold. Think about what we've talked about and let's meet next week. I'll be anxious to hear what you have to say.

Myra: Look, you've given me a lot to think about. It has been a long time since anyone gave me such a direct reaction and honest feedback. Usually people in the school keep their distance and treat me with kid gloves. I'm going home to think this over.

Like Ellen, Myra needs to be asked direct questions by her mentor, questions that will allow and encourage her to reflect on the negative aspects of her situation. We all have a better opportunity to communicate our hidden feelings when the questions are open ended but hit on the issues we are struggling with. We may wish to evade these questions but because they ask for the truth, we want to answer. Our defenses are down. A nascent trust can create a window of opportunity. Sometimes our initial stance, like Myra's, is to want to fight and challenge our would-be helper. But if the questioning has sincerity and clarity, we are disarmed. Linda, with her skillful questions, becomes a friend, not the enemy. Myra is suddenly free from her defensiveness and open to reality.

Reality for Myra becomes a little clearer in this mentoring episode. The bottom line for her to grapple with is that presenting at conferences, being a star performer, has its price. It can be costly. Spending time on the road can be draining and depleting. Speaking to some educators at a conference who have spent the previous night carousing is not fun. As Myra describes, the entire scene has begun to wear on her. Teachers in her position slowly begin to lose their classroom-teacher persona and begin to focus on marketing and self-promotion. They enter a new reality.

Linda's wake-up call to Myra reminds us all of the price we may be paying and what we may be losing in seeking professional and personal growth. It reminds us that knocking on the wrong doors can lead to mischief and unmarked roads. There are risks involved in stretching ourselves too far and drawing our boundaries too wide. Linda wisely helps Myra decide for herself if she wishes to continue on the road she has chosen. Maybe that is the greatest gift of mentoring, to be able to ask the right questions, to get protégés to reflect on their situation, to guide them to either accept where they are and accept the consequences, or to begin a process of change that will, as Myra suggests, unburden and free them. Perhaps it will allow Myra to be a great teacher of kids again, not a star teacher looking for affirmation in places that are temporary and ill suited to long-term professional and personal growth.

THE COUNSELOR AS MENTOR

This final vignette focuses on the pain of dislocation, of losing familiar boundaries—one's students, colleagues, seat in the faculty room, and daily coffee break with pals. That is what happened to fifteen-year veteran physics teacher Jim McDonald. In June, after the rush of final exams and good-byes to favorite students, Jim is told by his department chair that he is being reassigned to the junior high. The reason? Some of the veteran teachers who were expected to retire have chosen not to. The department now has a surplus of teachers. In order for Jim to keep his job he would have to go along with the change. It's a simple matter of arithmetic, but not simple at all for Jim.

At first Jim was OK with the move. He took things in his stride and was not a person who made waves. He would go along with the reassignment. At least he had a job and maybe he could get back to the high school once his more senior colleagues retired. The real impact of the change did not immediately hit him. Cleaning out his room, saying his good-byes, went on with little emotion, certainly no anger or resentment. He was told of the change after the year-end faculty party. For him, it was unlike a retirement—he never got to hear the speeches about how much he influenced his students, helped them enjoy physics, and excelled as a tennis coach, faculty advisor for the National Honor Society, and intramural sports coordinator. He was exiting alone, out the door with no fanfare or thanks. This kind of exiting happens to thousands of teachers each year. Reassigned: a nonemotional word, isn't it? It doesn't describe the emotional pain, the anxiety, the sense that everything the teacher worked for so hard has suddenly vanished. As I suggested in chapter 3, renewing yourself is often not easy, even under the best of conditions. How do you renew yourself in foreign territory? You leave an assignment where you know the boundaries. Then suddenly you arrive in a new school where you don't know the staff, don't have experience teaching at that level, don't know the students, and don't have a routine. Will your teaching skills work here? Will you be given time to adjust and get settled in?

At first, Jim did not anticipate these fears and concerns, but by August the real impact of the move set in. He received his teaching schedule in the mail, along with the curriculum outline and textbook list. He was assigned to three grade-seven earth science classes and two grade-eight biology classes, both subjects he had never taught before. He had less than four weeks to prepare. There would be a one-day orientation workshop designed to help him adjust to his new school. There was also a personal letter from counselor Ivy Harrison; she indicated that she would be Jim's mentor for the school year. In this capacity she would observe Jim's classes and hold follow-up conferences. The basic thrust of the program was to help Jim adjust to his new environment and find his best teaching self. Ivy would seek Jim out at the new teacher orientation so they could get to know each other. Although the letter was very thoughtful, the mentoring program sounded like just one more thing Jim had to do. It was a new program and for now was offered only in the junior high. If he had remained in the high school he wouldn't have to be dealing with any of this—new curriculum, new kids, new staff, and now mentoring. His resentment and anger began to grow. He feared this change was not going to be easy.

And it wasn't. In spite of getting some helpful hints at the orientation meeting run by principal Brad Foley and meeting Ivy Harrison (she seemed like a very helpful person who was serious about her mentoring role), things got off to a bad start. Jim quickly learned that his students were different. They were like little kids, talking, jabbering, acting out. They weren't like his high school students who were for the most part serious, high-achieving students. His high school classes had been almost like college classes, with quiet discussion and reflection. There were no behavioral problems. The students were intent on getting into good colleges and were not about to risk their chances for good grades and letters of recommendation. It was a quiet, highly professional routine; Jim was in charge and he had few distractions.

Junior high students, being early adolescents, don't focus on being quiet or reflecting. They make mischief, bully each other, and make the teacher pay for wavering or hesitating. If they sense fear or uncertainty, they pounce. There were certainly some talented students in Jim's new classes, kids who were studious and knew how to behave. But for the main part of his first month, Jim was constantly thrown into a disciplinarian mode. Much of his teaching persona centered on control. In a few short months he had gone from having a professor-like teaching persona that focused on real learning to being a disciplinarian with a few precious moments left over for real teaching.

It began to wear on Jim. Each day seemed endless, with the same issues of control disrupting the day. He had to continually stress to the students that he was in charge, not them. He was further handicapped by not knowing the students. What kinds of students were they? What interests did they have? What were their home lives like? It was such a slow process and there was no safe harbor for him. In the faculty room, teachers clustered in groups. During his visits few teachers noticed or acknowledged him except for some other new teachers. He had gone to a local bar where the junior high teachers hung out on Friday nights but he felt like an outsider. Everything seemed so wrong after seeming so right in the high school. He even thought about going back to his old haunts on Friday to have a drink with the high school staff, but he didn't belong there either. He knew he should take it one day at a time and maybe he would get the hang of the place. But what if he didn't? This was not where he wanted to spend the rest of his career. Who wants to control little kids all day?

Ivy had been a member of the school counseling staff for five years. While not a veteran, she was tough and clear on her role. She represented a new wave of school counselors, not like the ones from the sixties and seventies who thought of themselves as primarily there to assign students to classes and solve academic problems. Ivy was different. She believed in a proactive counseling role, in helping students solve their nonacademic and personal problems as well as their academic issues. She also believed in educating and supporting parents so they could be more effective in the child-rearing process. And she believed in helping teachers become more effective by improving their skills and their ability to work with all their students. As an African American, she knew about isolation and labeling. She was committed to promoting programs that improved diversity and inclusion. She was an educational leader who had a number of skills and resources. She had highly developed one-on-one counseling, group facilitation, and program development skills. Each week she saw over one hundred students in one-on-one conferences and problem-solving groups and co-led a ninth grade tobacco prevention group with P.E. teacher Shawn Mallory. She also led a parents' support group on Wednesday evenings and a "How to be an Effective Teacher-Advisor" staff development workshop on Tuesday afternoons. The main focus of the teacher-advisor workshop was to help teachers become more effective listeners and helpers.

Given these resources and skills, she was a natural selection for the mentoring team. She had demonstrated that she was able to listen to the concerns of teachers and help them solve classroom problems, and often personal problems that impacted negatively on their work. Principal Brad Foley was able to free up Ivy's schedule by working out an arrangement with a nearby university's counselor-education program. They assigned a master's degree candidate with individual and group counseling skills to the school on a half-day basis as a permanent sub who could take over Ivy's grade-seven counseling duties. Ivy still led the eighth and ninth grade programs and was available to support the new counselor. In turn, Ivy would join the adjunct counselor-education teaching staff serving as a visiting fellow in a summer counseling institute.

At least on paper, Ivy seems a good match for Jim. Yes, they are different. Ivy is African American, twenty-nine years old, trained in communications, and a rising star in her field and the school. Jim has an Irish-American background, is entering middle-age, trained in science; he found himself, one might say, to be a falling star. Both enjoyed students, aspired to be master teachers and educators, and had good track records. They had successes under their belts. Their first interaction took place in October, one month into Jim's junior high career. Their mentoring relationship focuses on several mentoring characteristics I mentioned in chapter 3:

Mentors understand that bad times can happen to every teacher. These bad times can be sudden, tumultuous, and even career threatening.

Mentors understand that renewing themselves is not always easy.

Mentors have a sense of history, of the good work that has gone on in
the past by caring teachers, the creative responses to changing needs
and times, and the good work that goes on in their school each day.

After Ivy had a chance to observe Jim's classes, they met for a conference.

Ivy: Hi, Jim. Glad we could meet. You've got a hectic schedule and so do I,
but this is great. We have some quiet time to talk. I enjoyed observing your
classes. It must be such a change for you from teaching juniors and seniors,
mature young men and women, at least most of them. It's different here, isn't
it? You have these preteens—their sexual awareness is developing as they go
through all of their physical and emotional changes. They're little kids one day
and they mature, they think, the next, with no real life experiences to guide
them. Kids at this level make mistakes, some of them big ones. Their newly
found freedom can lead them down many wrong roads—drinking, drugs,
smoking, early sex. It's an emotional cauldron here. Teachers have to work extremely hard to keep their kids focused on the subject matter. It seems a constant effort to keep the kids' boundaries defined and knowable. I notice how
hard you are working at that process. I sense it must be different in the high
school, although I'm no expert. Most high school kids, I believe—you'll have
to set me straight if I'm wrong—know how to control themselves and set
boundaries for their school behavior by the time they reach eleventh and
twelfth grade. As teacher, you don't have to spend half of your class time
maintaining control and discipline. It's different here. I think you're finding
that. I admire that you haven't backed off the challenges the students are
throwing at you. It takes three or four months just to get them in line. You're
a respected, veteran teacher, and I see you have great skills, but this is a new
set up. It will take some time for you to adjust to the kids, and them to you, but
I think you're doing just fine. Do you remember what happened to Ed Frankl?
He retired last year but you and he share a similar experience. He came to the
junior high four years ago. "Reluctantly" would be the kind word to use. He,
like you, had been an outstanding high school teacher, winner of the social
studies teacher of the year award in 1995. His first months were a nightmare,
worse than yours. But he hung in there and by the end of the year he was in the
groove. He got to know the faculty and found friendship and support. I remember him telling me that the last years of his career were the most enjoyable. He didn't have to deal with all the pressure of state exams and grade hun-
gry college-bound seniors and their parents. Life, he said, was simpler and
more enjoyable at the junior high level. What seemed like a career disaster

turned out to be an opportunity for renewal. The same thing could happen to you. Hang in there. Keep your expectations low for now. Take it day by day."

Jim: Well, let me tell you I appreciate your every word. It's nice to hear some good stuff. It has been a major change for me. Every day is a new challenge and I'm learning as I go along. It just seems to move so fast here. It's all go-go-go and there's no quiet time for learning like I had at the high school. And there are no real conversations and questioning. My kids in physics class were like adults. They asked great questions. In retrospect it was a piece of cake. Here, if I do succeed in creating some kind of order—and in some classes that's questionable—the kids just sit there. I have to ask all the questions. Sometimes I think to myself, "Hello? Doesn't anyone have a brain here except for a couple of the nerdy kids?" I try to keep myself in check and not get angry with the kids or myself. My wife says things will get better eventually and she says, and I have my doubts about this, that I'll be a better teacher for this experience. I wouldn't take any bets on that one.

Ivy: Hey, maybe she's right. It's good that you have her support. I know enough about change to know that you're probably missing your colleagues at the high school as well as the kids. You've been asked to make a major career change, to give up a teaching life you've worked hard at for fifteen years. You're being asked not only to teach a different grade level but also to form a whole new set of relationships, all in a matter of a few short months and with no real training. Everything has changed for you. I'm not saying you are, but I would sense that you might be feeling some resentment at this reassignment. And I sense you might be feeling some loneliness as well. I see you struggling to make some connections in the faculty room and at our Friday afternoon get-togethers. It's not easy. Most of us have been here a while and, in spite of our best judgment, we tend to hang out with certain groups. We're like the kids, really, forming little groups—the jocks, the nerds, the party people, the young marrieds, the divorcees. You're not a new teacher but still it will take a while for you to find your spot. It's great that your wife is supportive but sometimes that's not enough. I like to think that we can develop a friendship and good mentoring relationship. You're beginning anew here but your high school career needs to be honored and remembered. From what I hear about the way your reassignment was handled, it didn't allow time for some much needed affirmation and good-byes. That must have been tough. Saying good-bye to what once was, particularly if it was successful, is always hard. It takes time for the shadows to clear. But the bottom line is that you, and I, know you had a great high school career and you were a model teacher and student advisor. No one can take that away from you. OK, you didn't get the gold watch and accolades when you left. But you know, and your colleagues know, that you made a huge difference. Hang on to the good you did. You earned it.

But now that part of your life is over. Sure, maybe you were dealt a bad hand but that's the way it is. It's time to move on and focus, as you are, on today. Luckily, from what I can see, you're not a whiner or angry guy. You're not burdened with the kinds of negative stuff that would make you a candidate for burnout. You're trying to learn this new job and get to know the kids. You may think you are adjusting too slowly but I think you're right on schedule. I wouldn't change one thing you are doing, at least not right now. Let's continue our meetings. I think things will continue to improve. All I ask is that you try to think of yourself more as a beginner. Put aside, if you can, what you were like in the high school, what the kids were like, and what your colleagues were like. Bury those memories in some safe place for a while. Feel good that you are more than surviving here. Many teachers don't.

Jim: I think you're right on target on a lot of things. I do feel many of the things you're suggesting. And I have been looking back a lot. I guess I can't help that; it's not easy to put those feelings and memories aside. But I agree with you that no one here, teachers or kids, is going to read my resume and press releases. No one cares that I had almost one hundred percent of my students pass the state physics exams each year. No one cares that my students regularly won the county science contest in physics. To them I'm just the new guy on the block. I have to show them that I have the right stuff to make it here. The burden of proof, as always, is on the newcomer. And you're right; that's who I am. That's my new identity. No one cares if I am the former great high school physics teacher. Yesterday's news doesn't count. That clears up some of the mist for me. It's hard to think of myself as a beginner again, but it is so. Thanks, I'll sleep a little better tonight.

Beginning again is never easy. Ivy focuses Jim on the reality of his situation. He is in a new and difficult role and yes, the way he arrived there was less than ideal. He could rightfully be angry and resentful. He could even use his resentment to fuel a career-long vengeance that could consume him, make him bitter with himself, his students, and maybe with his family. But Ivy wisely suggests that he is made of better material than that. He had already chosen not to go down this road. Having harnessed his would-be demons, his job now is twofold. He must put his dreams of returning to the high school on hold for a while, and he must continue the course of learning new skills, the requirements of his new job, and more about this new breed of students. And Ivy is right. Jim is doing OK.

Both Ivy and Jim get the feedback they need. Jim is made aware that he is a newcomer again. Ivy learns that she is in step with Jim's feelings and suggests a necessary course of action that holds the possibility of bringing about new opportunities for success.

Effective one-on-one mentoring can help create a school climate that encourages lifelong learning for teachers. It is the first step in building an ongoing renewal process. Other steps are needed as well:

The themes communicated by protégés in the mentoring process need to be identified; they provide useful data in planning ongoing workshops and staff development efforts in the school.

Mentored teachers need to be encouraged to lead workshops designed to train colleagues in the best professional practices, workshops that highlight the personal hobbies and successes of teachers, and workshops that can add a little novelty and joy to the teachers' daily routine.

Mentored teachers need to be encouraged to serve as mentors themselves. Mentored teachers are a valuable resource, not only as trainers for colleagues but also as one-on-one mentors. It's called putting our best practices and resources to work.

Mentored teachers also can be the primary resource in creating a school-wide mentoring network. That means passing on mentoring skills to other members of the school community such as support staff and students. Both of these groups are ideally positioned to help struggling students. All too often they lack the training or are advised that this is not their role. Simple training led by skilled mentor-teachers can ready them to pass on simple, useful advice.

A skilled mentoring team can use these themes listed above to identify topics and build them into their ongoing renewal program They provide an accurate compass of the direction the team needs to follow to keep the learning pot boiling. In a sense, these themes help identify the curriculum for workshops to provide additional learning and support beyond the mentoring process, workshops presented by team members, mentored teachers, and community and university resources. Teachers need learning hubs that are attractive, easily accessible, and focused on pertinent topics. The mentors in the vignettes presented in this chapter generated ongoing workshop topics in mentoring conversations with protégés Tom, Ellen,

Shawn, Myra, and Jim. These workshop topics can be separated into two categories: classroom issues and professional/personal issues:

1. Classroom issues:
    a. How to identify teachers' talents and areas of strength in the classroom
    b. How to identify areas in which teachers are experiencing difficulty
    c. How to pinpoint the skills teachers need to improve
    d. Understanding adolescent development
    e. Developing effective discipline skills
    f. Developing effective listening skills
    g. How teachers hold effective classroom discussions
    h. How teachers work effectively with students in groups
    i. How teachers hold successful one-on-one conferences with students and parents
    j. How teachers handle crisis situations
    k. How teachers identify and solve classroom problems
    l. How teachers get helpful feedback from colleagues
    m. How to assess which students teachers tend to avoid and how to make a plan to include them
    n. How to assess which students teachers tend to spend too much time with and how to make a plan to reduce the level of interaction with them
    o. How to design an attractive classroom setting
    p. How to be an effective advisor to students and help them to solve personal problems
    q. How to identify and refer troubled students and parents to reliable sources of support
2. Professional and personal issues:
    a. How to say "no" to too many outside the classroom responsibilities
    b. How to stay well, physically and emotionally
    c. How to identify ongoing career renewal activities to avoid burnout
    d. Understanding the aging process
    e. How to intervene and give useful feedback to colleagues who are struggling
    f. How to identify possible mentoring skills. Can you visualize yourself as a mentor?

Ongoing renewal opportunities should be attractive, easily accessible, and focused on topics that are real and needed by teachers. In addition, they should be enjoyable experiences that are held in a comfortable professional setting with the necessary props of coffee and snacks. These workshops can be built on some of the classroom and professional/personal themes identified above or they can be built on the spontaneous ideas and needs of creative staff; for example, one teacher sharing her Ph.D. research or another talking about the article on discipline she coauthored. The themes and topics don't have to be classroom related. Teachers need a little novelty, a little joy, and a little relaxation during their day. Non-school related topics shared by teachers add spice to the daily routine and it's a wonderful morale boosting exercise—a way for colleagues to know the personal side of each other's lives.

These forums don't have to follow the often stale after-school training model so often employed in a school's staff development efforts. Workshops can be held on a voluntary basis before school, during free periods, at lunch, or after school. The famous line in the film *Field of Dreams* applies here: "If you build it they will come." Creative administrators like Brad Foley and Linda Alvarez can seek out funding resources to allow substitution services for teachers who are willing to put themselves on the line and lead workshops. This process encourages the notion of a teacher as trainer of colleagues, a career alternative that's not costly but is highly effective. Getting teachers to take on such a leadership role will not be easy. At first it may seem to them to be an unnatural and self-serving role. Teachers don't talk a lot about their professional and personal successes. Putting their skills and resources on public display and promoting themselves as skilled professionals who know much about their craft does not come easily. Stepping out of the group to model effective teaching techniques requires risk and courage.

Administrators like Brad Foley and Linda Alvarez can encourage and support this kind of risk-taking behavior. They understand that it is a necessary extension of the one-on-one mentoring program. Well-trained teachers are a valuable resource, a necessary resource to provide ongoing training for colleagues. Administrators like Brad and Linda serve as antennas to identify outstanding teachers who can be brought on board as teachers of teachers. This process provides an ongoing way to expand the learning community within the school, acquiring new talent that can help prevent stagnation, reach resisting groups, and expand the constituency of teacher learners. It will be an ongoing process of forging new alliances and networks.

Every day schools across America are losing the valuable training resources of successful teachers. Many teachers have outstanding helping and training skills that can be used to help struggling colleagues. Many have participated in recent skill-building programs such as mentoring, conferences, and workshops. They come back to their schools eager to share what they know, but often no one asks what they've learned. Once excited to share, they slowly lose interest and retreat to the boundaries of their classrooms. No one harnesses or uses their new learning and energy. There is no vehicle in place for them to share with and teach colleagues who need stimulation. Both the newly skilled teachers and their colleagues lose out on the opportunity for growth. This is not cost effective; the monies and time spent on training are limited to a single individual. The new learning never gets any exposure. Millions of dollars are spent each year on programs, conferences, and workshops to help improve teacher effectiveness, but too often these newly trained teachers are not asked, encouraged, or required to share their new learning. Money and resources are lost.

The same process can occur with newly mentored protégés unless they are encouraged to become mentors themselves. Again, many teachers do not see themselves as leaders or as having the skills to help colleagues. It's part of the group norm that teachers follow in most schools. The boundaries are fixed and based in the classroom. But moving outside of the classroom and becoming a mentor alters these boundaries and in a sense sets the mentored protégés free. They are free to be a resource for colleagues, to be of service, to see that others have an opportunity for renewal, as well.

To help expand the pool of mentors and avoid the stagnation that often comes when a new program settles in, the mentoring team needs antenna to identify newly mentored teachers who seem to have the right skills to join the program. Mentoring, when done right, is a taxing process. In addition to skill, it requires energy and the will to win, to jump from the ledge into new, uncharted territory. It can be draining. Because of this, being a mentor should not be a lifetime job. Team members will leave for many reasons and new talent needs to be identified and brought on board. It's an ongoing process of beginning and ending, with newly mentored protégés taking over the reins again and again.

We now have some understanding of what kinds of themes and issues take place in one-on-one mentoring conversations and how mentoring teams can use this data to build ongoing learning hubs such as teacher-led workshops. We also have an understanding that mentoring teams need to tap into the skills of newly mentored protégés and encourage them to come on board as mentors themselves. To do otherwise, I say, is irresponsible. Teams need every resource within the school community to establish a climate that offers ongoing renewal. Teachers and mentors can't depend on outside resources alone. Too often outsiders don't understand the unique issues in individual schools. The reality a mentoring team embraces is that educational issues need to be addressed primarily by members within their own school community.

A mentoring team can easily transfer the mentoring skills identified here to other members of the school community, such as support staff and students. How can mentors transfer these skills, making mentoring a whole-school process? After all, support staff and students are themselves valuable resources who can, with minimal training, intervene to help troubled students, and serve as additional antennas for a school committed to caring, inclusion, and community building.

A mentoring team can harness the skills and energy of recently mentored teachers to offer short term training to support staff, often labeled the "nonprofessional" staff: cafeteria workers, hall monitors, secretaries, security personnel, teacher aides, and so on. They can all play a critical role in creating positive interaction with students. They are on the front lines of the school and often the first people to spot trouble—students smoking in the bathroom, cutting classes, drinking at a school dance or sports event. Many school support staff have spent years in close contact with adolescents and they get to know students in a very intimate, unthreatening way. Students often confide in them and seek advice and information on personal issues. While many support staff may lack degrees, certificates, and formal training, many have learned through experience how to be helpful. In their roles they have one clear advantage—they are not perceived by students as "professional staff" or a threat. Rather, they are friends, neighbors, and confidantes who will not reveal a secret. Because they are easily accessible and usually trusted by students, they can serve as positive role models and trusted adults. They can serve, in a true sense, as a vital antenna to identify and guide teens to reliable sources of help within the school and community.

I suggest that formal training that helps ground them in practices and skills that work can enhance the resource of support staff. Many of the mentoring skills I describe in chapter 3 can be transformed into a formal, short term training workshop led by teachers committed to sharing and passing on their newly learned skills. A simple curriculum for such training could include a number of elements:

Identifying areas of strength in helping and guiding students. What do you do well?
Identifying areas that are not effective in helping and guiding students? What skills need improvement?
Adolescent development
Particular concerns and issues of adolescence
How to build trusting relationships
How to hold effective one-on-one discussions
How to hold group discussions
How to be an effective listener
How to give nonjudgmental but accurate feedback
How to address and sometimes confront, risky student behaviors (alcohol, tobacco, drugs, eating disorders, family problems, and so on)
How to assess student problems that present a critical health or safety issue and thus require immediate intervention by school staff
How to refer students to reliable sources of help in the school and community
How to create ongoing opportunities for professional growth

The notion of everyone in the school as a learner and of ongoing activities made available to ensure lifelong learning is a critical part of this book's message. To limit learning and professional growth only to teachers, administrators, and counselors leaves out important members of the school community—the support staff—and places them in a subservient role, suggesting that what they do requires minimal or no formal training. That perception changes when we begin to offer them the opportunity for ongoing training and professional growth. In acknowledging their skill and value to the school community, we bring them on board as allies and partners and in the process expand their boundaries. Professional opportunities should not be limited to or the sole domain of the professionals in our schools. Effective training for every staff member should be the goal.

To make mentoring a whole-school process, the mentoring team can also transfer skills to students. Kids are smart. They observe the adults in their school—the teachers, counselors, and administrators—and they see how they treat one another. They see how students are treated, as well. If some teachers and students are looked down on, they know it. They understand that the in-groups of teachers and kids get the praise and the outgroups get the ridicule and put-downs. The put-downs are not always purposeful or meant to hurt someone. It's just that someone has to be the target, the enemy, the scapegoat. That's school for many kids. Jim Moriarty, whom we met in an earlier vignette, knows that he is one of those kids on the outside. He is a relative newcomer with few friends, failing in school, has parents who are divorced, isn't into sports or clubs, is a smoker, a truant, and known to the staff as a troubled kid. He is not on the top-ten list of troubled kids in school; he can still be reached, but the odds against that are increasing each day. He knows he is different from the jocks and the preps. He is on the outside looking in.

But all that separation, the building of barriers and boundaries, the isolation of some school community members, can change when a mentoring program begins and takes hold. Kids are apt to observe something much different, a building of a strong sense of school community, a school that counts every teacher and student and considers them useful community members with special gifts. Many teachers and students have gifts that are hidden, because no one ever asked them to be share. As teachers begin to be listened to, helped with their problem solving and skill development, and encouraged to serve as mentors for colleagues, they begin to use these newly acquired skills with students. Students are no longer seen as belonging to separate groups but as individuals with hopes, dreams, and possibilities. And teachers, now that mentoring supports them and makes them aware of their classroom dynamics, can observe and see, often for the first time, the walls that have been built up among kids as well as kids and teachers.

Caring schools in which students care for, support, and respect each other do not develop overnight and without hard work by many members of the school community. These schools evolve because the adults in the school model these behaviors. Kids are quick learners and they too—with a little information, training, and expectation—can become mentors, as well.

Let's return to the story of Jim Moriarty and teacher Tom Murray. Since the incident with Jim's father, good things have happened. Tom Murray took Brad Foley's advice and moved Jim's desk to the front of the room. He also began having lunch with Jim once a week. Using the same listening skills that Brad modeled in their mentoring sessions, Tom learned a great deal about Jim's life. It's been a tough road for Jim. He has been in five schools and lived in three states. His father has been in and out of drug and alcohol rehab many times and never seemed to settle down. There were always fights and violence between his mother and father but his mother refused to leave despite Jim's pleading and fear that something bad was going to happen one day. Jim's older brothers all dropped out of school and moved out as soon as they were old enough. School had always been a problem for Jim. He was unable to learn the basic skills because he moved around so much. With moving so much, he could never fit in at the new schools and was always on the outside with both his schoolwork and relationships. One day, he just gave up. He was failing and had only a few friends in the band. It was easier to pretend he was sick and stay home than deal with class. His mother gave up on getting him to school He went just often enough that child protective services didn't get involved and bug his mother.

Once Tom began to take an interest in Jim, things changed dramatically. Jim started coming to school on a regular basis, doing his work, and keeping his counseling appointments. Tom got him into the social studies club and encouraged him to try out for the basketball team. One day in their session, Jim surprised Tom by saying, "I wish I could help other kids like you do. I know they have some programs in schools where kids get to help other kids. Do you think you and I could do something like that?" Tom was taken aback. Sure, he wanted to help Jim, but starting a mentoring program was out of his league. Tom promised Jim that he would think about it. At his next mentoring session with Brad Foley, Tom brought up Jim's idea. Brad, always looking for ways to promote a mentoring philosophy in the school, grabbed the idea.

Look, Tom, this is another opportunity to help Jim and other kids. Jim is ready to help others as he has been helped by you and Gregg. Sure, you're uneasy about starting a big program. Why not start with a small group of seventh graders, maybe about fifteen? You and Jim can plan out a training program for kids to be mentors using the same skills you've used with Jim. Make it a six to eight week program with meetings once a week. We'll rotate the meetings so they don't miss too much time in any one class. I'd be glad to help. When you're ready, we'll announce it to the staff, kids, and parents. As far as expectations, once kids get through the training, let's keep it simple. We can give them certificates for completing the mentoring training. Then let's turn them loose and ask only that they try to be helpful and useful to other kids. You and Jim can meet with them as a group once a week, hear their stories, support their efforts, and continue to teach them mentoring skills as the need arises. You know they'll be able to help some kids but others will reject their efforts. Failure, as you know, is part of the mentoring program.

It's early December now. Let's plan to start a small program after February break. By May, after a six- to eight-week training period and then practice time as mentors, we should have a better handle on how to train kids as mentors and where we can go with the program. For me, this completes the circle. I've got my administrative staff focusing on mentoring teachers, teachers mentoring each other and kids, and now kids helping each other. I've seen some real changes on the part of teachers who have been hard on kids. Maybe by mentoring, the kids will lessen the tension between the groups in the school. That's a good goal. I say go for it. Get back to Jim and work out topics for a training program. And keep a diary on the program as you go along. Who knows, maybe you could write a book about this and be a big-time conference speaker. This is good stuff that other teachers need to know about. The University School of Education is starting a Ph.D. program in leadership next fall. I'm teaching some of the introductory courses. Give some thought to applying. I'll get you the information. This mentoring program could be an excellent dissertation topic. I'll make sure you get some consultant money for planning the program. If you get it going, I'll also give you some release time to manage the project."

Tom and Jim went to work and came up with an eight-session training program. At Jim's suggestion they also asked Janine to be involved. Jim felt she would attract some kids who might otherwise avoid the project. They agreed on a list of topics to be addressed during the eight training sessions:

1: Why do I want to kelp other kids?
2: What are my strengths as a helper?
3: What are my weaknesses as a helper?
4: What kids do I want to help?

5: What problems areas do I want to help kids with?
6: What kids do I have trouble helping?
7: What problems do I avoid dealing with?
8: Where do I begin making plans to help?

Training students to mentor and help each other is a natural consequence of a teacher mentoring program. It gives everyone in the school a
chance to get on board and be a useful citizen of the school community.
It helps send the message that everyone in the school counts and we will
make every effort not to turn our backs on each other. Remember, our
working definition of mentor is "a wise, loyal friend, a teacher, a coach."
That's a role that can be played by students in advising peers who lack effective academic and personal problem solving skills.

I believe that these vignettes, constructed from my own real-life experiences in schools, help expose the angst that teachers and mentors experience in their everyday roles. After all, the words—renewal, professional
development, lifelong learning, intervention to help students at risk—are
neutral, unemotional words that do not describe what goes on in the
process of mentoring and helping colleagues. They lack the image of the
heat of the battle and the sweat and turmoil that novice and veteran teachers can experience in their classrooms, and mentors can experience in trying to help and guide their protégés. These words, without the images of
the real lives of teachers Tom Murray, Ellen Turner, Shawn Mallory,
Myra Fryman, and Jim McDonald, do us a disservice. The words alone
could make the mentors of these vignettes—principal Brad Foley, teacher
Frank Bronkowski, department chair Randy Edwards, assistant principal
Linda Alvarez, and counselor Ivy Harrison—unprepared for the tough issues that mentoring presents. Schools cannot ignore the fact that a
teacher's search for renewal and growth is a difficult journey. These vignettes help elucidate the perils involved in pragmatic, everyday mentoring. They also make clear the possibilities and positive alternatives that
mentoring can yield. Effective mentoring can help create an environment
in which teachers have a chance to turn their professional lives around.

This is not Mentoring 101 with a simple list of the things mentors
should accomplish. Rather, it has been stories of teachers trying to right
their careers with the help of mentors who are skilled and unafraid of going beyond mere suggestion into territory that leaves the teachers vulner-

able to the involvement of their mentor. The strength of effective mentoring builds on the notion that the responsibility for teachers changing their negative behaviors rests with the teachers themselves. The role of mentors is to help teachers become aware of their ill-conceived practices and identify approaches that are effective. Mentors give their protégés data on which they can base new, self-affirming decisions about their classroom management, their students, and their own careers. This data and feedback provide sources of new direction that can, as these vignettes demonstrate, alter the wrong directions of gifted teachers.

NOTES

1. Cary Goldberg, "Betraying a Trust: Teacher-Student Sex is Not Unusual," *New York Times,* 21 May 1995, L37.
2. "Mr. Holland's Opus," Hollywood Pictures, 1995.

7

Making the Case for a Whole-School Mentoring Program

In this final chapter, I summarize the important issues about instituting a whole-school mentoring program in our nation's schools. Three important principles guide these issues. First, there is a great need for mentoring teachers in our nation's schools. Second, the mentoring program I have described can be implemented without the addition of staff or major resources. Third, mentoring skills can also be taught to students, thereby creating a whole-school mentoring program in which no teacher or student falls through the cracks. Here are the issues administrators need to understand:

1. The pressing need to provide mentoring for teachers at all levels of their career development—novice, midcareer, and veteran teachers.
2. The need for administrators to play a leadership role in the mentoring process.
3. The need for the mentoring team to accurately assess the school's willingness to welcome change and new programs.
4. The need to understand what educational leaders and researchers say about mentoring. Do they favor the kind of mentoring model I recommend?
5. Examples of mentoring programs now in action around the country.
6. Mentoring as a vital part of building a strong school community.

ISSUE #1: THE PRESSING NEED TO PROVIDE MENTORING FOR TEACHERS AT ALL LEVELS OF THEIR CAREER DEVELOPMENT

I believe the mentoring model presented here, and its accompanying potential to expand learning opportunities for support staff and students, presents a positive and cost-effective way for administrators to respond to their staff's need for ongoing renewal. This model addresses the learning needs not only of novice teachers like Shawn Mallory and Tom Murray but also veterans like Ellen Turner, Myra Fryman, and Jim McDonald. It also addresses the need and opportunity for skilled educational leaders like principal Brad Foley, teacher Frank Bronkowski, department chair Randy Edwards, assistant principal Linda Alvarez, and counselor Ivy Harrison to become mentors, creating not only a vehicle to help and support teachers but also an exciting new career alternative.

Mentoring can make a difference in the professional and personal lives of teachers who want to be effective but who may encounter bad times. Teachers lose their way sometimes, even the best and the brightest of them. New teachers usually struggle to learn the ropes. Some of the lessons, as we saw in the cases of Tom Murray and Shawn Mallory, are subtle and difficult to learn. Teachers often naively assume that if they survive their first few years, they are set for life. As we saw in the cases of Ellen Turner, Myra Fryman, and Jim McDonald, new issues frequently emerge for teachers, professional and personal issues that throw them off course and cause them to question their effectiveness. Without intervention and mentoring, they can become another case of attrition, professional lives lost that might have been saved.

Tom, Shawn, Ellen, Myra, and Jim do not, I believe, represent the most at-risk teachers. They have been formally trained as teachers, have been part of a teacher induction program, have had successful classroom experience and now, if problems emerge, have the support and safety net of a trained mentoring team, an easily accessible school-based help and support mechanism that will assist them. As the need for new teachers accelerates nationally, a growing number of teachers enter the field with little or no formal education, internship experience, or induction program, and no mentoring team available to intervene. These new teachers are often not education majors; they may be retirees or college graduates who enter the classroom as a second or third career. They begin teaching with little or no training and support in how to manage a classroom and interact with students. Are they doomed to failure? Not all of them, but clearly the odds are not in their favor. We might rightfully ask why school boards and administrators go along with such a situation, allowing well intentioned but poorly trained would-be teachers to be exposed to the hazards and risks of the classroom. In a sense, school boards and administrators are encouraging a process that props up a warm body in front of the classroom and hopes for the best while knowing that the would-be teacher, the students, and the school could lose.

What follows is a vivid description of how two unprepared and unsupported teachers fared in the classroom. Bill Gaulman and Erica Lavrack had little or no formal training, no induction, and no mentoring. Bill Gaulman's teaching career began in early August in an old brick, two-story school north of Ybor City. It ended in September. In a matter of weeks Bill fell prey to a punishing combination. The hours were too long and not enough students were interested in learning. He developed a knot in his stomach that wouldn't go away. The word that came to mind was "overwhelmed," said Gaulman, a man whose background included being a Marine and a New York City firefighter. "People told me to just get through the first year," he said. "I thought, I don't know if I can get through this week." Erica Lavrack also started teaching at the beginning of the school year. She resigned on her second day. She was given a class of emotionally handicapped children, although she had never handled a classroom before. Her qualifications? A degree in psychology and the fact that the Hillsborough schools desperately needed teachers for special education classes. She reports, "The kids were nice enough but they were running all over the place. There was no way I could teach them anything if I couldn't get them to sit down. I didn't know what to do."

The stories of Gaulman and Lavrack are surprisingly common. Florida desperately needs to attract teachers; an estimated 12,500 teachers are needed each year. But Florida has another problem—keeping teachers from quitting. Many new and veteran teachers become disillusioned and start planning their exit. As Martha Howell, assistant superintendent for the Pinellas County schools, suggests, "If we don't give them the support they need, we lose them."[1]

One can argue that if Bill Gaulman and Erica Lavrack had preservice training they would have been better prepared to face the realities of the classroom. But Florida school districts are increasingly hiring noneducation majors, retirees, and college graduates who enter the classroom as a second or third career. They begin teaching without the benefit of internships and training to handle classroom situations. Teachers like Bill Gaulman and Erica Lavrack are growing in number as schools' need to have warm bodies in front of the classroom reaches a level of national crisis. These would-be teachers need effective intervention and mentoring, probably more than Tom, Ellen, Shawn, Myra, and Jim, because of their lack of preparation. They are, in a sense, the most at-risk teachers.

ISSUE #2: THE NEED FOR ADMINISTRATORS TO PLAY A LEADERSHIP ROLE IN THE MENTORING PROCESS

In making the case that mentoring is needed in our schools, I stress that concerned building administrators cannot do the job alone. They have a lot on their plates already. With the recent national emphasis on reform and producing effective teachers, their job definitions may be shifting away from a management and problem solving role to an instructional leader and facilitator role. Mentoring requires time for observations, follow-up one-on-one conferencing, and ongoing support. Realistically, a school-based team, as I have described, is required. A progression of steps needs to be successfully followed to reach our goal of implementing a school-wide mentoring process. Interestingly enough, three important elements in the mentoring model I am suggesting—newly mentored teachers becoming mentors, transferring mentoring skills to support staff, and transferring mentoring skills to students—are rarely addressed. Their significance in helping develop a supportive school community should not be underestimated.

Administrators need to follow the following important steps:

1. Become sold on the mentoring process and how it can help you, the principal, as well as assistant principals, department chairs, counselors, teacher leaders, teachers, support staff, and students.
2. Assess your mentoring skills and train yourself in areas in which you need improvement.
3. Form and train your mentoring team and sell the program to staff.
4. Intervene and mentor teachers.
5. Encourage newly mentored teachers to become mentors themselves.
6. Transfer mentoring skills to support staff.
7. Transfer mentoring skills to students.

ISSUE #3: THE NEED FOR THE MENTORING TEAM TO ACCURATELY ASSESS THE SCHOOL'S WILLINGNESS TO WELCOME CHANGE AND NEW PROGRAMS

This process requires an understanding of how new programs have fared in the school in the past. In many schools, there is a graveyard full of failed programs, begun with good intentions, commitment, and resources, that faltered along the way. They were torpedoed by not anticipating resistance, inadequate community building and political skills, and ignoring problems that arose. Pam Robbins suggests that program planners understand those critical factors that can have a major effect on program design, implementation, and maintenance.[2] While Robbins' focus is on coaching, I believe the same critical factors apply to mentoring. I believe Robbins' suggestions serve to reinforce my plea that administrators who set out to develop mentoring programs best be aware of the school's history in developing new programs, where resistance to change will likely arise, and possess a finely honed set of political, planning, and communication skills to help navigate the program through expected and unexpected barriers. While the vignettes offer a vision of Brad Foley as a supportive and skilled principal, there will be many schools in which the potential program leaders need to be tested with the following questions:

1. What is the pre-existing climate of collegiality? Is there a history of staff working together and supporting each other? Is this fertile territory to begin growing a new program? If not, building collegiality will take time, patience, and support.
2. Are there norms supporting risk-taking and experimentation? For mentoring to succeed, the school culture must encourage teachers to take risks and try new approaches. Risk-taking needs to be modeled throughout the school by the principal and school leaders. Administrators can't ask teachers to risk trying out new approaches while they remain safe in one spot.
3. Has the supervisory experience been a pleasant or unpleasant one for teachers? Mentoring has a focus of assisting, not evaluating or assessing. It is useful to remember that a teacher's experience with teaching in front of another adult will affect his or her feelings about teaching in front of a colleague and mentor. If the previous experi-

ence has not been rewarding and nurturing, mentors will have to develop new, supportive conditions.

4. What is the school's track record regarding staff development? Has there been a series of failed efforts to bring about change and reform? Is the school's graveyard of failed education programs running out of space? Mentoring needs to be seen by staff as useful, growth promoting, and enjoyable, not as just one more task added to the day. Staff need to be sold on the process and their input valued. Teachers tend to remember staff development interventions that did little for them.

5. What are the core values of the school? What do members of the school community think is important? Is rugged individualism prized or is value placed on working together, sharing ideas and supporting each other? Mentoring has a good chance to thrive in a school community that respects lifelong learning, creativity, and working together.

6. Does leadership support mentoring? Administrative support is a major factor in developing the success of mentoring programs. Support needs to be long-term. Administrators who are initially sold on mentoring may get cold feet confronted by problems and resistance. New programs need to be able to count on the leader for cover as well as participation and funding.

7. What else is going on? As Robbins wisely suggests, it is useful to examine what the program must compete with in terms of time, focus, and resources. There is a right and wrong time to begin a new program such as mentoring that will have a great impact on the way teachers interact and behave. Administrators need to weigh the odds for success and failure of such projects. They need to take a critical look at how many projects are already going on in the school and determine if the staff has the psychological and physical energy required for the new effort. They also need to consider if the school has the necessary resources. Successful administrators usually have a good sense of timing and know when the school needs a new focus. The key is to look for ways to integrate new programs such as mentoring with other efforts, such as restructuring.

8. Will the bureaucratic structure of the school support mentoring activities? To what extent will the bureaucratic structure promote or inhibit the program?

9. What are the existing structures of collaboration in the school? If the staff has a history of working together, mentoring will not represent a major departure from the norm.
10. What is the nature of decision making in the school? Does the staff have ownership in the school? Are they used to working together and being involved in shared decisions? Is it real participation that seeks the collective input of every staff member or is it only on paper?
11. How flexible is school culture? Do new ideas like mentoring have a chance to be incorporated into the school? Good ideas and intentions don't survive in a culture that is not open to change and fresh ideas.

These questions, if answered honestly, help pave the way for action. They provide useful antenna on how to proceed by helping sharpen mentors' vision as to where potential problems and opportunities lie. Considering these questions can move the mentoring team beyond good ideas and good intentions to the real issues they can expect to confront. It's good to know what is possible and it's good to know where the barriers lie.

ISSUE #4: THE NEED TO UNDERSTAND WHAT EDUCATIONAL LEADERS AND RESEARCHERS SAY ABOUT MENTORING

Let's hear what educational leader Lee Shulman, mentor advocate James Rowley, and practitioning mentor Mary Brooks have to say.

In an interview with Carol Tell, Lee Shulman, president of the Carnegie Foundation for the Advancement of Teaching, makes the following points regarding mentoring and the changing role of administrators.[3]

Carol Tell questions Shulman about his view of teacher evaluation. "As you know, a perennial debate in education involves the connection between evaluation and improvement. Some argue that evaluation needs to be treated separately to enhance teachers' knowledge and skills. Others think that given the current emphasis on measurable results, we must align evaluation with professional development and school improvement. How do you feel about making these distinctions? Do you think there will always be tensions?" Shulman replies, "Somebody once asked me, why are there tensions between theory and practice in the education of professionals? And my answer is that there have to be tensions. One of the ways we make the tension worse [for educators] is to put both the job of nurturer and the task of monitor in the hands of the same person. . . . When evaluating teachers and tying rewards to those evaluations, we should try, within limits of responsibility, to separate and delegate the twin functions of monitor and mentor to different individuals."

Tell also asked Shulman, "So a mentor should never have an evaluative role?" Shulman replied, "Well, never say never. If you were my mentor, and it was your job to help me learn to be a really accomplished teacher, you would have access—through observations and conversations—to views and perspectives of me that nobody else had. . . . There is a point at which it would be unethical for you to withhold information from those who represented the accountability side of the equation. But as mentor, you would have to explain that to me. You would have to explain to me that 99 percent of the time you are my buddy, my friend, my supporter. But there could be a case in which you observed me doing or not doing something that so violated the fundamental expectations of the role that you would have no recourse but to make the observation part of the general evaluative data."

Tell queries Shulman about the evaluation of principals. "We talk a lot about the evaluations of teachers, but no so much about the evaluation of principals and administrators. Do you know of any moves afoot to revamp the evaluation of those educators?" Shulman answers, "With regard to principals, my own view is that the principal is the lead teacher. The word principal is not only a noun, but also an adjective, the first word of a two-word title: principal teacher. Principals, therefore, should be highly accomplished teachers who have the capacity to manage, organize, lead, and develop the capabilities of other teachers."

I believe Shulman's comments about mentoring and his vision of a mentoring program fit well with my mentoring model and vision of the changing role of administrator/principal. In my model the mentor is available to assist the protégé. Shulman suggests the mentor is available to nurture, and be a friend and a supporter. Mentors are available to help the protégé learn to be a very accomplished teacher, to be nurturing and not to solely monitor, assess, or evaluate. In the vignettes in this book, principal Brad Foley is available to assist and support Tom Murray; it's a helping role and one that lacks a formal evaluation component.

In my model, as represented in the vignette focusing on teacher Shawn Mallory and department chair Randy Edwards, mentoring and close observation help prevent a situation that might have had dire consequences for a teacher's career and the well being of his or her students. Without the quick and skilled intervention of Randy Edwards, the innocent relationship between Shawn and Aileen could have moved beyond professional boundaries into a romantic relationship. Mentoring and heeding early warning signs proved to be an effective mechanism for help.

Shulman also offers cautionary advice about the limits of some aspects of the mentoring role when he responds to Tell's query, "So a mentor should never have an evaluative role?" Shulman answers, "But as a mentor you would have to remind me that ninety-nine percent of the time you are my buddy, my friend, my supporter. But there could be a case in which you observed me doing something or not doing something that so violated the fundamental expectations of the role that you would have no recourse but to make that observation part of the more evaluative data."

Let's use the example of Shawn to reinforce Shulman's point. Shawn, a new and inexperienced teacher, did not forsee the hazards involved in getting too close to a student. But thanks to Randy's observations and skillful intervention, Shawn learned an important lesson about student/teacher relationships: Keep a professional distance. Don't become a friend or surrogate parent. Shawn's experience easily could have had an unhappy or even career-thwarting ending. For example, what if Shawn rebutted Randy's interventions and continued to become involved with Aileen as a friend, surrogate parent, or even a lover? Eventually, Randy would have had to approach principal Brad Foley and share his situation. As Shulman suggests, "He would have no recourse but to make the observations part of the general evaluative data," in other words, of Shawn's formal record. A record that could lead to Shawn's dismissal of the behavior continued. Ninety-nine percent of the time mentors like Randy are friends and supporters of their protégés, but when information surfaces that involves the safety and well-being of teachers, students, and parents, it needs to be addressed. In this case, Randy's mentoring served as a deterrent to Shawn's perceived or real risky behavior.

James B. Rowley, associate professor at University of Dayton, suggests that good mentors have the following qualities:[4]

- Good mentors are committed to the role of mentoring. They are highly committed to the task of helping beginning teachers find success and gratification in their work. Committed mentors understand that persistence is as important in mentoring as it is in classroom teaching. Such commitment flows naturally from a resolute belief that mentors are capable of making a significant and positive impact on the life of another. The belief is not grounded in a naïve conception of what it means to be a mentor. Rather, it is anchored in the knowledge that mentoring can be a challenging endeavor requiring significant investments of time and energy. Good programs require formal mentor training as a prerequisite to mentoring.

- Good mentors are accepting of the beginning teacher. They recognize the power of accepting the beginning teacher as a developing person and professional. Accepting mentors do not judge or reject mentees as being poorly prepared, overconfident, naïve, or defensive. Mentors view these traits as changes to overcome in their efforts to deliver meaningful support. How can we encourage mentors to be more accepting of new teachers? A training program that engages prospective mentors in reflecting on the qualities of effective helpers is an excellent place to begin. It should be training that helps prospective mentors understand the problems and concerns of beginning teachers as well as teachers at all other stages and ages, training that can cause mentors to revisit their own first years of teaching.

- Good mentors are skilled at providing instructional support. They are willing to coach beginning teachers to improve their performance. Many mentors stop short of providing quality instructional support. Among the factors contributing to this problem is a school culture that does not encourage teachers to observe one another in the classroom. What can be done to prepare mentors to provide instructional support? Mentor training should equip mentors with knowledge, skills, and dispositions for effective coaching. We need to give mentors and mentees the opportunity to participate in preconference, classroom observations, and postconferences that lead to quality clinical support.

- Good mentors are effective in different interpersonal contexts. They recognize that each mentoring relationship occurs in a unique interpersonal context. Just as good teachers adjust their teaching behaviors and communications to meet the needs of individual students, good mentors adjust their mentoring communications to meet the needs of individual mentees. To make such adjustments, good mentors must possess a deep understanding of their own communication styles and a willingness to objectively observe the behavior of the mentee. How can we help mentors acquire such self-knowledge and adopt a positive disposition toward adjusting their mentoring behaviors? Mentor training programs that engage mentors in completing and reflecting on self inventories that provide insight into their leadership or supervisory styles are particularly helpful.

- Good mentors are a model of continuous learning. Good mentors are transparent about their own search for better answers and more effective solutions to their own problems. They model this commitment by their openness to learn from colleagues, including beginning teachers, and by their willingness to pursue professional growth through a variety of means. How can we ensure that mentors continue their own professional growth and development? Quality entry-year programs establish clear criteria for mentor selection that include a commitment to initial and ongoing mentor training. Program leaders work hard to give veteran mentors frequent opportunities to participate in high quality professional growth experiences that can enhance their work as mentors.

- Good mentors communicate hope and optimism. They capitalize on opportunities to affirm the human potential of their mentees. They do so in private conversations and in public settings. Good mentors share their own struggles and how they overcame them and always they do so in a genuine and caring way that engenders trust. What can we do to ensure that beginning teachers are supported by mentors capable of communicating hope and optimism? Quality programs take the necessary precaution of avoiding the use of veteran teachers who have lost their positive outlook. If teachers and administrators value mentoring and take it seriously, mentoring will attract caring and committed teachers who demonstrate hope and optimism for the future by their willingness to help new teachers discover the same joy and satisfaction that they have found in their own careers.

I believe Rowley's comments regarding the qualities of a good mentor fit well with my mentoring model.

Brad Foley, Frank Bronkowski, Randy Edwards, Linda Alvarez, and Ivy Harrison are all committed to their mentoring work. They realize the endeavor requires a significant investment of time and energy. The mentor training program and self inventories helped them focus on the need to take care of themselves, to be physically and emotionally up to the task. Their knowledge of the importance of self-care was easily transferred to their protégés who were neglecting their well-being.

My mentoring model also calls for the mentor to be an effective listener, to be nonjudgmental, to provide useful feedback, to be accepting, and to act as a guide for teacher improvement. For example, Frank Bronkowski refrains from making judgments about Ellen Turner's rapidly deteriorating professional and personal life. He listens and gives useful and accurate feedback. He provides breathing space in which Ellen can gather herself, acquire new awareness, and plan, with Frank, concrete ways to take back her classroom and professional and personal self.

My mentoring model calls for the mentor to be skilled in providing instructional support. Brad Foley, as a good mentor, is quickly able to identify Tom Murray's strengths and the areas that need improvement. He is able to show Tom how to improve some methods of instruction that if left unattended would hinder Tom's classroom success. Brad communicates these thorny issues in a nonthreatening, supportive way, more as a friend than a supervisor.

My mentoring model also fits well with Rowley's suggestion that each mentoring relationship is unique and good mentors need to adjust their mentoring communications to meet the needs of individual mentees. We need to look no further than mentors Randy Edwards, Linda Alvarez, and Ivy Harrison to see that each protégé brings his or her own professional and personal issues to the mentoring relationship. Teachers Shawn Mallory, Myra Fryman, and Jim McDonald are each in a unique experience. The same approach, Mentoring 101, cannot be used in every case. Protégés, with their unique stories and needs, force mentors to adjust, and sometimes learn new skills or use an intervention approach they are reluctant to call on. For example, Linda Alvarez must strongly confront Myra Fryman to make her see her dilemma. Soft words, going along quietly, being nice— these things don't work with Myra. Fastballs have to be thrown in order for Myra to see that her star role is, in reality, not very satisfying. Mentors need many different skills to fit their many different protégés.

In my model, mentors are also continuous learners. They seek out and create learning opportunities and hubs, not only for their protégés but for themselves, as well. Randy Edwards pursues his connection with a local university medical school and his interest in research about teacher sexual abuse. Ivy Harrison becomes an adjunct professor in counseling in exchange for internship help. Linda Alvarez champions issues related to diversity and inclusion. Brad Foley creates ongoing learning networks with community and educational resources. Frank Bronkowski coauthors books on teen issues. These mentors were chosen not only for their excellent track record, skills, and commitment, but also for their intellectual curiosity. They are learners.

Finally, in my model, mentors know how to bring a sense of joy, energy, humor, and lightness to the mentoring relationship. In many of the vignettes, the mentors involved are able to offer hope and optimism. Things can improve. Brad Foley lets Tom Murray know that he can deal with hostile situations like the confrontation with Jim's father. Be optimistic, he tells Tom. Frank Bronkowski does the same for Ellen Turner: shift your weight; things can change; lighten up; do simple things like bringing in flowers and pictures of your family; create a little joy for yourself. And Randy Edwards, responding to Shawn Mallory's sudden concern for his career, says he'll provide cover for Shawn. Lighten up, he says. This has been a valuable learning experience. Ivy Harrison, representing the truly empathetic and caring mentor, tells Jim McDonald he is doing OK; keep expectations low; one day at a time; this too will pass; keep working on the issues; I'll be here with you.

Mary Brooks is site coordinator for the Beginning Teacher Mentor Program in West Des Moines, Iowa community schools. She describes the responsibilities of mentors in the following ways:

Get involved in solving specific problems about curriculum, instruction, and relationships, offering plenty of feedback.
Provide opportunity for classroom visits with follow-up feedback.
Express positive feelings about teaching and help beginning teachers attain those same feelings. Address the new teacher's thoughts about being a teacher.
Assist with the new teacher's understanding and management of authority.
Listen to daily concerns, progress, and questions.
Serve as a source of ideas.

Be easily accessible, trustworthy, and understanding.
Offer assistance on classroom management.
Demonstrate professional competence.
Help expand the beginning teacher's repertoire of teaching strategies.
Show awareness of, commitment to, and familiarity with the new teacher's classroom.
Schedule time willingly with the beginning teacher.
Provide a task-oriented focus established through a two-way interchange about goals and procedures.

Brooks also provides a job description of a mentor that includes what she calls "demonstrated skills: professional competency, effective verbal and non-verbal communication, and interpersonal skills of caring, kindness, and understanding."[5]

My mentoring model includes many of the same responsibilities and job descriptions as Brooks'. In my training model and vignettes, mentors use the full arsenal of skills available to them: problem solving, classroom observations and feedback, expression of positive feelings about teaching, pointing out positive activities of teachers, helping teachers cope with practical details, serving as a source of ideas, remaining accessible and trustworthy, and being generally caring, kind, and understanding. As Brooks suggests, this process produced a win-win situation. As my model suggests, it need not be limited to offering support to beginning teachers. Teachers at every stage of development need support and sometimes intervention.

Nathalie Gehrke also supports my notion of teachers, department chairs, and counselors assuming leadership roles in supporting classroom teachers. Kathleen Devaney offers an inclusive list of leadership skills that teachers might be called upon to exercise in emerging school organizations. Clearly, these areas are consistent with my notion of mentors as school leaders:

Continuing to teach and improve one's own teaching.
Organizing and leading peer reviews of school practice.
Providing curriculum development knowledge.
Participating in school-level decision making.
Leading in-service education and assisting other teachers.

Certainly the successful teaching experiences of mentors Frank Bronkowski and Randy Edwards prepared them for advising and guiding veteran teacher Ellen Turner and novice Shawn Mallory. Mentoring presents an emerging opportunity for teachers to assume such a leadership role. It's a positive career opportunity for both skilled teachers and those in need of support. As Gehrke suggests, mentors must be able to provide not only good role modeling, but also offer the kind of help necessary to establish the beginner as a competent professional. They must know about teaching children and about teaching adults. They must have a level of expertise that goes beyond being a comforter and a source of practical information.[6]

Holly Bartunek also offers support to the notion of classroom teachers as school-based teacher/educators. She suggests that school-based teacher/educator positions open an avenue of teacher growth. In this role, the classroom teacher is offered opportunities that expand and enhance professional development. Bartunek suggests the following strategies:

Promote and support peer teacher growth.
Experience empowerment by facilitating local change.
Assume a leadership role without leaving the classroom.
Develop teaching behaviors that blend clinical skills with practitioner-translated research and history.[7]

This revitalization of the teaching role with new responsibilities benefits the school process and its participants. In terms of mentoring as a potential school-based teacher educator role, Bartunek suggests that mentoring programs are rooted in the belief that adults have the capacity for continued growth and learning and that this development can be influenced by specific types of interventions that both support and challenge them. As I mentioned earlier, a critical focus of her argument is the understanding of the teacher's career as moving within a cycle that includes distinct stages: preservice, induction, competency building, enthusiastic and growing, career frustration, stable and stagnant, career wind-down, and career exit. These stages are dynamically influenced, either singularly or in combination, by personal environmental factors such as family demands, crises, cumulative experience, and individual dispositions and by organizational environmental factors such as administrative style.

Clearly mentors Frank and Randy have added vitality and novelty by becoming school-based teacher educators, with one foot in the classroom and one foot in the mentoring program. Their mentor training program has helped focus them on the important role that aging and career development issues play in teachers' lives, both personally and professionally. As seen in Ellen Turner's case, family demands and crises do happen. A career that was once enthusiastic and growing winds up with career frustrations. Ellen is lucky, unlike Florida teachers Bill Gaulman and Erica Lavrack. Ellen has access to a well-trained mentor in Frank Bronkowski. The same holds true for Jim McDonald. The counselor and mentor Ivy Harrison, while not a classroom teacher, also has a new opportunity for professional growth, with one foot in the counseling office and one foot in the mentoring program. She, too, is well trained and ready to help Jim with his "career frustration."

Roland Barth also adds credence to my argument that mentoring creates a unique opportunity for teachers to assume a leadership role in their schools, a role that offers a career alternative, novelty, and, as Barth rightfully points out, an element of risk. Barth suggests that teachers who become leaders experience personal and professional satisfaction, a reduction in isolation, a sense of instrumentality, and new learning. They become investors in the school rather than mere tenants; they become professionals. Barth describes attributes of teachers who are leaders:

> They get to sit at the table with grown-ups as first class citizens rather than remain the subordinate in a world full of subordinates.
> They enjoy variety, even relief, from the often relentless tedium of the classroom.
> They have an opportunity to work with and influence the lives of adults as well as youngsters.[8]

Barth also points out that moving from classroom teacher, a subordinate role equal with peers, to a leadership position such as mentoring can be unsettling and even risky. Barth suggests that in a very real way teachers who choose to confine their work as educators to the classroom win. They have more time and energy to devote to their teaching, to each of their students, and to their responsibilities outside of school. They are immune from interpersonal conflicts with other teachers and the principal. They enjoy a measure of safety in the relatively risk-free sanctuary of the classroom, where they may be accountable for pupil achievement but not their own achievement as a leader. And they may enjoy a measure of sanity each day in the often turbulent and chaotic world of the school.

For teachers who assume leadership, the outcome is less clear. They choose to supplement their work as classroom teachers by taking on responsibility, some of the time, for some of the issues that are integral to the health and character of the entire school. By participating in a larger arena, these teachers lose what the larger group wins: time, energy, freedom from interpersonal hassles, and immunity from public criticism for efforts that may not succeed. They probably lose, as well, a measure of their sanity in their days at school and at home.

But Barth suggests that the risks are worth it. The teachers who assume a leadership role such as mentoring win something more important. They experience a reduction in isolation, the personal and professional satisfaction that comes from improving their schools, a sense of instrumentality, investment, and membership in the school community, and gain knowledge about schools, the process of change, and themselves. All of these positive experiences spill over into their classroom teaching. Again, these teachers become owners and investors in the school rather than mere tenants. They become professionals.

Yes, the mentoring model I advocate does have elements of risk and isolation in it. It's new territory. Mentors are no longer just one of the crowd. In becoming mentors they are in a way leaving their school family. The routines, professional and personal boundaries, and rewards all change. Dissonance and anxiety may ensue. Leaving a role they know well for something new does, and should, make them feel they may be losing something in the process. As mentor Frank Bronkowski says, he is new at the game and still learning, but he wants to help. The way is not clear or known but he is on the road, seizing a new opportunity for growth and service. He has a good track record and the will to succeed. These resources will help as he searches for the new rewards that a leadership role such as mentoring can provide. Barth reminds us that with our nation's schools under relentless scrutiny, a remarkable space exists for teachers to fill. Many teachers want to lead and schools badly need their ideas, intervention, energy, and leadership.

ISSUE #5: EXAMPLES OF MENTORING PROGRAMS NOW IN ACTION AROUND THE COUNTRY

Mentoring teams and school administrators can learn from several examples of mentoring programs in action throughout the country. Administrators considering implementing a mentoring program do not have to reinvent the wheel. They can tap into many excellent mentoring programs in action throughout the country. Establishing contaçt with leaders of these programs also provides an instant resource for information and networking. What follows is just a sampling of the many fine programs in place:

1. Rochester, New York: The tidal wave that washes over first year teachers when they dive into the classroom for the first time can be enough to throw them back on the beach and send them home. The lifesavers for these aspiring educators are often their union colleagues, especially their teacher mentors. Few do it better than the Rochester Teachers Association, a critical part of the Rochester Public Schools Career in Teaching Program. The mentor-intern program was established in 1986 by the Rochester Teachers Association in cooperation with the city school district and has become a national model for improving teacher retention and preparing new teachers for urban schools. The 2000 school year produced the largest program in its fifteen-year history with 205 lead teacher mentors serving more than six hundred interns. Nearly all of the interns had no prior teaching experience. The support helped maintain a ninety-three percent retention rate during the year. Even more impressive, eighty-six percent of all the two thousand teachers who have been interns in the program since 1986 are still teaching. Before the program began, the district's retention rate was around sixty percent. In the Rochester program, aspiring mentors need recommendations. Mentors also need seven years in the district, a desire to continue learning, respect for the profession, and the quality of empathy. Carl O'Connell, Rochester Teachers Association mentor program coordinator, reports, "Can you imagine how many teachers would have been lost to the district and city if we hadn't been here? I've never seen a program that has done so much for our kids, for our administration, and for our colleagues. . . . We've had thirteen

years to put this all together. We have a list of warning signs we watch for—a lack of confidence, discouragement, frequent absences, etc. We always try to fix the problem, not blame."[9]

2. North Bellmore, New York: The North Bellmore Teacher Center on Long Island offers a mentoring that holds training sessions twice a month on communication, adult learning styles, peer coaching, and weaning. Susan Weinstein, director of the teacher center, stresses the need to provide training for mentors. She wisely suggests, "Just because you are a good teacher doesn't mean you [will be] a good mentor."

3. Dumont, New Jersey: Dumont has a mentoring program for first-year teachers at the Honiss Elementary School. It is a program to help new teachers weather the classroom, what school principal Richard S. Sterberg describes vividly: "There is this onslaught, what I call the violation of expectations, the minute they arrive. There is no way to experience it except by living through it." It's a support program for teachers like new eighth-grade science teacher Pam Nathan, who quickly discovers the gap between idealism and reality. Asking students to pass papers up to the front of the room can be an invitation to chaos. Students, some as tall as she, sass back when she asks for quiet. Many teachers, some of whom taught not only her but her mother, "tsk-tsk" when she tries something new. Asking for new textbooks becomes more work than seeking a presidential pardon. There are plenty of days when Nathan feels like quitting. That she has not is in no small measure thanks to seventh-grade science teacher Linda Merschtina, who was assigned as her mentor when Nathan arrived in September. Merschtina quickly became her confidential source of reassurance and tips on how to deal with parents, colleagues, and unruly students.

   The program at Dumont is part of a statewide requirement of a year of formal, structured mentoring for new teachers, a program that state officials are now proposing to extend to two years. Already fifteen school districts in Bergen County, including Dumont, have started pilot two-year mentoring induction programs. The job description for a mentor at Dumont includes terms like "coach, prober, empathizer, communicator, promoter of risk-taking, diplomat, nurturer, observer, counselor, motivator, and goal-setter."[10]

4. Centerville, Ohio: The success of the Centerville mentoring program for new teachers depends on systemic support of the mentoring program. For Mindy Cline, a kindergarten teacher, that support takes the form of mentor Barb Roberts, who smoothed her initial transition into teaching. From the mundane to the philosophical, Roberts lent a hand—and an ear—in Cline's new classroom. She helped Cline arrange her room, reviewed the early lesson plans, and introduced her to other school staff. Even though Cline had participated in a five-year preparation program with a year-long internship, she still benefited from Roberts' gentle guidance. As a requirement of the Centerville program, Roberts and Cline observed each other's teaching. They also had four days of release time, which they used to visit other schools and gather instructional ideas. During the course of her induction year, Cline frequently sought Roberts' input on her classroom practices. "Barb made me feel really successful, but she also let me fall a few times. . . . She supported me yet she gave me the space to try new things and see how they worked." At one point, Cline experienced classroom management difficulties and sought Roberts' assistance. Together they devised a new classroom management program and within three weeks Cline's class exhibited significant improvement. "Barb also helps me to avoid burning out. She saw that I was constantly working quite late; she advised me to go home. She told me that I might have flawless bulletin boards, but if I was physically exhausted, I wouldn't be very good for students."

Roberts, who serves on the Centerville school district mentoring committee, believes the success of mentoring hinges on systemic support. The union local negotiated release time and a $1000 stipend for mentor teachers. Roberts says the stipends and incentives are real boosts for mentors. And formalizing the program gives it credibility and communicates that the program is valued. For Cline the stipend also makes a difference. "Knowing she was being paid kept me from feeling I was imposing on her." Roberts also believes mentors require specialized professional development. "Educators need to be trained to effectively help new teachers." In Centerville, experienced teachers apply to become mentors and participate in course work. Each year the district mentoring committee gives careful consideration to the matches between mentors and new teachers. Mindy Cline believes she benefited from the careful selection process. "As a reading resource teacher, Barb really understood my content concerns, but because she wasn't a member of my teaching team I felt comfortable seeking her advice on my team's dynamics."[11]

5. Glastonbury, Connecticut: The school day ended for Tom Griffin's twenty-six students nearly an hour ago, but the fourth-grade teacher is still in his classroom. He sits at a squat table across from his mentor, Elaine Ahnell. Ten weeks into his first teaching job, the twenty-nine year old rookie has a lot on his mind. In short order, the two educators cover the logistics of parent-teacher conferences and how to divide the students into different reading groups based on their ability. Ahnell, a twenty-nine year veteran at Hebron Avenue Elementary School, shares examples of her students' work from a lesson Griffin plans to replicate in the coming days. These weekly sessions make a long day even longer but Griffin says he wouldn't want to go through his first year without them. "Elaine is my keel. If I didn't have this, I'd be up until two o'clock in the morning, scared." But these mentoring meetings are more than hand-holding sessions. They're a part of Connecticut's comprehensive program for inducting teachers into the profession. By providing them with ample support and guidance, the state is betting that new teachers like Griffin will not only survive their first year but will also grow to be highly skilled educators. This program, Beginning Educators Support and Training (BEST), is part of the $300 million comprehensive Education Enhancement Act passed in 1986. New teachers must successfully complete the program within three years of beginning their first jobs before they can move beyond Connecticut's initial license. BEST requires that districts give each new teacher a mentor or team of mentors for at least the first year of the program. In terms of training, the state gives each of its mentors three days of workshops in which the educators learn what the program requires of new teachers, such as Connecticut's Common Core of Teaching, a set of standards spelling out the skills and knowledge expected of teachers in each subject area and grade level.

Tom Griffin says having a mentor across the hall who is also a fourth grade teacher has been a major asset as he tries to find the right balance in setting expectations that are big enough for his students but not so high that they become lost. Although his first year has been a lot of work, more than he expected, he's convinced he made the right choice of a career.[12]

The mentoring programs in Rochester, Dumont, Centerville, and Glastonbury represent some of the many mentoring programs that are being developed throughout the country. The state of California has a Beginning Teacher Support and Assessment Program in which mentors, called "providers," develop trusting relationships with their novices by meeting formally and informally on a regular basis. The providers are selected for their competency in the classroom and for their communication skills.[13] The state of Kentucky Teacher Internship Program also represents a major effort to provide mentoring. Legislation passed in 1985 requires all first-year teachers to receive a level of support that develops a strong, lifelong career foundation. The program guides each new teacher through a structured process of assistance and assessment with the active involvement of a committee of seasoned educators, a mentor teacher, a university representative and the school principal.[14] In Columbus, Ohio, public schools established the Peer Assistance and Review (PAR) Program in 1986. The PAR Program was developed collaboratively by representatives from the teachers' union and district administrators to help new teachers and those experiencing difficulty on the job become effective. PAR mentors, called "consultants," are experienced teachers who remember what it is like to be new. A panel of administrators, teachers. and union officials select these consultants and release them from their classroom teaching duties for up to three years. All new teachers are required to enroll in PAR. Interns must successfully complete the one-year program to have their contracts renewed. The mentors conduct preschool orientation meetings, and once school starts make weekly visits to the interns' classrooms and keep in touch through individual conferences. The goal is to establish a supportive relationship that can provide an avenue to help improve teaching strategies and solve nonteaching problems.[15]

Research concerning these mentoring programs had shown positive results. In the California program, researchers Barbara Storm, Jean Wing, Theresa Jinks, Kathleen Banks and Patricia Cavazos found that most of the program's teachers said that mentoring played a significant role in the professional growth of new teachers. Specifically, the program's design helped new teachers hone their practice—planning lessons, for example—and reflect on the effectiveness of instruction. Mentors also found that working with beginning teachers engaged them in reflection about their own instructional practices.[16]

Some words of caution need to be said in terms of implementing mentoring programs. In spite of the growing need for mentoring teachers at all levels of career development and some early evidence that effective mentoring reduces attrition, we still must heed the early warning signs I cited in previous chapters. Let me remind the reader that problems can occur if program members do not pay attention to the hazards and risks involved in the selection and training of mentors and establishing a philosophy and process that focus on assisting teachers. Be alert to the following risks:

Not every experienced master teacher can become an effective mentor. Working intimately with colleagues demands an entirely new set of skills. Selecting veteran teachers on the basis of popularity, political power, and desire alone isn't enough.

Mentors require well planned training in how to help and support colleagues. Not recognizing the pitfalls that can occur in intimate relationships and not being trained in how to respond can leave new mentors at risk and vulnerable.

Mentoring programs that confuse assistance with assessment can quickly backfire. Mentoring programs that initially set out to assist and support teachers through a trusting, loyal, and collegial relationship can sometimes take on an evaluative role, a role that monitors performance. The mentoring team needs to be sure of their program's goals and state them clearly. Don't tell protégés that mentors are there to assist and then begin making classroom observations part of a formal evaluation process. Loyalty can be abused in a pressured school climate. When loyalty goes down the drain, so does the mentoring program.

ISSUE #6: MENTORING AS A VITAL PART OF BUILDING A STRONG SCHOOL COMMUNITY

In *Habits of the Heart*, Robert Bellah suggests that a community is a "group of people who are socially interdependent, who participate together in discussions and decision making, and who share certain practices that both define the community and are nurtured by it."[17] Building a strong community cannot occur in schools where teachers are isolated and lack ways to come together in positive fashions that build self-esteem and encourage learning and renewal throughout their careers. How can they be positive role models, mentors for students, support staff, and parents, when they lack experienced guides and mentors to offer them support?

I believe a mentoring program that focuses on the mentor as a loyal and trustworthy friend, advisor, coach, and teacher can reshape our schools and can create a caring community that fosters the notion that we are all our brothers' keepers. We are responsible and responsive to the glaring problems of teachers like Ellen Turner and students like Jim Moriarty. We are responsible and responsive to the subtle but just as pressing problems of teachers like Myra Fryman and Shawn Mallory, and student Aileen Lopez. Mentoring, when offered as real assistance and support, is a mechanism to reduce isolation and apathy and, as Bellah suggests, create a "certain practice that both defines the community and is nurtured by it." It is a way for both staff and students to be connected. It shifts schools from being a community that defines itself by grade level and subject taught to a community of unique but coupled citizens who bring their own gifts and needs to school each day, eager to share, learn, and be supported. This community encourages each member's voice to be heard and stand for something, and values service to others by becoming involved when its members see troubled colleagues or students.

Offering assistance and support, sometimes requiring tough love and feedback, may be a more powerful tool than formal assessment and evaluation. Promoting conditions that create trust, encourage risk, allow for an experience of failure, and focus on the need to improve, even an inch at a time, can pay off in the long run with improved performance for every member of the school community—administrators, department chairs, counselors, teachers, support staff, students, and even parents.

When people like Mindy Cline are helped and given space to test their own wings, they learn many lessons. They become more effective teachers as well as ideally positioned to help colleagues who need renewal. Who can really predict the future in the life of a community? Who knows when Cline's mentor Barb Roberts may also need renewal and rebirth? One hopes Cline would step in to return the care and support she received.

One hopes that kind of intervention would be part of the community norm in their school, part of the work ethic and ethos. Who knows when Glastonbury, Connecticut teacher Tom Griffin might be called on to be a mentor for Elaine Ahnell? His room is across the hall from hers; he'll know if things begin to not go well for her. Will he intervene? Is that kind of behavior encouraged, part of the community norm and work ethic and ethos, at Hebron Avenue Elementary School? These are the kinds of expectations, responsibilities, and responses we want to create and encourage in our school community, responses that rest on a community norm that calls for action, intervention, and support at all times and for every member of the community.

When students like Jim Moriarty have help and space to test their own wings, they too learn valuable lessons. When gifted students suddenly find themselves at risk, they will need the support of peers like Jim who have faced their problems and learned to move on, becoming more independent and self-sufficient and aware of his peers—thanks to Tom Murray's intervention. Jim has become a member of a caring school community and is ideally positioned to help a peer in trouble work through tough times. Is the community norm of the school supportive of students sharing a concern and helping troubled peers? I believe we need the proactive responses of students like Jim to help create and encourage expectations, responsibilities, and responses that support practices, as Bellah suggests, that both "define the community and are nurtured by it," practices that encourage commitment and caring.

In a caring, conscious school community, members learn to be unafraid of the trouble, pain, and struggle of fellow community members. They learn to embrace the human condition in its many forms, even the dark sides. In fact, the dark sides really show the community the curriculum for mentoring intervention, where the troubles lie and where their intervention should aim. It may seem easier to ignore the star teacher Myra Fryman because she can be hostile and has political connections and clout. It may seem easier to let Ellen Turner slowly twist in the wind until the rope snaps. By intervening, however, mentors send a powerful message to the whole school community that life and the people in the school are precious and worth caring about, even when the caring may not come easy.

I know mentors like Brad Foley, Frank Bronkowski, Randy Edwards, Linda Alvarez, and Ivy Harrison. They exist in the real world. I also know teachers like Tom Murray, Ellen Turner, Shawn Mallory, Myra Fryman, and Jim McDonald. I have met and observed them, and I know from first-hand experience that mentoring can work. It can work if two important variables are put into play: the trust of the mentoring relationship and the skills of the mentor. I know students like Jim and Janine who can benefit from Tom Murray's intervention. They, too, can be part of a cyclical mentoring process that does not stop at the teacher's door. Students and support staff can acquire the same mentoring skills.

Is such a caring, whole-school mentoring program too much to hope for? Pie in the sky? No. Everything I suggest in this book is doable by ordinary folks like you and me. It just takes some assessment of helping and mentoring skills, self-training, skill acquisition, and a plan for mentor training and program implementation. Yes, establishing a successful program takes political skills, the ability to deal with resistance, and selling the program to make it work. However, people like you and me can do these things. Keep it simple. Follow the path.

Education has once again become a top priority for the American people. Proposals for education reform—competency testing for students and teachers, creating a system of national standards, reforming or eliminating tenure, school choice options such as vouchers and charter schools—are sweeping the country. Critics of public schools say the schools are not capable of reforming themselves and that the public needs alternatives. Many believe that vouchers are the best way to help children who are locked in urban schools that don't work. Many teachers and administrators say they can manage education reform if critics stop blasting them and undermining their work, and if the public starts providing the level of funding and staffing they need to address the multitude of issues that today's students are bringing into the schools. Teachers say that vouchers and other education reform proposals are, in reality, efforts to privatize and weaken public education and establish a system of semiprivate schools in America.

The energy behind many of these proposals to improve public schools is welcome and long overdue. Proposals to help urban students and teachers who are locked into schools that are decaying, unsafe, and without computers and science labs are to be applauded. But the proposals seem far removed from what happens in the daily life of teachers in classrooms throughout the country. Even if all of these education reforms were enacted tomorrow, the reality is that teachers in the classrooms—whether in a charter school, a magnet school, or a school attended by voucher students—still will be faced with the challenge of how to develop their craft over a lifetime career. They will need to learn how to adapt, change, and respond successfully to the students' and their own professional needs.

If educational leaders are truly going to reform our schools, we will need ongoing mentoring so that teachers can learn, in easily accessible ways, how to aspire to become, and actually become, skilled and competent teachers, no matter what kind of education reform model takes center stage. The bulk of this mentoring will have to go on in local schools, where teachers are found each day and are available for ongoing training. The mentoring process itself will have to be led by school administrators who have the power, the position, and the resources to mount such an effort. To really make a dent in improving teacher effectiveness and reaching out to resistant groups, administrators will have to form a mentoring team composed of known and respected school leaders, experienced educators who have developed their craft and who can model and demonstrate for their peers how to be an effective teacher.

The danger in rushing to reform is that we may be overlooking two important factors that are necessary in developing effective teachers. First, teaching is a craft that is developed over a lifetime. A critical question, and one noticeably absent in the debate about which road to take in education reform, is, "What are the characteristics of teachers who master their craft?" How do they, through a process of accumulated classroom experience, often with many failures and some successes, develop a body of knowledge and a special set of skills that work for them, their students, and for parents?

A second factor that is extremely important to reformers is how to use the experience of successful school leaders—administrators, department chairs, and teacher and counselor leaders—to retrain colleagues who are locked into outmoded and unsuccessful practices. What does it take to translate and transfer what constitutes effective teaching practices to teachers who are less than effective? What are the characteristics of educators who are able to successfully share their knowledge and experience with teachers who aren't quite making it? How do they get these teachers to trust and believe they can start again? There are teachers in every school who seem to stay the same and never develop their craft, using the same skills and methods learned early in their careers despite a changing world and radically different student needs. At the same time, many of these teachers are talented and they aspire, in spite of their resistance, to be better at their craft. What is missing for them in the workplace is a mentoring process that connects their aspirations with intervention and training that can open up their classrooms and professional lives to new energy and teaching options. Again, to quote Stephen Sondheim, "What I found out in my experience is that everyone is talented. It's just that some people get it developed and some don't. Developing your talent takes work." Developing into an effective teacher takes a steady dose of hard work. Teachers must proceed to rekindle the spirit and enthusiasm of sub-par teachers so they can once again begin to work hard to raise their level of skill and competency.

Clearly, educators who are successful in their schools and have the skills to mentor and retrain their colleagues are our major resource for rekindling spirits and raising competency. National movements, education department dictates, and attempts to influence the daily work of teachers by experts espousing their own solutions are often seen as threatening, faddish, and self-serving vehicles. We would be wise to remind ourselves that well-trained educators are ideally positioned to train, not tell, teachers to embrace the notion that developing their craft requires a lifelong process of acquiring knowledge, of adapting or abandoning what falls short of their goal, and of acquiring a new set of skills that works for today's schoolwide community.

In closing, let me reiterate the three important principles that administrators need to keep in mind as they embark on a mentoring program. First, there is a great need to create a safe and supportive mentoring environment in which teachers at every career stage have the opportunity to learn and in some cases turn their professional lives around. Whenever possible, these mentoring programs should take place in the schools in which teachers work. Easy access and availability for help and support are key components in establishing a mentoring program.

Second, mentoring programs can be implemented without an increase in staff or resources. Staff in place can become skilled mentors if they are provided with the hands-on training I suggest in this book. Many administrators, department chairpersons, counselors, and teacher leaders are looking for exciting career alternatives in which they can learn new skills and offer needed services without giving up their regular positions.

Finally, mentoring skills can be passed on from mentored teachers to their students, creating a whole-school mentoring process. In the aftermath of the terrorist attacks on the World Trade Centers in New York, many students are searching for ways to be of service to their peers, school, and community. Learning the skills to intervene and help others is important not only to our students, but to our nation.

In a real sense, an effective mentoring program can help teachers believe in themselves and avoid the trap of defining themselves as just a cog in the wheel, with nothing unique about them. This is a sad state of mind that a wise mentor knows can be avoided with support, insight, self-care, risk, and a belief in and enjoyment of the work of teaching. A mentoring program in which skills are passed on to students can also help those students who see themselves as having nothing unique about them. Mentoring can change low self-esteem and lack of worth by offering programs in which students can learn to be of use and value—programs in which they will be noticed, affirmed, and can begin to believe in themselves. Simply put, mentoring provides turnaround opportunities for the whole school community.

NOTES

1. This and previous two quotes from Stephen Hegarty, "Some Newcomers Find Teaching to Be Too Tough," *Naples Daily News,* 28 January 2001, 8D.

2. Pam Robbins, *How to Plan and Implement a Peer Coaching Program* (Alexandria, Va.: Association for Supervision and Curriculum Development [ASCD], 1991), 44–54.

3. Carol Tell, "Appreciating Good Teaching," *Educational Leadership* 58(5) (February 2001): 8–11.

4. James B. Rowley, "The Good Mentor," *Educational Leadership* 56(8) (May 1999): 20–21.

5. Mary Brooks, "Mentors Matter," in *A Better Beginning,* ed. Marge Scherer (Alexandria, Va.: Association for Supervision and Curriculum Development [ASCD], 1999), 53–56.

6. Nathalie Gehrke, "Developing Teachers' Leadership Skills," *ERIC,* 1990, http://www.ericsp.org/pages/digests/dev_teacher_leadership_90–5.html (23 April 2001).

7. Holly Bartunek, "Classroom Teacher as Teacher Educator," *ERIC*, 1989, http://www.ericsp.org/pages/digests/classroom_teacher_edu_89–7.html (20 April 2001).

8. Roland Barth, "Teacher Leader," *Kappan* 82(6) (February 2001): 443–9.

9. Clarisse Butler and Ned Hoskins, "Why Mentoring Really Matters," *New York Teacher* (25 April 2001): 10–11.

10. Kate Zernike, "Helping New Teachers Survive the Hardest Years," *New York Times,* 14 February 2001, B11.

11. Joan Montgomery-Halford, "Easing the Way for New Teachers," *Educational Leadership* 55(5) (February 1998): 34–36.

12. Jeff Archer, "Earning Their Stripes," *Education Week* (January 2000), http://www.edweek.org/sreports/qc00/templates/article.cfm?slug=onestate.htm& keywords (20 April 2001).

13. Margaret Oleve, Amy Jackson, and Charlotte Danielson, "Investing in Beginning Teachers—The California Model," *Educational Leadership* 56(8) (May 1999): 41–44.

14. Sharon Brennan, William Thames, and Richard Roberts, "In Kentucky . . . Mentoring with a Mission," *Educational Leadership* 56(8) (May 1999): 52.

15. Patricia Stedman and Sandra A. Stroot, "Teachers Helping Teachers," *Educational Leadership* 55(5) (February 1998): 37–38.

16. Barbara Storm, Jean Wing, Theresa Jinks, Kathleen Banks, and Patricia Cavazos, "CFASST [California Formatie Assessment and Support System for Teachers] (field review) Implementation 1999–2000: A Formative Evaluation Report," Princeton, NJ: Educational Testing Service.

17. Robert Bellah et al., *Habits of the Heart* (New York: Harper & Row, 1985), 333.

Bibliography

Andrews, Fred. "Learning to Celebrate Water-Cooler Gossip." *New York Times,* 25 February 2001, BU6.

Araton, Harvey. "At Age 30, Mullin's World Takes Strange New Twists." *New York Times,* 14 January 1994, C6.

Archer, Jeff. "Earning Their Stripes." *Education Week* (January 2000). http://www.edweek.org/sreports/qc00/templates/article.cfm?slug=onestate.htm&keywords (15 March 2001).

Balliett, Whitney. "King Louis." *The New Yorker* (8 August 1994): 69.

———. "Cecil." *The New Yorker* (5 May 1986): 104.

———. "Miles." *The New Yorker* (4 December 1989): 156.

Barth, Roland. "Teacher Leaders." *Kappan* 86:2 (February 2001): 443–49.

Bartunek, Holly. "Classroom Teacher as Teacher Educator." *ERIC,* 1989. http://www.ericsp.org/pages/digests/classroom_teacher_edu_89–7.html (20 March 2001).

Bellah, Robert, Richard Madsen, William Sullivan, Ann Swidler, and Steven Tipton, *Habits of the Heart.* New York: Harper & Row, 1985.

Berkow, Ira. "The Legend Continues . . . Bird Shoots for Greatness." *New York Times,* 10 August 1997, sec. 8, p.1.

Berliner, David C. "Improving the Quality of the Teaching Force." *Educational Leadership* 58(8) (May 2001): 10–11.

Blair, Julie. "Teachers' Idealism Tempered by Frustration, Survey Finds." *Education Week,* 31 May 2000, 6.

Brennan, Sharon, William Thames, and Richard Roberts. "In Kentucky . . . Mentoring with a Mission." *Educational Leadership* 56(8) (May 1999): 52.

Brooks, Mary. "Mentors Matter." In *A Better Beginning,* edited by Marge Scherer. Alexandria, Va.: Association for Supervision and Curriculum Development (ASCD), 1999.

Butler, Clarisse and Ned Hoskins. "Why Mentoring Really Matters." *New York Teacher* (25 April 2001): 10–11.

Ciavonne, Jean. "Dandelions, Pine-Cone Turkey, and Abraham Lincoln." *Kappan* 66(2) (October 1984): 142–43.

Coleman, Cy. "It's Not Where You Start." In the Broadway musical *Follies,* 1972.

Combs, Arthur, Donald L. Avila, and William W. Purkey. *Helping Relationships: Basic Concepts for the Helping Profession.* Boston: Allyn & Bacon, 1971.

Cruickshank, Donald, Deborah Bainer, Joshue Cruz, Jr., Carmen Giebelhaus, Joy D. McCullough, Kim K. Mentcalf, and Richard Reynolds. *Preparing America's Teachers.* Bloomington, IN: Phi Delta Kappa Foundation, 1996.

Dunning, Jennifer. "Twyla Tharp Finds Value as a Cause for Dancing." *New York Times,* 12 January 1995, C1, C13.

Education Research Service. "Is There a Shortage of Qualified Candidates for Openings in the Principalship? An Exploratory Study." NAESP [National Association of Elementary School Pricipals] Online, 1998, http://www.naesp.org/misc/edweek_article_2–23.htm (20 April 2001).

Ellington, Duke. "Do Nothin' Till You Hear from Me." Louis Armstrong and Duke Ellington. Capitol Records, 3 April 1961.

Erickson, Steve. "Neil Young . . . On a Good Day." *New York Times,* 30 July 2000, sec. 6, p. 26.

Etzioni, Emitai. *The Spirit of Community.* New York: Crown, 1993.

Faulkner, David. "For Yastrzemski, the Fire Still Burns." *New York Times,* 14 October 1986, C3.

Ferrandino, V. L. and G. N. Tirolli. "Our Time Has Come." *NAESP Online.* http://www.naesp.org/misc/edweek_article_2–23-00.html (23 February 2000)

Gehrke, Nathalie. "Developing Teachers' Leadership Skills." *ERIC,* 1990. http://www.naesp.org/misc/edweek_article_2–23-00.html (23 April 2001).

Gilman, David A. and Barbara Lanman-Givens. "Where Have all the Principals Gone?" *Educational Leadership* 58(8) (May 2001): 73.

Gladwell, Malcolm. "Designs for Working." *The New Yorker* (8 December 2000): 60–70.

Glauber, Bob. "Simms: I'd Retire If . . . " *Newsday,* 19 October 1991, Newspapers & Newswires Section, p. 85.

Goldberg, Cary. "Betraying a Trust: Teacher Student Sex is Not Unusual, Experts Say." *New York Times,* 21 May 1995, L37.

Goodnough, Abby. "Teaching by the Book, No Asides Allowed." *New York Times,* 23 May 2000, A1, L37.

Hammer, Michael and James Champy. *Reengineering the Corporation.* New York: HarperCollins, 1993.

Hegarty, Stephen. "Some Newcomers Find Teaching to be Too Tough." *Naples Daily News,* 28 January 2001, 8D.

Holland, Holly. "KERA, A Tale of One Teacher." *Kappan* 79(4) (December 1997): 265–71.

Holloway, John S. "The Benefits of Mentoring." *Educational Leadership* 58(8) (May 2001): 85–86.

Hollywood Pictures. "Mr. Holland's Opus."

Jacobson, Steve. "A Complement to Sutton's Life." *Newsday,* 7 January 1998, A75.

———. "Complex Illness Hits Harnisch." *Newsday,* 6 August 1997, A71.

James, Caryn. "Death, Mighty Thou Art; So To, a Compassionate Heart." *New York Times,* 23 March 2001, E1.

Keiffer-Brown, Susan and Kathleen Ware, "Growing Great Teachers in Cincinnati." *Educational Leadership* 58(8) (May 2001): 56–58.

King, Matthew. "If These Walls Could Talk." *Educational Leadership* 58(5) (February 2001): 64–65.

Lahr, John. "The Imperfectionist." *The New Yorker* (12 September 1992): 68.

———. "Sinatra's Song." *The New Yorker* (3 November 1997): 77.

———. "Making It Real . . . How Mike Nichols Recreated Comedy and Himself." *The New Yorker* (21 February 2000): 197.

———. "Been Here and Gone . . . How August Wilson Brought a Century of Black American Culture to the Stage." *The New Yorker* (16 April 2000): 49–65.

Lemmon, Jack and Kevin Spacey. "A Couple of Winners Talk Awards and Acting." *New York Times,* 12 March 2000, Sec. 2A, 2.

Letters to the Editor, "The Education of Donna Moffett." *New York Times,* 29 May 2001, A14.

Lopate, Phillip. "Learning to Love the Ardent Chaos of Cassavetes." *New York Times,* 10 August 1997, H11.

Macaulay, Alastair. "Happy Hooligan." *The New Yorker* (27 April 1992): 89.

McCay, Elizabeth. "The Learning Needs of Principals." *Educational Leadership* 58(8) (May 2001): 75–76.

Montgomery-Halford, Joan. "Easing the Way for New Teachers." *Educational Leadership* 55(5) (February 1998): 34–36.

NEA Teacher Quality Fact Sheet. "Teaching." http://www.nea.org/teaching/ shortage.html (20 April 2001).

Oleve, Margaret, Amy Jackson, and Charlotte Danielson. "Investing in Beginning Teachers—The California Model." *Educational Leadership* (May 1999): 41–44.

Rehak, Melanie. "Things Fall Together." *New York Times,* 26 March 2000, sec. 6, 36.

Riding, Alan. "The Joy of a Comeback that Leaves the Past Behind." *New York Times,* 29 April 2001, AR3.

————. "Looking at a France That's Seldom Seen." *New York Times,* 27 August 2000, AR17.

Robbins, Pam. *How to Plan and Implement a Peer Coaching Program.* Alexandria, Va.: Association for Supervision and Curriculum Development (ASCD), 1991.

Routtencutter, Helen. "Andre Previn." *The New Yorker* (12 January 1983): 43.

Rowley, James B. "The Good Mentor." *Educational Leadership* 56(8) (May 1999): 20–21.

Saint Exupery, Antoine. *Wind, Sand, and Stars.* New York: Reynolds & Hitchcock, 1939.

Sarason, Seymour. *Creation of Settings.* San Francisco: Jossey Bass, 1972.

Schiff, Stephen. "Stephen Sondheim." *The New Yorker* (8 March 1993): 77.

Seuss, Dr. *Oh, the Places You'll Go.* New York: Random House, 1990.

Solomon, Andrew. "The Jazz Martyr." *New York Times,* 9 February 1997, sec. 6, pp. 34–38.

Sondheim, Stephen. "I'm Still Here." In the Broadway musical *Follies,* 1972.

Spacey, Kevin. "An Example, A Mentor, An Actor Above All." *New York Times,* 4 January 2001, AR6.

Stedman, Patricia and Sandra A. Stroot. "Teachers Helping Teachers." *Educational Leadership* 55(5) (February 1998): 37–38.

Steinbeck, John. *East of Eden.* New York: Viking Press, 1952.

Steinberg, Jacques. "Clashing over Education's One True Faith." *New York Times,* 14 December 1997, sec. 4, 1.

Storms, Barbara, J. Wings, T. Jinks, K. Banks and P. Cavazos. "CFASST [California Formative Assessment and Support System for Teachers] (field review) Implementation 1999–2000: A Formative Evaluation Report." Princeton, NJ: Educational Testing Service, 2000.

Teachout, Terry. "Still Full of Jazz, Still Pouring It Out." *New York Times,* 19 December 1999, AR 44.

Tell, Carol. "Appreciating Good Teaching." *Educational Leadership* 58(5) (February 2001): 8–11.

Temes, Peter. "The End of School Reform." *Education Week.* 2001. http://www.edweek.org/ew/ewstory.cfm?Slug=29temes.h20 (4 April 2001).

Thomas, George. "Jets Discover Their Coach's Joyful Energy." *New York Times,* 17 May 2001, D5.

Weintraub, Bernie. "Looking Back at Two Classics." *New York Times,* 23 January 1998, E8.

Zernike, Kate. "Helping New Teachers Survive the Hardest Years." *New York Times,* 14 February 2001, B11.

Zipkin, Amy. "In Tight Labor Market Bosses Find Value in Being Nice." *New York Times,* 31 May 2000, C1.

Index

About the Author

William L. Fibkins is an education consultant, writer, and lecturer specializing in training school administrators, teacher leaders, and school counselors on how to develop school-based teacher training and student support services. His training programs include leadership and peer counseling training for student leaders and alcohol, drug, and tobacco intervention program for at-risk students. Fibkins holds degrees in education, counselor education, and school administration from Syracuse University and the University of Massachusetts.

Fibkins's publications include, *What Schools Should Do to Help Kids Stop Smoking, The Empowering School . . . Getting Everyone on Board to Help Teenagers, The Teacher-As-Helper Training Manual, Preventing Teacher Sexual Misconduct,* and *Tobacco Interventions.* He is also the author of numerous professional monographs on restructuring secondary schools, training secondary teachers to be advisors, implementing group counseling programs, restructuring secondary school guidance services, and developing school-based health centers to address teen health issues.

Fibkins's in-school experience includes serving as the director of the Stony Brook University-Bay Shore Public School teacher training center, school-community project director for the Queens College-Louis Armstrong Intermediate School, and founder of the student assistance counseling program for the Shoreham-Wading River, New York school district.